Theological Education in Contemporary Africa

Theological Education in Contemporary Africa

Zapf Chancery Tertiary Level Publications

A Guide to Academic Writing by C. B. Peter (1994)
Africa in the 21st Century by Eric M. Aseka (1996)
Women in Development by Egara Kabaji (1997)
Introducing Social Science: A Guidebook by J. H. van Doorne (2000)
Elementary Statistics by J. H. van Doorne (2001)
Iteso Survival Rites on the Birth of Twins by Festus B. Omusolo (2001)
The Church in the New Millennium: Three Studies in the Acts of the Apostles by John Stott (2002)
Introduction to Philosophy in an African Perspective by Cletus N. Chukwu (2002)
Participatory Monitoring and Evaluation by Francis W. Mulwa and Simon N. Nguluu (2003)
Applied Ethics and HIV/AIDS in Africa by Cletus N. Chukwu (2003)
For God and Humanity: 100 Years of St. Paul's United Theological College Edited by Emily Onyango (2003)
Establishing and Managing School Libraries and Resource Centres by Margaret Makenzi and Raymond Ongus (2003)
Introduction to the Study of Religion by Nehemiah Nyaundi (2003)
A Guest in God's World: Memories of Madagascar by Patricia McGregor (2004)
Introduction to Critical Thinking by J. Kahiga Kiruki (2004)
Computer Programming: Theory and Practice by Gerald Injendi (In Press)
Dying Voice (An Anthropological Novel) by Andrew K. Tanui (In Press)
Theological Education in Contemporary Africa edited by Grant LeMarquand and Joseph D. Galgalo (2004)

Theological Education in Contemporary Africa

Edited by
Grant LeMarquand
Joseph D. Galgalo

Zapf Chancery
Eldoret, Kenya

First Published 2004
© St. Paul's United Theological College
All rights reserved.

Cover concept and design by
Grant LeMarquand, Joseph D. Galgalo and C. B. Peter

Typesetting, layout and design by
C. B. Peter

Printed by
Kijabe Printing Press,
P. O. Box 40,
Kijabe.

Published by

Zapf Chancery Research Consultants and Publishers,
P. O. Box 4988,
Eldoret, Kenya.
Email: zapfchancerykenya@yahoo.co.uk
Mobile: 0721-222 311 or 0733-915 814

ISBN 9966-9742-6-1

Cover Picture
Woodcarving of *Jesus Calming the Storm*. The Prince of Peace Benedictine Monastery, Tigoni, PO Box 900, Limuru, Kenya. Used with permission.

This book has been printed on fully recyclable, environment-friendly paper.

Contents

Introduction   *(Joseph Galgalo and Grant LeMarquand)*..........1

Part One: Theological Foundations

Chapter One: The Teaching of Theology in Africa: Some Reflections on Sources, Methods and Curriculum *(Joseph D. Galgalo)*........................5

Chapter Two: The Binding Power of the Text and the Context in which we Preach *(Jonas Pasztor)*.................29

Chapter Three: Current Issues in Biblical Interpretation *(Musa W. Dube)*................................39

Chapter Four: Learning to Read the Bible in Limuru: Textual and Hermeneutical Reflections of a Non-African Guest *(Grant LeMarquand)*............................63

Chapter Five: Ecumenism and Theological Education in Africa *(Nyambura J. Njoroge)*.....................83

Part Two: Contemporary Issues

HIV/AIDS

Chapter Six: Theological Education: HIV/AIDS and Other Challenges in the New Millennium *(Musa W. Dube)*..............................105

Chapter Seven: The Challenges Posed by HIV/AIDS: A Way Forward for Educators *(Maryann N. Mwangi)*......................131

Chapter Eight: Beyond "Victim Theology": Reconstructing Theological Education in an Era of HIV/AIDS in Africa *(Peter Mageto)*...............147

RELIGIOUS PLURALISM

Chapter Nine: Christian Theological Education in the Context of the Religiously Pluralistic Continent of Africa *(Johnson A. Mbillah)*.......167

Chapter Ten: Approaches to teaching Islam in the Twenty First Century *(John Chesworth)*......181

THE MARGINALIZED

Chapter Eleven: Biblical Reflections on a Panel Discussion on 'Disability' *(Grant LeMarquand)*...................211

Chapter Twelve: Theological Education and the Youth in the Family, Church, and School *(Josphine Gitome)*..........219

THEOLOGICAL PAEDAGOGY

Chapter Thirteen: Challenges of Theological Education in the Twenty-First Century *(Sammy Githuku)*.........227

Chapter Fourteen: Residential, and Distance Approaches to Theological Education *(Godfrey Nguru)*.........237

Part Three: Postscript

Chapter Fifteen: Final Statement of the Conference..................249

List of Contributors..255

Introduction

Theological education needs to be a priority for the churches in Africa in the coming generation. The Christian faith has taken root and has grown so quickly on the African continent that it has been difficult for the churches to train and provide pastoral leadership for congregations.

Those who provide theological training are often all too aware that the job could be done better: more theological teachers are needed, better libraries and facilities should be built, more encouragement to do research and writing are essential. Perhaps most importantly, the African context must be taken seriously.

The essays in this book only scratch the surface of the many concerns of theological educators, theological students and church leaders. A number of issues that have received attention in the past (the importance of African traditional religion for African theology and practice, culture and inculturation, liberation and the sad legacy of colonialism, the often-alleged irrelevancy of missionary Christianity for Africa, the paternalism of western Christianity vis-à-vis the infant church in Africa) are not highlighted in this book. Certainly these issues appear in many of the essays, but they are in the background.

In the foreground are subjects of current and pressing need. In the book these issues are divided into two categories: 'Theological Foundations' and 'Contemporary Issues.'

Part One addresses 'Theological Foundations.' The five essays in this section deal with the Bible, Theology and Ecumenism. The subjects of theological methods, contextual hermeneutics, and appropriate curriculum are given special attention. Of course even foundational issues cannot be discussed in a vacuum and so each of the essays addresses these foundational subjects in the light of African realities.

Part Two deals with 'Contemporary Issues.' It is particularly in this section that the traditional themes in African theology have been somewhat displaced by concerns which are today very pressing indeed. Three essays are devoted to the question of HIV/AIDS. This disease, which has devastated the African continent, demands a theological and practical response from those who claim to follow Jesus Christ. If the churches do not respond to this crisis with energy and determination we should not be surprised if the next generation wonders whether the Gospel has the power which we claim that it has. Two essays address the question of Islam and Muslim-Christian Relations in Africa. The resurgence of Islam in the world today is a concern of many. For those who believe in Jesus, this is a challenge which demands much wisdom and love. How should we respond to our Muslim neighbours? What are appropriate and thoughtful ways to share the love of Christ? Two further essays appear under the title of 'The Marginalized.' This could, of course, be a much large section. Those who suffer from AIDS could be included in this number, and one might have expected to see at least one essay on the place of women. In this volume, however, the 'disabled' and youth are highlighted. Both groups are clearly in need of the attention of the churches, and both groups are clearly misunderstood and neglected. The final section of Part Two contains essays, which focus attention on 'Theological Paedagogy.' All of the other contributions to this volume make suggestions and arguments about curriculum, resources, and issues of concern for theological educators. The causal aim of this book is that these essays may help us to reflect in an intentional way on the implications of contemporary realities for the future of theological education.

Work on this book has been collaborative from the start, and it remains for us to thank many people who have been involved in assisting us. In the first place, Joseph Galgalo would like to thank

Introduction 3

Grant LeMarquand for undertaking the lion's share of the spadework for the book. Both of us would like to thank all of those who contributed to the book, and the administration of St. Paul's United Theological College for organising the theological consultation at which the chapters in this volume were first presented as individual papers. Special thanks go to Professor Godfrey Nguru and Dr. Esther Mombo in this regard, and to three postgraduate students at St. Paul's – Msonda Bowa, Onesphore N. Ngabo and Stephen Nduati for their diligent recording of all the proceedings during the presentations. The administration and the contributors' energy and enthusiasm are a sign of the growing vitality of the theological enterprise in Kenya. Many thanks also go to Grant's students at Trinity Episcopal School for Ministry, Ambridge, Pennsylvania in the U.S.A., especially Bud Brooker, Daniel Cave, and Rosa Richards who acted as proofreaders in the last stages of putting this book together. They were very helpful and have saved the editors from some embarrassing mistakes! They are, of course, not responsible for any remaining errors in the final manuscript, for which the editors take full responsibility. We also owe thanks to Church Mission Publishing Company, Hartford, Connecticut, USA, for their generous grant without which this book could not have been published. We further wish to thank M/S Zapf Chancery Research Consultants and Publishers for their good work. Lastly special thanks are due to John Chesworth who has remained a true friend and endured not only facilitating the communication between Grant and Joseph (the two editors) but also sacrificially made available the use of his e-mail facility.

We cannot forget to give thanks and praise to God as we acknowledge his blessing in the success of this project. It is to God's glory and to all sincere efforts in the promotion of theological education in Africa that we dedicate this book.

Grant LeMarquand
Joseph D. Galgalo

CHAPTER ONE

The Teaching of Theology in Africa: Some Reflections on Sources, Methods and Curriculum

Joseph D. Galgalo

Introduction

This paper is a general discussion of how theology is taught in Africa with special reference to theological method, its sources, and content (curriculum). I am aware that Africa is a vast continent and its geographical, cultural and social diversity, among other factors, makes it very difficult to speak in any general way that can adequately cover the concerns and issues arising from these vast contextual differences. Whilst fully conscious of this gap I will still use this broad reference in addressing the topic assuming some basis in existing similarities and shared experiences of the peoples of Africa across their vast cultural and regional divides. Particular examples, however, will be mentioned as may be necessary and their uniqueness acknowledged. We may also need to note that the learning and teaching of theology as an academic discipline continuously happens at both informal, as well as highly structured formal levels. The mode of transmission has been both oral as well as written. The task of theological reflection and its teaching has not always been the exclusive privilege of seminaries, theological institutions or universities, but is a task carried out by the faithful who share their faith experiences in whatever forum is available to them. This of course includes revival fellowships, women's groups, youth groups, choir practices, occasional seminars and retreats, quasi-formal Theological Education by Extension programmes, and so on. It is not a wonder that profound theological reflection often draws its inspiration not from the theological resources of the renowned and established academies, but rather from the humble environs of catechism classes and cell group studies.

It is very interesting to study the kind of theological learning and teaching that goes on in such informal set-ups, but time and space will not allow us to do an in-depth treatment of both formal and informal contexts within which theology is taught and learnt. I shall therefore limit my discussions to the formal teaching of theology in Africa, and my focus will especially be on institutions that provide theological education at a higher level of learning. We shall further ease our task by examining only three elements, namely, the sources, methods and content, as mentioned earlier. These—especially the first two—are, in my opinion, the determining factors in the way the subject or the discipline is presented or taught. We shall treat these three in the order just mentioned.

Sources[1]

The first Pan African Conference of Third World Theologians, meeting in Accra, Ghana from December 17-23, 1977, listed the following five elements in their final communiqué as the sources of African theology: "The Bible and Christian heritage, African anthropology, African traditional religions and other African realities."[2] While endorsing this as indisputable, we must also point out that the key to understanding the sources for African theology largely lies in understanding some epochs in the history of African Christianity and their direct bearing on the reception, interpretation, and owning of the Christian faith in Africa. Some social, political, economic and cultural realities impinge on the ongoing processes of

---

[1] The material for this section and the next has been largely lifted out of a chapter of my forthcoming book, *"African Christology."*

[2] Kofi Appiah-Kubi and Sergio Torres, ed., *African Theology en Route* (Maryknoll: Orbis, 1979), 192ff.

owning the received dogmas, traditions, and the perceived relationship between that which is received and the context. I shall here only point out some sources of inspiration for African theology rather than the actual source materials *per se*.

A range of factors has influenced the direction in which African theologising has been taking shape for some time now. The social and political realities of contemporary Africa and the need to relate the Christian message of salvation in ways understandable and relevant to Africa have, for example, given rise to two dominant strands of theology: Black theology and contextual theology, or theology of inculturation.[3] The content and method of this theologising draws inspiration from a number of sources, especially history, the scriptures, culture and context. The longstanding theological tradition of the West, received in the historical context of Western imperialism and colonization, has also provided a dartboard of sorts, against which African theology has been played. A perceived irrelevancy of western theology for an 'African Christianity' provides the motivation to search for an alternative theological schema. This affirms, as John Parratt notes, the "belief that Christian theology in Africa, whether oral or written, must serve the needs of the church if it is to be of any value. Theology therefore is essentially a practical task ..."[4] and as such this motive puts a special spin on methodological choices. Let us briefly look at the crucible within which the framework of approaches has been moulded and taken shape.

History
There is a somewhat complicated story of the birth, death, and rebirth of Christianity in Africa. The initial contact between Christianity and the African continent, as far back as the first century, remained essentially a Mediterranean affair. It never reached down to sub-Saharan Africa. Indeed, most of North African Christianity died of several maladies including heresies, schisms and onslaught by Islam.

---

[3] Emmanuel Martey *African Theology: Inculturation and Liberation* (Maryknoll: Orbis, 1995), xi.
[4] *A Reader in African Christian Theology* (London, SPCK, 1987), 147.

What was left of early African Christianity in Egypt and Ethiopia survived in spite of centuries of isolation and other challenges. Mother Africa had to wait for the birth of another baby to carry on this Christian name. With the arrival of the Portuguese in the 15th c. an ill-fated flirtation with Christianity followed. This was unfortunately an affair characterised by exploitation, abuse, and domination meted out by this purported herald of the gospel. The seeds of mistrust and doubt in the salvific significance of the message of Christianity were firmly planted in the minds of the Africans who bore the brunt of this abusive relationship. The irony is that there was a resultant owning of the message while Africa, at the same time, disowned the messenger. The message too had to be cleaned of its taint, repackaged and presented in ways an African could identify with, domesticate, and own.

The story of Beatrice Kimpa Vita is perhaps an archetype of a theological trend born out of and nurtured by experiences of Africans under oppression. Her baptismal name Beatrice, was a contradiction in terms as far as her identity was concerned – as an African with a 'foreign' name, she was effectively rendered a foreigner in her own home; but the struggle with her 'impaired' identity inspired her theology. The fresh way she looked at the 'good news' earned her a place in history as the mother of African theology. She rejected the Jesus Christ that was presented and interpreted to Africans through the eyes of the white oppressor. She preached that Jesus was indeed an African – the Black Messiah, and that he was always on the side of the oppressed. All his disciples were also black, and like their master, were champions of the course of the downtrodden. Despite these efforts at inculturation, Christianity born out of this abusive relationship slept with its older sibling only to wait in hope for a new rebirth.

This was not to happen until the advent of the so-called "age of missions" that helped to establish Christianity in almost all parts of Africa. This historical epoch culminated in the rise of nationalism and the founding of independent African states. The war against colonialism, and the search for African selfhood inspired in its own way a brand of theology which is typically reactionary against the West and its theology. Themes fostering the African aspirations gave birth to theologies that emphasize Africanisation, indigenisation and decolonisation of the church and inculturation of Christianity. The nationalism that inspired these theologies often brought the issue of African identity into sharp focus. This in turn, intimately connected with African culture, provoking such questions as the compatibility of the gospel with culture, the best method of relating one to the other, and the place and authority of the gospel within the context of African realities. Answers to these vexing questions were sought in African realities, but more so in the Bible, which has become the primary source of African theology and is therefore having a great bearing on the way theology is taught.

Scripture
Fashole-Luke writes, "the Bible is the basic and the primary source for the development of African Christian theologies."[5] His assertion finds consensus among many writers on the subject. Mercy Amba Oduyoye, highlighting the common sources for "all Africans who theologise," comments that, "[the] first of course is the Bible."[6] Kwesi Dickson not only identifies the Bible as the invaluable foundation for African theology, but also advocates that it should be accorded the most prominent place among all other sources.[7] J.S. Mbiti,[8] writing back in 1986, while recognising and commending the major role the Bible is playing in the construction of theology in Africa, equally laments how some theological trends such as 'liberation', have very little biblical basis. He noted that writing, oral

---

[5]"The Quest for African Christian Theologies," in *Third World Theologies*, ed. G.H. Anderson and T.F. Stransky (NY: Paulist Press, 1976), 135-150.

[6]*Hearing and Knowing: Theological Reflections on Christianity in Africa* (Maryknoll: Orbis, 1986), 51.

[7] "Towards a Theologia Africana," in *New Testament Christianity for Africa and the World,* ed. Fashole-Luke and Mark Glasswell; London: SPCK, 1974), 204.

[8]*Bible and Theology in African Christianity* (Nairobi, Oxford University Press, 1986).

communication, and symbolic representations are three ways of theological expression in Africa. Comparing the use of the Bible in written and oral communication, he concludes that, the Bible "exerts a greater impact on oral theology than on what can be gathered in the extremely sparse published materials."[9] His specific contention is that, "there is a serious tendency for some theological debates to be propagated without full or clear biblical grounding."[10] Regardless of the limited use of the Bible in some areas, Mbiti points out the important fact that, "many, if not all, of the concerns of African theology lend themselves to biblical illumination."[11] Underscoring the need for adequate engagement with the Bible, he insists that, "as long as we keep the scriptures close to our minds and hearts, our theology will render viable and relevant service to the church, and adequately communicate the word of the Lord to the peoples of our times."[12]

A lot has happened since Mbiti first published these words in 1979, and later in 1986. The question to ask today is perhaps not about the adequacy of the use of the Bible in African theology but of the way it is used or abused by different interpreters. The Bible has undoubtedly become the most basic resource text both for those who can read it for themselves and for the hearers. It has become great inspiration for theological reflection, providing models and tools for constructing or deconstructing theological systems, socio-political structures, moral and ethical perceptions, and cultural norms, among other things. Distinctive hermeneutical principles have been developed and pursued to achieve intended goals, resulting in, generally speaking, literalist, inculturationist, liberationist, and feminist readings of the Bible. We may also note that it has neither been accorded primacy nor supremacy by all its readers at all times. While views that uncritically endorse the Bible as the literal word of God

---

[9] Mbiti, *Bible and Theology*, 59.
[10] Ibid, 59.
[11] Ibid., 60.
[12] Ibid, 63; Mbiti, "The Biblical Basis for Present Trends in African Theology," in *African Theology en Route*," 91.

abound, there are also voices, critical to the extreme, calling for its radical revision in order to adapt the Bible suitably to the African context.[13]

A good example here, perhaps, is found in some extreme feminist readings of the Bible. These are of course varied, but most approaches within this category are generally counter-cultural, especially critical of those strongly patriarchal aspects of culture within Africa that seem to perpetuate male dominance. The Bible is used to confront cultural expectations, which are perceived as biased against women.[14] Some interpreters even suggest that the Bible should be supplemented by other texts if it fails adequately to address the issues of the oppression of women due to its patriarchal bias. Gloria Kehilwe Plaatjie, writing from her post-apartheid South African perspective, makes precisely this point:

> In [the] background of entrenched apartheid and patriarchal oppression against and marginalization of black women, it is clear that the Bible as a sacred, authoritative, and analytical text for social consciousness and change is not enough. The Bible itself indulges in both patriarchal and apartheid oppression. Black women ought to know that the country's post-apartheid constitution is another authoritative and sacred text.[15]

It is evident that the issue is no longer the use or lack of use or reading of the Bible but of *how* it is used or read. This is also true in

---

[13]See especially the case of Canaan Banana and his proposal for the rewriting of the Bible. The thesis entitled, '*The Case for a New Bible*,' was initially delivered as a seminar paper to the Department of Religious Studies, Classics and Philosophy at the University of Zimbabwe, June 14, 1991 and published in the same year and under the same title by Mambo Press, Gweru. Cf. also the responses in *"Rewriting" the Bible: The Real Issues,* ed. I. Mukonyora, *et al.* (Mambo: Gweru Press, 1993).

[14]See, for example, Musimbi R. A. Kanyoro, "Cultural Hermeneutics: An African Contribution," in *Other Ways of Reading: African Women and the Bible,* ed. Musa Dube (Geneva: WCC Publications / Atlanta: SBL, 2001), 101-13.

[15]"Towards a Post-apartheid Black Feminist Reading of the Bible: A Case of Luke 2:36-38," in *Other Ways of Reading,* 114 -42, see 135.

spite of the existence of the different levels of the biblical readership. Indeed some scholars distinguish "trained and untrained readers"[16] and go on to elucidate how the Bible is read either "existentially or contextually,"[17] regardless of the category of the reader. At both these levels, the use of the Bible has been prominent. Different approaches are applied in its interpretation, and are accordingly shaped or determined by either context or general realities in life. In any case, the Bible is an expedient source, if not the ultimate source, for theological enterprise in Africa. We also need to note that changing situations in Africa have constantly influenced different approaches to biblical hermeneutics in Africa. Culture is also used as a tool of interpretation. If the Bible illuminates culture, culture provides the linguistic and conceptual framework for the illumination of the Bible. We shall now turn to see the role of culture and cultural worldviews, in inspiring and influencing theological reflection in Africa.

Culture

Mercy Amba Oduyoye rightly observes that, "a living Christian faith in Africa cannot but interact with African Culture." She also explains how this reality influences the development of a distinctively "Christian theology that one may describe as African."[18] Justin Ukpong makes a similar point when he emphasises the importance of "re-expressing the original Christian message in an African cultural

---

[16] See Gerald West, *Biblical Hermeneutics of Liberation: Modes of Reading the Bible in the South African Context* (Pietermaritzburg: Cluster / Maryknoll: Orbis, 1995); "The Interface between Trained Readers and Ordinary Readers in Liberation Hermeneutics. A Case Study: Mark 10:17-22," *Neotestimentica* 27/1 (1993): 165-80; "Constructing Critical and Contextual Readings with Ordinary Readers: Mark 5:21-6:1," *Journal of Theology for Southern Africa*, 92 (1995): 60-69; "Reading the Bible Differently: Giving Shape to the Discourse of the Dominated," *Semeia,* 73 (1996): 21-41.

[17] Gloria Plaatjie, "Towards a Post-apartheid Black Feminist Reading of the Bible: A Case of Luke 2:36-38," in *Other Ways of Reading*, 117.

[18] "The Value of African Religious Beliefs and Practices for Christian Theology," in *African Theology en Route*, 109-16, see 110.

milieu," and that in the process of faith encountering culture, the result is "a new theological expression that is African and Christian."[19] Expressing this same sentiment, John Pobee asserts that the primary task of African theology is "to translate Christianity into genuine African categories."[20] In the effort to realise this goal, some theologians have engaged in the search for a master hermeneutical key, or a set of key cultural elements, to help understand the African worldview. The key could then hopefully be used for the ultimate goal of constructing a grand theological system for Africa. As nowhere else, this is perhaps best expressed in Bénézet Bujo's prescriptive proposal. He urges that, "what the church needs to do today is to uncover the vital elements of African culture which are stamped on the African soul."[21] He further proposes what the likely procedure should be, that "anyone who wants to construct an African theology must take the basic elements of the African tradition and interpret them in the light of the Bible and the Fathers."[22] Bujo indeed highly commends some Catholic pioneers in African theology such as Placide Tempels, Vincent Mulago, Alexis Kagame, Alfred Vanneste, and Tharcisse Tshibangu, for their efforts in this direction. Their works, each in its own way, is an attempt at discovering a cultural element that may be used as an effective hermeneutical key for incarnating the gospel in the African world.

It has often been noted that Placide Tempels' publication of *Bantu Philosophy*[23] is a significant step in this direction. John Parratt writes that, "it was the first attempt to come to grips, other than in a purely descriptive way, with African thought forms, and to treat

---

[19] Justin Ukpong, *African Theologies Now: A Profile* (Eldoret: Gaba Publications, 1984), 30.

[20] *Towards an African Theology* (Nashville: Abingdon, 1979), 17.

[21] *African Theology in its Social Context* (Nairobi: St. Paul Publications, 1992), 68.

[22] Bujo, *African Theology in its Social Context*, 68.

[23] Originally published as *La Philosophie Bantoue* (Elizabethville, 1945); the English translation did not appear until 1952.

them both analytically and as a coherent system."[24] Bujo explains that Tempels "analysed the fundamental elements of African cultural tradition in order to get at the thought-categories and the religion of the people of Africa."[25] In his search, Tempels arrived at the conclusion that, the hermeneutical key to understanding the African worldview is the concept of "vital force" or "life force." He proposed that this concept was basic to African thought and that it could be a unifying element in interpreting African philosophy and religion, as well as a means by which the Christian faith could be effectively communicated to the African person. Tempels was not alone in either proposing the search for a basic thought category to help formulate theology in ways relevant to African reality or to use this particular category. Many including Tharcisse Tshibangu,[26] Alfred Vanneste,[27] and A. Ngindu Mushete[28] have tried to do so.

The quest of this fundamental principle has also been sought in other concepts such as what Vincent Mulago called the 'vital union.'[29] This idea draws its inspiration from the concept of family, personal relationships, way of life and social structure of the Bantu people. Similarly Julien Pénoukou speaks of what he called 'the cosmotheadric relationship.' Building on the cosmology of the Ewe-Mina people, he explains their idea of a cosmotheadric vision of reality in which God, humanity, and the world are united. This

---

[24] *Reinventing Christianity* (Grand Rapids: Eerdmans, 1995), 10.

[25] Bujo, *African Theology in its Social Context*, 56.

[26] Tshibangu's ideas are mainly formulated in two of his works: "Vers une théologie de couleur africaine?" *Revue du Clergé Africain* 15 (1960): 333-46; *Le propos d'une théologie africaine* (Kinshasa), 1974.

[27] See especially the dialogue with Tshibangu in the *Revue du Clergé Africain* 15 (1960), entitled, "Débat sur la "theologie africaine."

[28] "Unité et pluralité de la théologie," *Revue du Clergé Africaine* 22 (1967): 593-615.

[29] Une visage africaine de Christianisme: L'union vitale bantu face à l'unité vitale ecclésiale (Paris, 1965); "Symbolisme dans les religions traditionnelles africaines et sacramentalisme," *Revue du Clergé Africaine* 27 (1972): 467-502; "Eléments fondamentaux de la religion africaine," in *Religions africaines et christianisme*, 1 (1979): 45-49.

symbiotic co-existence of the universe is grounded in a unitary vision of relationship, a kind of 'ontological solidarity,' between all empirical and supra-empirical realities, especially the Supreme Being and the cosmos. He holds that the human person is the '"organic medium"... the procreator who mediates all relationships of being between creator and creature."[30] He applies this concept especially in his African Christology where Christ is explained in the light of this traditional worldview. Examples of this kind could be multiplied. These are enough to lead us to conclude that African theology has sought to engage critically with culture, sustaining a reflective process that can make the gospel message meaningful and fruitful for the mission and service of the church.

While the efforts of these individual theologians and many others are commendable, it is also evident that the search for a grand hermeneutical key cannot so far be said to be a success. Whereas the search for a fundamental philosophical principle to aid in discovering a point of confluence of the African cultural categories is a step in the right direction, it is perhaps overly optimistic to expect that such a principle would be limited to a single conceptual category. A nexus of ideas may yield better results if held together and, of course, we have no reason to assume the existence of a uniform worldview across the diverse socio-cultural contexts of Africa. The effort is further complicated and undermined by the dynamism of culture, and changing African social realities. With western forms of education, philosophical and ethical orientation, and the very fast pace in which lifestyles and social allegiances are changing, and not least owing to speedy globalisation, it is increasingly becoming difficult to identify what may pass for 'an authentic African culture.' The boon is that in institutions of theological education where the works of these African 'divines' are taught as part of an 'African theology' course, they have served positively by inspiring critical thinking.

---

[30]"Realité africaine et salut en Jésus Christ," *Spiritus* 23/.88 (1982): 374ff; "Christologie au village," in *Chemins de la christologie africaine*, Paris, 1956.

Context

The types of African theology - Black, inculturation, liberation, and feminist theologies - are largely contextual, in other words, they are, especially in terms of their agenda and method, determined by the context. In the beginning, for example, African theology was mainly reactive, criticizing the ills of colonialism and western imperialism, the faults of the foreign missionaries, and the alleged distortion of the gospel of Christ. This is reflected in almost all the earliest colloquia, conferences, debates and writings.[31] This 'combative approach' came to a symbolic climax in the moratorium debate at the AACC conference of 1974, which called for the withdrawal of foreign missionaries and the Africanisation of the church leadership. Indeed, no western missionary worker was invited to attend the Dar-es-Salaam conference convened two years later. With time, the reactive approach simply fell out of vogue and new challenges, as determined by changing times and situations, took the centre stage. In South Africa, for example, the struggle against apartheid - the oppression and systematic marginalization of Blacks - concentrated on the question of Black Power, Black dignity, Black identity, as well as issues of social justice, equality, poverty, and of God's involvement with a world where one class of the human race is regarded as less human by another.[32]

It is evident that the context bears more on the way one theologises, than has perhaps been recognised previously. Cultural worldviews or thought forms are naturally drawn from our repertoires for self-expression, but it is indeed the *context* that furnishes us with

---

[31]For example, *First International Conference of Africanists* (London: 1964); the conference took place in 1962 in Accra, Ghana; E. Fashole-Luke, *et al.* eds. *Christianity in Independent Africa* (Papers from the conference held in 1975 at Jos, Nigeria) (London, 1978); Sergio Torres, *et al.* ed. *The Emergent Gospel, Theology from the Underside of History* (Papers from the Ecumenical dialogue of Third World Theologians held at Dar-es-Salaam, 1976 (Maryknoll: Orbis, 1978).

[32]See, for example, Basil Moore, ed. *Black Theology: The South African Voice* (Papers from various conferences held in South Africa, 1971) (London, C. Hurst Publishers, 1973).

the agenda, and how we express the substance or content of our theology. Just as we can express ourselves only in concepts, languages, and nuances acquired from our orientation in life, so we only formulate our theology in the context of realities within our experience. When we critically examine this point in the light of curriculum and the mode of delivery or teaching of theology in our institutions of higher learning, the context is not often given the prominence it deserves in the setting of theological agenda. This happens, not least, because of our 'western orientation' and the enormous influence still exercised by 'expatriates' who teach theology in Africa. Incidentally, the medium of instruction for the teaching of theology in Africa is still almost entirely in foreign tongues. Ironically, for those who write theology from within or for the African context, the *context*, perhaps inevitably provides them with a linguistic and conceptual frame of reference, even when they do not write in their own languages. Many institutions are now realising that contextual realities such as neo-colonialism and exploitation, dictatorial and oppressive governance, poverty, social inequality and injustice, hunger and diseases, especially HIV/AIDS, are bound to impinge on theological reflection. Incipient secularism, urbanization, the erosion of cultural values and disintegration of the traditional social systems that go with it, further compound the situation in Africa. The question of how to respond theologically to these and other issues is now beginning to find a place within many theological curricula.

Methods

John Parratt has noted that, "the Bible and Christian tradition, African culture and religion, and socio-political situation,"[33] are the three basic factors that continually shape theological method in Africa. They are the primary sources of inspiration for theological engagement in Africa. They have, right from the start of a sustained theological undertaking in Africa going back to the 1950s, influenced the hermeneutics that typically emphasise one or the other of socio-political, cultural or spiritual need as context or situation may demand. It has been pointed out that these factors have given rise to distinctive types of African theology. Ngindu Mushete[34] identifies three such types or what he called "currents that typify theology in Africa." These are missionary theology, African, and Black theologies.[35] He elaborates that the second type namely, African theology, developed in two distinct stages, with each stage employing a different approach. The two stages are, in his words, "theology of adaptation, which centres around stepping stones in the development of African Christianity," and what "might be called a more critical African theology."[36] Mushete has noted that adaptation is primarily a method of 'evangelisation' that attempts to incarnate the gospel message by appealing to the worldview and the socio-political milieu of the recipient culture.

While 'the theology of adaptation,' has gone a long way in influencing the Africanisation of the church in Africa, Mushete gives a critique of how it suffers from a kind of "concordism." That is, it essentially fails to reconcile the two systems of thought that emerge and stand as two separate entities, when Christianity encounters a traditional religious-cultural system that it seeks to 'convert'.[37] The second stage, namely, the 'critical African theology' stands as a corrective to this shortcoming. It is an approach that takes revelation seriously, with the scriptures and tradition as its two chief witnesses, history and its role in theology, and the place of cultural and social analysis, in the construction of a sound and meaningful theology. In my view, Mushete makes a valid observation. We must, however, point out that, if the reflections are at a deeper level, the content and methodology basically remains the same. Either way, whether at adaptation or critical stage, the pertinent question remains of 'how best the gospel message may be incarnated into Africa.' It is this basic agenda that seems to have a great bearing on the matter of theological method in Africa.

---

[33] *Reinventing Christianity*, 2.
[34] "The History of Theology in Africa," *African Theology en Route*, 23-35.
[35] Mushete, "History of Theology", 23.
[36] Mushete, "History of Theology", 27.
[37] Mushete, "History of Theology", 28.

A slightly different way of looking at how theology has been done, and continues to be done, in Africa is proposed by Charles Nyamiti.[38] He stresses that there is not one but a number of theologies in Africa and therefore, a 'variety of theological approaches.'[39] He explains, however, that these "various approaches" ultimately give rise to only "two types of theology" which either employ an "inculturation method" or "liberation." With regard to the "inculturation method," he writes that, "various schools are found in this way of procedure."[40] He identifies what he calls the speculative or philosophical approach, and the socio-cultural and biblical approach. His 'speculative/philosophical' category could be seen to correspond to Mushete's 'critical theology-stage.' He explicates this as follows:

> The philosophical or speculative school is characterized by a critical and philosophical approach to African religions or socio-cultural realities, as well as biblical and traditional Christian teaching. Stress is put on the noetic aspect of theology, primarily understood as *intellectus fidei*. Both the Bible and church tradition are directly confronted with African traditional wisdom, problems, and aspirations. The approach to Christian mysteries is both ontological and functional, analytical and practical.[41]

This method, which he associates mainly with Catholic theologians, is shown as different from the 'socio-cultural and biblical' method which is generally existential or functional, seeking how the African traditional system of thought and life can be related to that presented by the Christian gospel. This first method, which he associates mainly with the Protestant theologians, emphasises the authority of the bible over that of the church tradition.[42] Nyamiti's analysis is helpful in its meticulous attention to detail, showing the specific concerns of what he sees as the different 'schools of thought.' He also draws attention to how the different schools prioritise their sources of

---

[38] "Contemporary African Christologies: Assessment and Practical Suggestions," in *Paths of African Theology,* ed. Rosino Gibellini (London: SCM Press, 1994), 62-77.

[39] Nyamiti, "Contemporary African Christologies", 64.

[40] Nyamiti, "Contemporary African Christologies", 64.

[41] Nyamiti, "Contemporary African Christologies", 64-5.

inspiration—Bible, Christian tradition, recipient culture and context, and so on—one over the other.

His second type—liberation is further categorized into two types: the South African Black theology and African liberation theology. The main factor that furnishes the liberation approach with a distinctive theological hermeneutic is the human condition and the situation that faces humanity e.g. racism, oppression, injustice, poverty etc. In as far as the application of the Christian message to these situations is concerned; it becomes clear that the basic concerns of inculturation and liberation converge. Only one fundamental difference may be noted: the departure point of liberation is that of the situation of the human person, but inculturation operates from the premises of the divine revelation and seeks to discover or propose how best this may encounter and transform culture.

The terms used to describe 'types' of theology in Africa are seen by some theologians, like James C Okoye,[43] as distinctive stages in theological development in Africa. However, these terms – indigenisation/adaptation, inculturation/liberation, contextualisation or reconstruction – are generally descriptive and are suggestive of the theological methods that are employed. All these categories whether adaptation, liberation, contextualisation or reconstruction, employ a method that seeks to take into account the aspirations and the thought-system of the African person. They are basically attempts at using the cultural and social thought-forms, language and contextual realities of Africa to interpret and apply the gospel message in ways relevant and meaningful for the appropriation of their particular faith experience. There is a need to clarify here that there is really only one general approach in the way 'African theology' has so far been done, namely, the quest to relate the gospel message to African socio-political and cultural realities. This reveals that the bottom line is simply inculturation or contextualisation. One may

---

[42] Nyamiti, "Contemporary African Christologies", 65.
[43] "Inculturation and Theology in Africa," *Mission Studies* 27/28 (1997), 67ff.

speak specifically of liberation, adaptation, or reconstruction not as distinctive methods but rather in reference to particular concerns and emphases of the one general method. *Mutatis mutandis*, the teaching of theology in Africa also takes a similar approach, the central concern being that of how to interpret and relate theological data in ways relevant and understandable to the African person.

While this is a valid concern, the pertinent question that needs to be asked in this regard concerns the superficial way in which most African theologians have related Christian theology and African realities. Unfortunately, the often-cosmetic way in which the corresponding concepts have been applied has greatly undermined the efficacy of the general method. It may be fruitful if more attention could be given to analysis of the context, especially the socio-political realities that Africans face in their daily lives, and the essence or the kernel of Christian gospel applied accordingly. The methodological framework should largely, in any case, be determined by unbiased social analysis, and a firm biblical foundation, which should inform the theological discourse thereof. Having said that, we must also point out that the 'enterprise' called 'African theology' has largely remained the efforts and products of individual scholars written mainly for the academy and with very little or no influence at all towards communicating with the general populace of the churches of Africa. Of even more concern is the fact that the greater bulk of their theology hardly finds a place and receives little attention within the academy itself. This is mainly because of these institutions' traditionally 'western oriented' theological curriculum, which we now turn to examine.

Curriculum

Here we have in mind the general content of theology that is taught in Africa. A quick survey of several curricula of theological institutions reveals a general scheme that adopts a sevenfold division of subject areas, modelled on the western conventional theological curriculum both in terms of structure and content. This will typically include Biblical Studies, Theology and Philosophy, Ecclesiastical History, Religion and Missiology, Practical and Pastoral Studies, and Ethics.[44] This 'inherited model' has been perpetuated or upheld for several reasons. The degree and the mode of application, and the extent of the contextualisation of what was inherited differ from institution to institution. The Catholic faculties are notably much more progressive and pro-inculturation than Protestant institutions.

This is mainly because of the nature of the Catholic ecclesiastical polity and policies toward relating the traditional dogma to the local realities. It is considered a matter of principle to present Christian truth within cultural expressions. As we examine in this section how curriculum determines the teaching of African theology, we particularly have in mind Protestant institutions rather than Catholic ones.

With regard to theological education in the Southern region of Africa, Paul H. Gundani and his colleagues write that, "The history of theological education in the region has basically been characterised by foreignness, that is, foreign theological content, methodology and languages ... Theological education in the region has been captive to the North Atlantic worldview, and is showing little signs of struggle out of this form of oppression."[45] The story can be repeated from region to region throughout Africa. Oppression might be too strong a word to express this reality, but there is no doubt of the reality of western dominance in how theology is taught in nearly all parts of Africa. The perpetuation of the 'inherited model' has its reasons but also several problems. Nearly every theological institution, regardless of this, typically adopts it. A detailed treatment of the reasons for adoption is not possible in the given time and space. We can only mention a few which, among other factors, include lack of commitment, confessionalism, and conservatism that prefers the

---

[44]Joseph Galgalo and Esther Mombo, "Theological Education and Ecumenical Formation: Some Challenges," *Ecumenical Formation* 98/99 (July/October 2002): 7-14.

status quo, lack of expertise, and not least, lack of vision and dynamic leadership. While these are 'internal' or 'African' factors, there also are 'external' factors that contribute to the continued use of the 'inherited model.' Lack of resources, especially human, has, for example, made African theological institutions heavily dependent on 'imported' theological teachers.[46] They cannot be blamed for teaching what they know and the way they know it, for they cannot help but draw on their conceptual and linguistic repertoire. Even where Africanisation in terms of human resources is slowly gaining ground, the theological teachers are mainly western trained. This has generally not helped in the Africanisation of the curriculum. Almost exclusively western-oriented library resources further compound this, and determine to a great extent the theological method in the teaching of theology as well as its essential content.

This means that the teaching of theology in Africa is basically a perpetuation of 'western theological models.' The biggest problem with this is the 'hermeneutical gap.' This phrase refers to the reality that meaning can only be transferred between contexts with great difficulty. Western theological resources are a product of a totally different context from that of Africa, born out of theological reflections inspired by different situations in life, and expressed distinctively in the context of those situations. It is very difficult if not impossible to overcome this hermeneutical gap and understand or interpret meaning between situations that are so different. This difficulty perhaps accounts for the existing dichotomy between the church and the academy, where theories learnt in the academic institutions rarely find adequate application in pastoral settings. There is often also an observable gulf between orthodoxy and orthopraxis, an indication that the doctrines learnt have not, and possibly cannot, be fully integrated into the thought system of the African recipients. This is mainly because of the 'foreignness' of the western-oriented

---

[45]"The State of Theological Education in Southern Africa: Issues and Concerns," *Ecumenical Formation* 98/99 (July/October 2002): 67-75.

[46]Gundani, et al, "The State of Theological Education", 67.

theology that is taught in Africa, and the method of its delivery. This raises the question of the effectiveness, if not the relevance, of much of the theological content and the methodology of much of the theological enterprise in Africa. Many institutions are slowly awakening to this reality and are changing accordingly in spite of the slow pace of such change. There is now increasingly a growing Africanisation of the curriculum and of human resources and, with this Africanisation, a theological discussion is emerging that engages with the African situation. In the light of this slow but sure change, the direction it is taking, and what already exists, four different models or approaches to theological teachings in Africa can be drawn.

The four models represent two extreme approaches at the opposite ends with two moderate positions in the middle. The first of the two extreme approaches is what we may call the *minimalist model*. This approach gives complete priority to the African culture, African existential realities, and action for social justice and equality. These African realities are presented as the absolute criteria or framework against which everything can be explained and understood. The Bible and the traditional Christian theological heritage receive minimal and in most cases superficial treatment if they are used at all. Indeed, these are only used when and if they support the exponent's theological propositions, and if they fit within the perceived African cultural framework. In this sense, the tools of the social sciences are used as the heuristic key to interpret the African worldview, which provides the basic framework for the resulting theological discourse. One characteristic feature of this approach is its overboard polemic against everything western despite the irony of using one or the other of the western languages for the articulation of its own theology.

The opposite extreme is what we may call *conservative traditionalist model* which, as the name suggests, advocates support for perpetuation of existing theological traditions and schools of thought, and is generally suspicious of innovations with regard to theological interpretation. This approach builds almost exclusively on the inherited 'western-oriented' curriculum model. This approach normally holds a particular view of what is traditional and, therefore, the normative version of theological doctrines, sources and methods which must be preserved and faithfully perpetuated. This model does not generally accommodate progressive views that advocate support for contextual frameworks. It is generally oblivious of the impotence of its 'archaic' forms and worldviews for effective engagement with contemporary issues. This model is perhaps nowhere rigidly applied, but there is no doubt that it is the most dominant model.

Two other models, both more moderate compared to the first two are the *open-model* and the *broad-based* or *maximalist models*. The first recognises the Bible and the African context as the basis of its theological discourse. It is open to borrowing from any other context but none are considered to be normative or even necessary for the construction of what normally is referred to as 'authentic African Christian theology.' This approach may be narrow or broad in its focus depending on how the curriculum is designed and applied in teaching it.

The *broad-based model* or *maximalist model* demands maximum use of the Bible, the traditional Christian heritage, especially the Fathers, and the African context. For all practical purposes, this broad-based approach does better than all the others; not only because of its level-headedness but also the willingness to learn from all contexts and making the best of it in applying its lessons as may be contextually relevant.

Conclusion

There is no doubt that the theological curriculum is the most important of all the factors in the teaching of theology. It determines the content and to some extent how that content should be taught. It should therefore be given the attention it deserves by all stakeholders in theological education in Africa. In doing this, we must carefully distinguish two things: the essential content of Christian theology and the mode in which that content is expressed. We have no quarrel with the content of the 'western model' *per se*, but suggest that the kernel of the Christian truth contained in that model, be re-expressed in the thought forms and ways relevant and appropriate to the African context. There is a great deal to learn from the great western theological tradition, and African Christians must not be carried away in a reactionary mode to deny themselves this great heritage that is as much rightfully theirs as it is for any other context. It is with this in mind that we recommend that the curriculum to be re-written with an eye on the Bible, the Fathers, Christian theological heritage, and the African context. While some things will be optional, there should be at least two imperatives: preservation and faithful transmission of the *Regula Fidei*, and the re-expression of Christian truth in contextually relevant and workable forms. We must also guard against sacrificing the essentials at the altar of communicability.

One thing needs to be pointed out that hitherto has not been mentioned. While the curriculum has all sorts of factors that determine its content, theology (and by this we mean theological reflection and practice) seems to have a life of its own. There is a natural dynamism about theology that is seen to be at work in the life of the believer as exercised in devotion, reflection and other faith experiences. This manifests itself in various forms of expressions of faith – including Pentecostalism, charismatic spirituality, and the spirituality of the African Instituted Churches, which are becoming definitive for the contours of African Christianity. These movements seem to be more in touch with African realities than the 'western oriented' theology produced in our theological institutions. The irony is that most of the leaders of this vibrant African Christianity lack formal theological training and yet are greatly successful, if numbers are anything to go by. There must be something that they are getting right, or that is at least workable, which makes their methods more effective and their theology more appealing than that produced in our theological institutions.

This is all the more reason for us to consider the re-writing of curricula, the review of our theological methods, and the way we teach theology in Africa to be urgent tasks. Our 'orthodoxy' must be brought in line with our spirituality. It is of little comfort to possess the necessary theoretical knowledge regarding sound doctrine when such knowledge cannot be brought to bear on our worship, life of faith, and everyday living. While the laying of a sound doctrinal basis cannot be compromised, it is equally imperative that we bring doctrinal propositions to bear on the corresponding pastoral contexts in ways relevant and practical for that context. Therefore teachers of theology in Africa must bear in mind these two things: correct doctrine, and the application or 'contextualisation' of that doctrine. We cannot have one without the other, for doctrine without context remains mere theory, and 'contextualizing' without correct doctrine is misleading.

CHAPTER TWO

The Binding Power of the Text and the Context in which We Preach

János Pásztor

My wife and I have been deeply moved by your invitation to take part and read a paper at this anniversary conference celebrating 100 years of faithful ministry of St. Paul's United Theological College. We have also been affected deeply by walking around the houses and gardens of the College, which was our home for six years. When I first came here I used to say that my Christian faith was formed in the life of the Reformed Church in Hungary, which during the tumultuous post-war years experienced a revival movement. After returning to Hungary I kept saying that my Christian conviction was strengthened and transformed by sharing fellowship with Christians, especially the lecturers and students, of this College. I was deeply aware of the truth of the old Latin saying - *docendo discimus* - we teach through learning and we learn by teaching. Teaching and studying is a two way interaction in which teachers learn from the students as well as the other way around.

The history of Christianity in East Africa, the people who have come to Christ, and the churches' response to the dynamic events of colonial times, followed by political and social *Uhuru*, have taught us and deepened our understanding of the truth of Romans 1:16 that the gospel is the power of God both in terms of individual lives and also in the community. In other words the interaction between the Gospel and the particular East African context brought out significant peculiar characteristics which have proved significant for my church and also for other parts of the One Body of Christ.

Thus when, immediately after my return to Hungary, I was appointed professor of theology at the Debrecen theological faculty of my own church, it was natural for me to emphasize in my teaching the significance of the "context." Shortly afterward students gave me the nickname: "Dr. Context" or just "the fellow with the context." The things I learned in Kenya have been with me ever since.

Now having been here for several days listening to the lively and excellent presentation in this Consultation I have become even more deeply conscious of the significance of the context in preaching and teaching. The presentations have brought up the serious problems and challenges the church faces here with HIV/AIDS, social problems, care for the handicapped, and relations with Islam without which your proclamation of the Gospel would be like "a resounding gong or a clanging cymbal." (1 Corinthians 13:1)

However, let us make it clear that it is not the context that gives new birth and changes our lives, but the Word of God — the Divine Word that always addresses humans in a context. The ancient experience that God has spoken (*Deus dixit*), was given to Abraham, to Moses, and to the great prophets of the Old Testament who prepared the way for the coming of the Messiah. That Word has always been spoken in the midst of life. God's revelation did not come to his people in a heavenly helicopter flying around *above* the heads of people, but always in the *midst* of life full of miseries, dangers, threats and expectations. Therefore we have to emphasize that the context is part of the Word-Event. In order to see this, we have to remind ourselves that God the Saviour is God the Creator. He brought about the world and humans within it, thereby launching by the Word the series of events. The Word created heaven and earth with its inhabitants. By creating humans according to His image and the combination of events and reflection upon those events, history was launched, which is both the result and the venue of that event.

The rebellion of humans against the Creator did not bring about the destruction of humankind and its history, but became the venue of further word-Events in which God acted to save rebellious humankind from final self-destruction. Furthermore, due to the fact that the Divine Word is not just a means of oral communication, but the Second Person of the Trinity the word-Event includes not only God's voice but the very God himself. Therefore can Isaiah say: "In all their distress he, too, was distressed." (63:9). That was also made clear when the Glory of God (כבוד־יהוה) went to the Babylonian concentration camp to dwell, with the deported people of Israel (Ezekiel 10:18 & 11:15-16). God was with them. This series of events led to the ultimate realization of the Word in the Incarnation: "The Word became flesh and dwelled among us. We have seen his glory" (John 1:14). God the Creator and Saviour of the world became part of his creation and took upon himself the sins and the sufferings of the world. It is the Cross of Christ in which we can fully behold the significance of the context: people humiliated and killed their Saviour God. The Cross raised by humans and the body of the Saviour hanging on it, show the destructive power of sin but also the even greater power of salvation which is the full reality and significance of the context.

As the title of this paper suggests, we have really to face two contexts: one is that of the Word-Event itself; the other is the context in which we live and preach in our own days.

On the one hand, what we have said about the theological significance of the context should make it clear for us that the thorough study of the text including its literary, social-political background is absolutely necessary for the understanding of the text.

At the same time, while doing this, we cannot step out of ourselves or out of the context in which we live. It is not possible to approach the text without ourselves being biased by our own situations and problems. Bultmann called this fact the "pre-understanding" of which we have to be aware. The pre-understanding can be so strong that our own thoughts, ideas, joy or tensions are forcefully read into the text. And so we must be cautious. We have to be clear that the feelings and analyses of our own time or those of the contemporary scene of the text do not give us the answer. The answer is given by the Word of God brought alive by the Holy Spirit. The intellectual work of analysing the text is not a replacement of the work of the Holy Spirit. At the same time the Holy Spirit does not replace this intellectual effort but saves it and directs it. Without this enlightening and encouraging work of the Holy Spirit our efforts are unable to lead us to the light.[1]

Under the guidance of the Spirit a dynamism develops in which the context is intrinsically bound up with the word and so the text and the context interact. The situation of the ancient days might enlighten certain problems of today. At the same time the experience of biblical times can help us to understand our own situation. This interaction is not limited to discovering certain similarities between then and now, although there are many. It also makes clear the differences. That is how the two horizons interact[2] and mutually enlighten one another under the guidance of the Holy Spirit. In the course of this dynamic event the preacher is drawn into the original Word-Event and becomes a contemporary of it, and then is able to take the congregation along. That is why St. Paul can write to the

---

[1] In the African context the serious study of the text makes it absolutely necessary to translate the Bible into local languages, not from English, but from the original text. As long as translators are dependent on the English Bible there is still a remnant of colonialism. It was a joy to meet the minister who is working on the revision of the translation of the New Testament from the Greek text into Kikuyu.

[2] Anthony C. Thiselton, *The Two Horizons: New Testament Hermeneutics and Philosophical Description with Special Reference to Heidegger, Bultmann, Gadamer and Wittgenstein* (Grand Rapids: Eerdmans, 1980).

Galatians: "Before your very eyes Jesus Christ was clearly portrayed as crucified" (Galatians 3:1). In the same way it was also sung by the descendants of the African slaves coming to Christ in America: "Were you there, when they crucified my Lord? Yes, I was there and my heart trembled" (Afro-American spiritual).

Therefore preacher and congregation should be one in their prayer in direct relation to the sermon:

Come Holy Ghost Our hearts inspire;
Let us Thine influence prove.

We have already stated that the Word-Event takes place in the world. Within the world, however, God has brought into life a new community, the Church, which is - in analogy with the creation of the world - both the result and the venue of the creating activity of the Word of God. The Church consists of people who have heard, accepted, and responded to the Word by their whole existence: body, soul, intellect, will, and emotions. After his resurrection Jesus Christ gave his peace to the disciples: he called them to himself and then sent them out into the world. Before the Day of Pentecost this group is in the process of being, as it were, in the mother's womb. The people who received this sending (John 20:21-22) represented the whole church of the future. "It is not ordination to a position of authority within the church for an internal ministry, but it is not excluded. The disciples, and the whole Church after them, carry on the mission of Christ which he received from the Father" - says Bishop Newbigin[3]. Accordingly the preacher is within this community, which has been given the mission, and not above it. At the same time he is in line with the servants of the word representing a historical succession and continuity which is guaranteed in some churches as the succession of bishops, by others

---

[3] Lesslie Newbigin, *The Light Has Come: An Exposition of the Fourth Gospel.*(Grand Rapids: Eerdmans, 1982), 270.

as the historical apostolic succession of the whole ministry.[4] The significance of the ministry of leadership is twofold: it enables the mission of the whole community (Ephesians 4:11-12), and also proclaims the Gospel with the full vigour of personal, oral communication in close communion with the whole church (Acts 2:14), which is itself an active participant of the same proclamation (Philippians 2:15-19).

The life and witness of the Church is summed up in Acts 2:37-47 which is the description of the communion (êïéíùíßá) of the disciples. This is both an ontological and a functional communion. It is ontological because the participants are in close union with Christ.[5] They died with Him in baptism in order that they might live in his resurrected life. To be in Christ (åí ×ñéóôþ) means to live a fully new life. It is also functional, because the people in Christ are continually engaged in listening to the apostolic teaching and taking part in the Eucharist, the prayers and taking care of one another (äéáêïíßá). The four functions cannot be separated from one another: the proclamation of the word in its fullness includes the proclamation of Christ in action through being fed by the body and blood of Christ (1Corinthians 11:26b).[6] It means the experience of being looked after and helped by the Lord. As we pass the bread and the wine we offer and share God's life-giving gifts with one another. And the whole movement is inconceivable without prayer. This is the life of the congregation in helping and maintaining one another. Thus their activity is part of the full proclamation of Christ.

The role of the ordained minister is crucial in all this. Here we are dealing with the task of continuing the apostolic teaching, but

---

[4]Hans Küng, *Die Kirche* (Freiburg-Basel-Wien: Herder, 1969), 408-429. Available also in English translation: *The Church*.

[5]Lesslie Newbigin, *The Gospel in a Pluralist Society* (London: SPCK, 1989), 117, 136.

[6]It has been made clear that the full Christian worship includes communion. This is based on the Scripture and was also emphasized by Calvin who said it was the invention of the Devil not to have communion every Sunday.

are reminded that the context is the congregation and fourfold activity is essential.

Last but not least, let us turn now to the subject of the text itself. The text is a portion of the Holy Scripture of Old and New Testaments. Each text is related to the other. Both parts proclaim Christ. The Old Testament does this in terms of preparation and promise. The Gospels proclaim the ultimate fulfilment of the promises in Christ. The Epistles reflect upon the Christ-Event and draw the theological and practical conclusions. Each text is to be examined in relation to all these aspects. If the Old Testament is neglected, it is easy - as has happened in the course of church history very often - to interpret a New Testament text using concepts and ideas alien to the Scriptures.[7]

In the history of preaching we often find so-called topical sermons which might take certain biblical concepts, but the preacher puts them together not according to the dynamic of the text, but follows wilfully his or her own logic. Some of these might make a good lecture on a biblical concept but such a sermon is outside of the binding power of the text. The temptation to fall into a trap of building upon human wisdom is too great. The most important problem here is that the preacher wants to be the master of the topic (as a rhetor is and should be) rather than being a servant of the Word as she or he should be.[8] The church fathers -

---

[7] In the Church of Europe heathen concepts were used as hermeneutical keys without testing those in the whole of Scripture. The most significant of these was and still is the dualism of Greek philosophy which divided creation into visible and invisible, the latter being regarded as truly real. The most extreme of these ideas was in the various Gnostic sects. According to these the God of the Old Testament is not identical with the Father of Jesus Christ who was conceived as coming to liberate humans from the bondage of bodily existence. That is why it is so significant that the Creed confesses the resurrection of the body and why, from the 2nd century onward, the Eucharistic liturgies included thanksgiving for both Creation and Redemption.

[8] Although the common practice was to preach a whole book in continuous reading (*lectio continua*), we must also acknowledge that there have been topical sermons faithfully enlightening aspects of the Gospel.

St. Augustine, St. Chrysostom, St. Bernard of Clairvaux, just as later the Reformers following their practice, preached textually-based sermons.

In talking about the binding power of the text we follow their example. The text preached is a well-defined portion of the Scriptures, which gives us the point of access in the Bible. In the course of my preparation I get involved in a text that speaks about a particular part of the One Christ-Event. It is my task to discover how an individual text is connected with and related to the One Event. It will, then, direct me, enlighten me, and lead me. Approaching the text without prayerful reliance on the Holy Spirit it is possible to be arbitrary with the text in various ways such as taking it out of the context[9] and putting it together with other portions artificially. This is manipulation. One can prove anything out of the Bible, but the Bible does not approve of many things.[10] The only way of avoiding the temptation to manipulation is obedient listening: "Speak, LORD, your servant is listening" (1Samuel 3:10). This listening takes place in prayerful and disciplined listening to the dynamics of the text. Every text in the Bible - even in the wisdom literature or apostolic teaching - is related to the One Event. The Name above every name has to be uttered. We preach Christ (2 Corinthians 4:5), but we do so within the particular movement of our text.

The question arises of how we preach Christ if the text does not mention the Name. This is to be discovered in the course of preparation. This question often arises in the case of Old Testament text.

In Europe there has been a traditional neglect of Old Testament texts by some preachers or a tendency to interpret them in the light

---

[9]This temptation is very strong in the case of short texts. If the context of the text is not taken into consideration, misinterpretation is very likely. If the context is taken into consideration it is seen to be a part of the text and should be read as such.

[10]A primitive example: It is written in Psalm 14: "There is no God", if the first part of verse 1 is left out: "The fool says in his heart."

of Greek philosophy. This temptation can be avoided by taking the Old Testament events seriously within their own context. They speak about God's dealing with His chosen people and offer many analogies with the New Testament. It is the same God who speaks and His dealing with His people shows the same characteristics as the New. The New Testament is not a replacement of the Old Testament or a dualistic spiritualization of the Old, but the continuation of the story of the People of God in the light of the ultimate fulfilment in Christ. There is a structural analogy between the two Testaments. Both witness to the encounter with God, who deeply hides and reveals Himself, This hidden and self-revealing God is at work in the Old Testament as in Jesus of Nazareth. His acts are of judgement and grace, in which grace overcomes judgement. There is a relation of correspondence (Gerhard von Rad). Therefore it is possible to discern God's ways of dealing with humans in both Testaments. There is an historical Exodus analogous to the coming eschatological one. There was a suffering Servant of the Lord in the Old Testament just as on the Cross. This is the basis of biblical typology as opposed to the mystical/ speculative typology of Eastern religions[11].

In the course of this consideration I must refer to the example of Karl Barth's teaching and practice of preaching. He was never a scholar closed in his study inventing doctrines for the church, but he proclaimed the Christ-Event as the only hope of humankind. He as a professor was a regular preacher in the Basel prison. He taught the text as an organic unity, as a body with its own inner dynamics. He believed that it was the task of the preacher to discover the movement of the text. In order to make this discovery we must once again refer to the importance of thorough exegesis under the enlightening guidance of the Holy Spirit. In doing this we shall find many analogies with our own situation and will

---

[11]Contrary to this, allegory is something not rooted in event, but in speculation. St. Paul speaks about allegory in Gal 4:21-31. However, even here he finds analogies, types, in Hagar and Isaac. J.B. Lightfoot, *Saint Paul's Epistle to the Galatians* (London: Macmillan, 1884), 180ff.

understand more and more deeply that Christ is the Saviour within our own situation who meets us in the context in which we live.

I hope I have been able to convey my conviction that we—ministers of the Word of God—have the privilege of being involved in the Word-Event which is Christ-Event, that every sermon we preach should be part of that which began when God spoke: "Let there be light" for us and for the people among whom and with whom we serve today in East Africa and elsewhere.

CHAPTER THREE

Current Issues in Biblical Interpretation

Musa W. Dube

Introduction

I have been asked to give a paper on 'current issues in biblical interpretation especially within the African continent.' I have discovered, however, that in the past four years there has been an explosion of such papers – a fact which itself tells us something important about what is currently going on.[1] Given this explosion of 'mapping' papers dealing with African biblical studies, I did not feel that I needed

---

[1] To list just a few, the *Journal of Theology for Southern Africa* 108 (2000) was a special issue, on *Reading the Bible in Africa*. One of the notable papers on current issues in African biblical studies in that issue is Justin Ukpong's "Developments in Biblical Interpretation in Africa." Part one of The *Bible in Africa: Transactions, Trajectories and Trends* (Leiden: Brill, 2000), a volume of 64 articles that I co-edited with Gerald West, features five evaluative articles on biblical studies in Africa. Here, we have Ukpong's paper re-presented (pp. 11-28); Gerald West's paper "Mapping African Biblical Interpretation: A Tentative Sketch," (pp. 29-53); Knut Holter's "Old Testament Scholarship in Sub-Saharan Africa, North of Limpopo River" (pp. 54-71); and Grant LeMarquand's, "New Testament Exegesis in Modern Africa" (pp. 72-102). Turning to a volume edited by Mary Getui, Knut Holter and Victor Zinkuratire, *On Interpreting the Old Testament in Africa* (New York: Peter Lang / Nairobi: Acton, 2001), we find Knut Holter's paper on "The Current State of Old Testament Scholarship in Africa: Where we are at the Turn of the Century?" (pp. 27-39). A volume that came out in 2002 opens with Chris Ukachukwu Manus' detailed paper on, "Methodological Approaches in Contemporary African Biblical Scholarship: The Case of West Africa." *Reading the Bible in the Global Village*, a volume that came from the Society of Biblical Literature International Meeting held

to write yet another paper on the same subject. Two aspects, however, have not been sufficiently highlighted.

First, there was a lack of an evaluative paper on Feminist biblical studies in Africa, which I believe represents the cutting edge at the moment.[2] The volume *Other Ways of Reading: African Women and the Bible*[3] is truly a ground breaking work not only in African biblical studies but in biblical studies in general. The particular contribution of African women is in terms of methodological and theoretical innovations as they begin to try and apply new methods and theories such as storytelling, divination, post-colonial, *bosadi*/womanhood, post-apartheid Black feminist readings and to address issues of gender and colonialism in African biblical translations. Nonetheless, I have found that most evaluative studies hardly do justice to African women's work. This is one paper that needs doing.

The second aspect that appeared missing was an evaluation that gives a clear worldwide map of biblical studies and how African biblical studies fits into that picture. What I will do in this presentation is the latter; namely I will speak about current issues in biblical studies globally and attempt to locate African biblical studies within that map. Yet there is another reason why I want to focus on this angle - because the teaching of biblical studies that uses Western methods in Africa is still using historical criticism almost exclusively, indicating little or no awareness of the major changes that have been taking place globally in the past forty years.

---

in Cape Town, features two 'mapping' papers, "Reading the Bible in a Global Village" (pp. 9-40), by Ukpong, and my own "Villagizing, Globalizing, and Biblical Studies: Issues and Challenges From African Readings" (pp. 41-64). Both of these papers are evaluative essays which highlight trends in African biblical studies and raise issues of concern.

[2]T. S. Maluleke., "Half a Century of African Theologies," *Journal of Theology for Southern Africa* 99 (1991): 4-22.

[3]Musa W. Dube, ed. (Geneva: WCC Publications / Atlanta: SBL, 2001).

Biblical Exegesis and Hermeneutics

In the past, scholars made a strict distinction between biblical exegesis and hermeneutics. Exegesis was the discipline of 'taking out meaning' from the text, which demanded that the interpreter should be neutral and disinterested. Readers were to avoid *eisegesis*, that is, reading into the text their own perspectives. The task of the reader/interpreter was to bring out the 'original meaning' of the text as the 'author intended' it. The exegete was thus trained in biblical languages and in the social context of the text, and was interested in the author or the world of the biblical text. The exegete further referred to other texts of the day which were related to the biblical text and context, for they could illumine the 'original meaning' of the text and the 'author's intention.' From this exegetical point of view, it was assumed, any of us, if properly trained to avoid *eisegesis*, could bring out the same meaning of the text. We could find one meaning.

Hermeneutics on the other hand was interpretation. It allowed the reader to examine the text with theological concerns for contemporary context. Such a division has been found to be false. Disinterested exegesis is not possible, for even the scholars who claimed to be reading as neutral subjects showed themselves to be reading through their particular social settings. The scholars who propounded and claimed to practise 'proper' exegesis were, by and large, white males of the so-called first world. Their supposedly neutral exegesis was found to be informed by their class, race, gender, and various church traditions. For example, even when scholars were supposedly doing a 'neutral' and disinterested exegesis, there were still Catholic, Lutheran, Anglican, Wesleyan scholars and their works varied, reflecting the influence of their church traditions. Further, their very insistence on a neutral reading that would produce one universal meaning regardless of cultural differences, showed itself to be an ideology that promoted such things as European imperialism and gender oppression.

The appearance of 'minority' readers on the scholarly scene at the end of the 1960s and beginning of the 70s was instrumental in changing biblical studies. Women and feminist readers found the so-called neutral exegesis to be gender biased, propounding readings that protected patriarchal institutions and reinforced the marginalization of women. Third World readers exposed this scholarship to be classist and imperialist, protecting the interests of the exploitative economic policies of their countries. Black African-American readers showed this neutral and scientific scholarship to be racist, suppressing the Black presence in the Bible. Homosexual readers exposed heterosexual readers as homophobic and oppressive to their sexual orientation. Migrants, refugees, or people who live in the Diaspora showed that the questions they bring to the text are not questions of a detached disinterested approach, but are indeed shaped by their social experiences of living in foreign lands, and, mostly, occupying positions of powerlessness. The debunking of the standard academic study of the Bible was thus directly linked to the coming in of minority readers from different social standing such as women, Two-Thirds World, African-Americans, homosexuals, immigrants, and so on. It is on these grounds that Fernando Segovia has described the current changes in biblical studies as a process of decolonization and liberation.[4]

Neutral and disinterested exegesis of the biblical text, designed to 'take out' the 'author's original meaning' has been declared to be impossible wishful thinking that only succeeds in imposing the interpretation of the powerful and suppressing powerless readers under the banner of objective reading. Such apparently neutral readings are now regarded as making a 'rhetorical claim,' intended to persuade readers. Such claims are not equivalent to producing 'facts.' Biblical scholarship today recognizes that all reading is interpretation, all reading is hermeneutics. In short, every interpreter inevitably uses her or his social standing or social location to bring out the meaning of the biblical text. All interpretation, therefore, is some form of construction of the text and of the self/reader.

---

[4]See Fernando Segovia, "And They Began to Speak in Other Tongues": Competing Modes of Discourse in Contemporary Biblical Criticism," pp. 1-32 in Fernando Segovia and Mary Ann Tolbert., *Reading From This Place Volume 1: Social Location and Biblical Interpretation in the United State* (Minneapolis: Fortress Press, 1995).

Social Location and Biblical Interpretation

By 'social location' I refer to the following factors: First, the social construction of one's biological factors. This includes gender, race, sexual orientation, ethnicity, motherhood, or any other physical or biological trait. Second, social location includes one's social standing in terms of the material factors of the world, one's position with regard to economic institutions of power. This includes family, church or religious affiliation, education, class, ethnicity and nationality.[5] An individual's social location includes, therefore, both the social construction of one's biological factors and of one's relation to material or economic institutions. These factors are, of course, closely intertwined.

Every person is obviously located differently depending on their varying social relations, their place in social structures, and social circumstances. For example, people of male gender, white race, heterosexuality, respected ethnic groups, mothers, and Christian religion, tend to be more or less empowered to speak and to be heard, for most societies give high values to social categories.[6] On the other hand, people of female gender, Black race, homosexuals, despised ethnic groups, barren women, short and fat people will be more or less disempowered, for most societies tend to give negative values to these features. People with these social factors are thus less empowered to speak, or to be heard in the society.

When it comes to material or economic institutions, those who are married, who belong to the Christian religion (especially if they are in mainline churches), who have a higher education, higher class, and are from 'first world' nations are generally empowered. On the other hand, an unmarried person, a non-Christian or member of an African

---

[5] See Mary Ann Tolbert, "The Politics and Poetics of Location," pp. 305-17 in *Reading From this Place Volume 1*, for further explanation of the concept of social location to which my exposition is highly indebted.

[6] Please note that the values accorded to various social factors are not the same in every society nor do they remain permanent. For example, while marriage was a source of empowerment in patriarchal worlds, in the current days, it may no longer signify empowerment since more and more women are now capable of entering the public arena and earning a living for themselves.

Independent Church, someone with a low education, or from a lower social class, or from a Third World nation is more or less disempowered. Such people do not have easy access to power that allows them to speak or to be heard—I am not saying they have no power. Most people have a mixture of social factors, which empowers and disempowers them. Some are more empowered than others.

So how and why is a reader's social location important in biblical studies? In the act of reading, every reader needs to understand her or his own social factors—where one is oppressed and where one is an oppressor; where one is empowered and where one is disempowered. Let me illustrate this by outlining the factors of my social location. To begin with that which empowers me, I am a mother of a son, married, educated, and middle class. I teach in the highest institution of learning in my country, the University of Botswana, and I belong to an established Christian church. I now work for a large ecumenical body, the World Council of Churches, with a huge title the "HIV/AIDS and theological consultant in mission." All these social factors lend me authority to speak and to be heard in my society and international forums. However, the following factors disempower me: my Blackness, Africanness, femaleness, my Third World status, lack of ethnic group in Botswana, and the fact that I also belong to African Religions.

With these varied social factors I am sometimes powerful and sometimes powerless, depending on where I am. For example, in my numerous travels, especially flying to Western countries, I become consciously aware of my Blackness and the mistrust it evokes. I am subjected to intense interrogation and searching, either because I am suspected of trying to go and work in a 'first world' country, or feared for bringing disease and drugs. In short my identity is complex and fluid. In some settings I will be disempowered, while in other settings I may be privileged, depending on which factors of my identity would be influential at that particular time. This complexity and fluidity of one's identity is a reality that is beginning to be emphasised in biblical scholarship today, for all the factors of one's social location come into play during the process of reading and all inform one's interpretation of the Bible.

The importance of social location in biblical interpretation pertains to the fact that we are all socially located. Our social standing inevitably informs how we interpret the world or any texts. What a reader sees in the text, what a reader does not see in the text, and what a reader expounds as the meaning of a text is dependent on one's class, gender, church, religion, education, training, race, sexual orientation, ethnic, family, first/third status and so on. Your social location informs your biblical interpretation. The implications of social location to all interpretation are also obvious: If we have people from a similar social group reading, they will interpret from their own point of view and suppress people and interpretations of different social locations. All groups, of various social locations, must, therefore, be actively involved in the institutions of biblical interpretation to avoid oppression and to enable meaningful dialogue to proceed.

The centrality of social location to interpretation also means that the process of reading and producing meaning involves more than the Bible, or texts. It also involves the reader and her or his world. It is a process whereby the reader and the text both produce meaning. Whereas in the past, biblical exegesis focused on studying the text and its social location alone, by encouraging the reader to assume a neutral stance we now need to study the reader as well, to understand the reader's context in order to understand and appreciate his or her interpretation, its strength and its shortcomings. In short, the reader has become an alive, active, and interested exegete.

Yet, as I said, the reader who is a teacher is also institutionally located in particular church, university, seminary, or religion and this will affect the type of educational training he or she gives to individuals. Institutions train people to read in certain ways which are approved by them. Let me venture to generalize here: I believe that most European biblical schools are still very much grounded in historical critical methods, which insists on neutrality and disinterested reading of biblical texts. It follows that people trained there will remain oblivious of other methods unless they make the effort to educate themselves further. People trained in this school of reading may not appreciate other ways of reading. In short, institutions give us certain presuppositions and questions that are brought to the text. Each method used determines the assumptions and questions a reader brings to the biblical texts. For example, questions asked by narrative criticism are different from those of source criticism. Each method of reading, therefore, determines to a large extent the kind of answers a reader will get from the process of interpretation. Learning various methods of reading is advantageous for several reasons. First, it allows a reader to choose a method that best suits the concerns of their social location. Second, it allows a reader to communicate with scholars writing from different methodological perspectives.

If one is sent to schools whose methods do not reflect openness to the diversity readers, or to be more blunt, school that use methods of upper class, white males, it may stifle one's interest in biblical studies since the methods are designed to ask questions of a certain class other than your own concerns and world.[7] This, I believe, partly explains the divergence of many Sub-Saharan African scholars, who were trained in the West as biblical exegetes in historical methods. The bulk of these scholars (you can name them: John Mbiti, John Pobee, Kwesi Dickson) diverted from historical critical training after graduate studies. They came to focus on inculturation hermeneutics and Black biblical hermeneutics. In the light of what is now known about historical criticism, it is now evident that most African scholars trained in historical criticism found that the methods they learnt did not allow them even to begin to ask questions about their social location, since that would amount to *eisegesis*. Fortunately, a wide range of methods of reading the Bible have now come into existence.

Methods and Theories in Biblical Interpretation

In the area of method, the field of biblical interpretation experienced an explosion of various methods and theories that are used in the process of producing meaning. This is attested by numerous books that have

---

[7]See Gerald West and Musa W. Dube, "An Introduction: How We Have Come to Read With," pp. 10-15 in *Semeia 73: "Reading With": An Exploration of the Interface Between Critical and Ordinary Readings of the Bible* (Atlanta: Scholars Press, 1996) where I discuss the professional death that comes upon Third World scholars who are trained in methods that stifle their own questions.

attempted to describe and apply the methods for the guild. Good examples of such books are: *To Each Its own Meaning: An Introduction to Biblical Criticisms and Their Applications* edited by Stephen L. McKenzie and Stephen Haynes;[8] *Mark and Method: New Approaches to Biblical Studies* edited by Janice Capel Anderson and Stephen Moore;[9] *The Postmodern Bible*;[10] *Judges and Method: New Approaches in Biblical Studies* edited by Gale A. Yee,[11] and *Searching the Scriptures* edited by Elisabeth Schüssler Fiorenza.[12] Following Fernando F. Segovia's classification, I will briefly summarize biblical methods and theories under three paradigms; namely: the Historical Paradigm, the Literary Paradigm and the Cultural Paradigm.[13] Each of these paradigms consists of various methods and theories of interpretation. Since my aim is not to repeat what has been well documented elsewhere, I shall just briefly describe and outline these methods and theories of reading the Bible.

Historical Paradigm
This paradigm consists of methods and theories that are now characterised as traditional exegesis. The methods advocated neutral and disinterested reading. The methods were concerned with bringing out the "original meaning' of the text or of the 'author's intention.' The method required that one should be familiar with the ancient biblical world that gave us the text and where the author resided. The scholar was meant to build a bridge across the cultural, time and space gap between the contemporary reader and the ancient texts. The text was thus seen as the 'means' or

---

[8](Louisville: Westminster / John Knox, 1993).
[9](Minneapolis: Fortress, 1992).
[10]The Bible and Culture Collective, *The Postmodern Bible* (New Haven and London: Yale University Press, 1995).
[11](Minneapolis: Fortress, 2003).
[12]Elisabeth Schüssler Fiorenza, *Searching the Scriptures. Volume 1: A Feminist Introduction* (New York: Crossroad, 1993).
[13]See Fernando Segovia, "And They Began to Speak in Other Tongues" pp. 1-32 in Fernando Segovia and Mary Ann Tolbert, eds. *Reading From This Place Volume 1: Social Location and Biblical Interpretation in the United States* (Minneapolis: Fortress Press, 1995) for further details of changes in biblical studies and the currents instigating them. My exposition is highly indebted to his.

'window' to the ancient world. Exegesis was thus an act of constantly trying to peer behind the text; an attempt to hear and see the ancient people in their daily lives. Up until the sixties the historical paradigm was the major approach that dominated biblical studies. It still remains the main approach of many schools of religion and seminaries. Under the umbrella of historical paradigm, the following methods are included: source criticism, textual criticism, form criticism, composition criticism, redaction criticism, canon criticism.

I am sure that many of you who have undergone biblical studies have learnt and applied these methods. For a long time these were the methods that marked academic biblical training. Indeed in many institutions, these are still regarded as the only method of biblical scholarship. However, this historical paradigm has shifted to include what is called a literary paradigm of biblical reading.

Literary Paradigm
The methods and theories of the literary paradigm entered biblical interpretation largely in the 1960s, coming from secular departments of literature. This paradigm notably laid emphasis on the text as a sufficient mode of communication used by the author to communicate to his or her audience or readers. Since the text was a sufficient medium of communication, biblical interpreters began to be trained in techniques and theories used by a narrative to communicate its message to its reader. This method asks such questions as, 'How does the story mean?'[14] It was no longer particularly important to study the ancient world behind the text or to seek the 'author's meaning' or 'the original meaning', unless one was using such methods as rhetorical analysis or examining ancient narrative genres. Readers were now largely concerned with the narrative world and how it functions. The literary paradigm focused on the world of the text itself and how it communicates to the reader

---

[14]See Elisabeth Malbon, "Narrative Criticism: How Does the Text Mean?" pp. 23-49 in Janice Capel Anderson and Stephen Moore eds. *Mark and Method: New Approaches to Biblical Studies* (Minneapolis: Fortress Press, 1992).

effectively or persuasively. This latter word suggests that the text was meant to have an 'effect' or to 'persuade' the reader, a fact that was exposing the requirement to be 'neutral', 'disinterested', and 'detached' to be a violent contradiction against 'the original intention' of the ancient author. Ancient authors (like all authors) used techniques to involve our minds and emotions to arouse a certain understanding from the reader. In short, biblical studies began to focus on both the text and the reader. The text as a medium of communication depended upon certain inherent qualities of the text.

As this paradigm developed, various theories of readers and texts introduced the question of who really produces meaning. 'How do people actually read?' 'Where is meaning found?' 'Is meaning in the text or in the reader?' Some theories gave more power to the text; others gave more power to the reader, while others gave a balance of power to both the text and the reader. In any case, focusing on the ancient world of the text and the author, behind the text; or seeking the original and intended meaning of the author, was no longer the exclusive focus of academic biblical studies. Exegetes could now be content to read on the surface of the text, to treat the text as a mirror and to resurrect the reader into life in the process of exegesis.

The literary paradigm includes the following methods and theories of reading: narrative (literary) criticism, ideological criticism, rhetorical criticism (ancient Greek rhetoric), genre criticism (biography, novel or Romance), structuralist theories, reader-response theories, psychoanalytical theories, postcolonial theories.

Cultural Paradigm
This paradigm tends to use sophisticated theories and models of analysis to read the text as a social artefact, to be decoded properly, in order to understand the social worlds that produced it. It recognises the presence of a real reader, only to suppress it in the process of producing meaning. The paradigm has contributed immensely in illuminating the social context that gave us the biblical text and the ideologies inscribed in the texts. The cultural paradigm includes the following methods and theories

of reading: social description, sociological analysis, Marxist readings, cultural anthropology, archaeological excavation and analysis.

The presuppositions and questions of some of these methods closely befriend the historical method, which insists on a neutral and disinterested reader, and whose main job is to let the ancient text speak in its own terms. Cultural anthropology's models of reading, for example, insist on a disinterested reader. Unlike historical criticism, these methods have their own theoretical sophistication in their investigation of the ancient text and its world.

Multiple Meanings of the Biblical Text

With these changes in biblical studies, it is now largely recognized that *there is no single meaning to any one particular text*. There can be as many interpretations of a biblical passage as there are its readers and the methods, that is, *multiple meanings*. Consequently, biblical studies is becoming concerned with such questions as 'determinacy and interdeterminacy of texts' and 'autobiographical' interpretation.[15] Further, if all reading is socially conditioned, academic interpretations may be no 'better' than readings of untrained readers. Subaltern interpretations are as important as the academic readings. This, however, does not mean than all readings or interpretations are equally useful. It does mean that we can no longer easily claim that academic readings are the only legitimate or less dangerous readings of the Bible, without perhaps, privileging a class of the educated.

Many of these new methods and concerns in biblical studies are discussed in the experimental journal of biblical studies called, *Semeia*. For example, *Semeia Volume 73*, entitled, "Reading With" African Overtures: The Exploration of the Interface Between Critical and Ordinary Readings of the Bible," is a volume that indicates the acknowledgement of non-academic readers of biblical texts in the academic arena. In other words, if all reading is a construction which takes place between the text and the self, what reason could there be to

---

[15]Janice Capel Anderson and Jeffrey Staley, eds. "Taking It Personally: Autobiographical Biblical Criticism," *Semeia* 72 (Atlanta: Scholars Press, 1995).

privilege academic readings? Academic readings are simply those readings which are carried out by those who have been trained to ask particular questions. The issue of the journal was also a victory for African scholars since they had a chance to make their voices heard in a scholarly forum of the West - a rare opportunity, given that biblical studies still operates within the one way traffic channel of the global economy.

One of the most recent methods of reading, which is also linked with minority readers, is a post-colonial approach. Post-colonial theories of reading see a link between texts and imperialism and they also seek to read from various perspectives to expose how texts promote imperialism and how the colonized also use texts to resist. Such readings also focus on the hybrid nature of cultures which resist imperial claims of superiority. In one of the latest issues of *Semeia, Volume 75,* postcolonial theories were formally introduced to the world of biblical scholarship. Obviously Postcolonialism is a subject that is closely related to our world in Africa and hence its theories of reading should be of considerable interest to African scholars and other Third World people. I happen to be interested in this methodological approach. Indeed, my dissertation was written from this theoretical perspective.[16]

Semeia 78: Reading the Bible as Women: Perspectives From Africa, Asia, and Latin America, discusses the reader, text and method as well as providing an introduction to non-Western biblical readers. The Third World social location of the scholars in this volume brings

---

[16]See Musa W. Dube Shomanah, "Towards a Postcolonial Feminist Interpretation of the Bible" (Ann Arbor: UMI, 1997) now published as Musa W. Dube, *Postcolonial Feminist Interpretation of the Bible* (St. Louis: Chalice Press, 2000). See also my two articles "Reading for Decolonization (John 4:1-42), pp. 37-59 in *Semeia 75: Postcolonialism and Scriptural Reading* (Atlanta: Scholars Press, 1996); and "Towards A Post-colonial Interpretation of the Bible" pp. 11-23 in *Semeia 78: Reading the Bible as Women: Perspectives From Africa Asia and Latin America* (Atlanta: Scholars Press, 1997): 11-23.

new questions to the texts and to the methods of academic biblical scholarship.

Ethics and Accountability in Biblical Studies

This explosion of readers, theories and methods in the past forty years has left biblical interpretation without an easily recognised central standard. It is therefore inevitable that a number of questions will be raised. 'Are all biblical interpretations equally important and valid?' 'How does one decide if a biblical reading is acceptable or unacceptable?' 'Does anything go?' These concerns have brought the question of the *ethics of biblical interpretation* onto the scene. An interpretation will be judged by its impact and persuasiveness. The question to ask now is, 'What is the use and contribution of this interpretation?' 'Does it further illuminate the meaning of the text?' 'Is it persuasive, or can it be defended?' 'Does this interpretation contribute to the liberation of the oppressed?' 'Is it oppressive to some other groups?' As it has been recently argued, a current trend in biblical studies affirms the 'legitimacy' of the interpretations of 'ordinary readers' from different social locations and seeks to encourage and promote such readings. What would happen, Glancy asks, if such a stance were taken in the case of 'real reader' like the racist Senator Davidson? An uncritical biblical pluralism that defers to popular readings without taking account of the social and political effects of those readings, she cautions, is likely to repeat and reinscribe the liabilities of the readings.[17]

Glancy's ethical concerns are legitimate. Many deadly interpretations have been propounded by popular readings. At the same time, critical scholars of the Bible have, and are still involved, in propounding some of the most deadly interpretations that re-inscribe imperialism, apartheid, anti-Semitism and gender discrimination partly because all interpretations are 'partial visions' and partly because most readers are unaware that they read from their social locations and for their own interest. Biblical studies thus recognises the diversity of readers

---
[17]Cheryl J. Exum and Stephen D. Moore, eds. *Biblical Studies/Cultural Studies: The Third Sheffield Colloquium* (Sheffield: Sheffield Academic Press, 1998), 37.

and interpretations but is struggling to come to terms with the reality that this diversity also entails 'accountability' to those of one's neighbour. *An acceptable reading, therefore, should not only be persuasive, useful, defensible, and contribute to knowledge – it must also be liberating.*

In sum, biblical studies is now characterised by readers from diverse backgrounds, who use diverse methods, and engage in intense dialogue and which requires accountability to other groups. Biblical interpretation is now about reading the text/s, reading the reader/s, reading the method/s, and a call to propound readings that strive to respect the human dignity of all people. Every biblical interpreter must, therefore, put the above questions to her or his reading of a text, regardless of the fact that one is a popular or critical reader. That ethical concerns have become an essential aspect of biblical interpretation is attested by the recent *Semeia 77: The Bible and Ethics of Reading,* which challenges every reader to interpret with 'the face of the other' and 'to face up to a weighty responsibility.'[18]

Biblical Interpretations in Africa

Almost all, if not all, Black African biblical scholars of the last twenty years were trained in Western schools of religion and seminaries steeped in the historical critical methods of biblical studies. Yet the assessment of their works indicates that most of them took a different approach from their training. Let me divide African biblical scholarship in two categories, as it is commonly done: Sub-Saharan scholars in countries above South Africa and South African scholarship.[19] The former hermeneutical approach has been given such names as indigenisation, inculturation, incarnation, Africanisation, contextualisation, and adaptation. This scholarship departed from the methods of Western schools in that it was not as concerned with recovering 'the author's original meaning' or attempting to be neutral and disinterested readers.

---

[18] Nolan Fewell and Gary Phillips, eds. "The Bible and Ethics of Reading" *Semeia* 77 (Atlanta: SBL 1997), 7-8.

[19] For a review of these African hermeneutical approaches see Emmanuel Martey, *African Theology: Inculturation and Liberation* (Maryknoll: Orbis Books, 1993).

Rather they had an African agenda at heart. They were also not as concerned about learning about the ancient world of the biblical authors.

Rather, the inculturation hermeneutics of African scholars has always consisted of interested readers and has always taken its own contexts as a point of reference in biblical interpretation.[20] Departing from the methods of their universities, seminaries, and teachers which called for disinterested exegesis which focused on the ancient biblical world, they concentrated on the African contexts, its cultures, and current concerns and how these African contexts compare with the biblical cultures. Scholars insisted on finding similarities between the Bible and African cultures. In short, African scholars were insisting that they would read the biblical text through their own social locations. A major aspect of this approach was an act of resistance against Western Christian imperialism, which had made a blanket dismissal of African culture as barbaric and ungodly. Inculturation hermeneutics was indeed a process of reading for decolonization that sought liberation by asserting their diversity and similarities of African cultures and Christian tradition. It was partly meant to debunk imperialist presentations of colonial Christianity, which legitimised the suppression of African and other world cultures.

It is important to note that inculturation took a wide range of methods of interpreting. It included, for example, those readers whose main concerns were evangelical and whose goal was to ensure that the gospel was spread to Africa in their own language and symbols. Some of these inculturation readers tended to be interested in turning African culture into a vehicle of spreading the gospel, rather than to recognize them as cultures in their own right. This perspective has been characterised as viewing African cultures as a 'preparation for the gospel.' At the other end, there were some African scholars, represented by the likes of Canaan Banana, who insisted that we must treat all creation as

---

[20]In so far as taking local contexts as the normative point of reference in concerned, African scholarship is similar to other Third World scholars. Moreover, it is also theological.

holy and concede that God has not been completely revealed through biblical cultures only or that God has stopped speaking to humanity today.[21] Banana called for a re-writing of the Bible, which would include adding and subtracting things from the Bible so that it would reflect the diversity of the world. Banana argued that the biblical canon was a result of human selection and choice, and argued that it can be revisited.

Let me state that the inculturation approach remains quite vibrant amongst African scholars outside of South Africa. Recently, I had the privilege of being a co-editor of the volume *Bible in Africa*,[22] a project that collected into one volume a wide selection of biblical interpretations. Those who wrote reviews of trends in African biblical scholarship pointed to the prevalence of inculturation hermeneutics in the past twenty years, and the individual papers that came from all the corners of the continent and beyond suggest that inculturation hermeneutics is dominant method being used in Africa. In this approach African scholars do not study the Bible primarily through the ancient context of its birth. They do not study the Bible against the background of the extra-canonical texts of Judaism. Rather, they study it together with the unwritten cultures/ 'scriptures' of Africa and within the contexts of Africa. In this way, they are engaged in Africanizing the Bible and putting it together with their cultural texts, and not above or uniquely distinct from other 'African cultural Scriptures.'

Yet I must add that the continued vitality of African inculturation biblical scholarship is more than just talking back to the imperialist discourse. Most importantly, inculturation hermeneutics reflects the fact that most African biblical interpreters recognise the presence of another authoritative canon; namely their cultures. From this perspective, it may

---

[21]Canaan, Banana, "The Case for a New Bible," pp.17-29 in L. Cox and I. Mukonyora., eds. *Rewriting the Bible: The Real Issues* (Gweru: Mambo Press, 1993). The volume also contains a number of responses to Banana's thesis.

[22]Gerald O. West and Musa W. Dube, *The Bible in Africa: Transactions Trajectories and Trends* (Leiden: Brill, 2000).

be expected that inculturation hermeneutics will be around for a long time.

Southern African Scholarship

Black South African biblical scholarship was also largely informed by its context, in this case the context of apartheid, the racial and economic oppression of Black people. The uniqueness of the oppression of apartheid on the African continent led Black scholars to develop a close affinity with African-American scholars, who had also suffered and still suffer from racial discrimination. Race is thus a very important category of analysis. Black South African biblical scholarship also made use of Marxist theories. Thus their biblical hermeneutics combined both Black consciousness and Marxist theories in their reading. An excellent example of this kind of study is Itumeleng Mosala's *Black Biblical Hermeneutics and Black Theology in South Africa*.[23] Here, once again, we can see that Black South African readers have always been alive, they have always read from their particular contexts, with the particular concerns of their social locations, and not from a 'disinterested' perspective.

South African biblical scholarship, however, includes a great deal of white biblical interpretation. These scholars have employed methods of the West effectively. Most of their reading made little or no reference to apartheid. This is beginning to change, however, as some white biblical scholars seek to read for liberation and in dialogue with African readers. Gerald West's work is exemplary in this movement.[24] This trend is indeed desirable and to be encouraged.

9. African Women in Biblical Studies

African women biblical scholars have been few. Teresa Okure was almost a lone voice for a long time. Okure, who wrote her dissertation on *The Johannine Approach to Mission: A Contextual Study of John*

---

[23] Itumeleng Mosala, *Black Biblical Hermeneutics and Black Theology in South Africa* (Grand Rapids: Eerdmans, 1989).

[24] See Gerald West, *Biblical Hermeneutics of Liberation: Modes of Reading the Bible in The South African Context.* New York: Orbis, 1991; "Reading With: An Exploration of the Interface Between Critical and Ordinary Readings of the Bible," *Semeia* 73.

4:1-42,[25] has contributed to inculturation biblical hermeneutics, African feminist interpretation, and in international forums of feminism. Her articles have dealt with social location and with recent feminist trends representing the voice of Africa.[26] Yet, I must add that Africa is too diverse even within each country to be represented by one voice. No one can and should be given the burden of speaking for all of Africa. Rather, the challenge is to train scholars around the continent who can speak from their specific cultures and countries. If a few scholars are given the unfair burden of speaking for the whole of Africa, other readers will soon say they are oppressed and misrepresented by the one who has been forced to speak for them but who happens to be from a different culture. It is therefore important that more biblical scholars should be trained, to enable them to speak from their specific places, and to avoid the imperialist generalization of speaking 'as Africans and for Africans.'

Yet there is a glimmer of hope. A few other African women scholars are coming up. Some have just completed their PhDs and some are about to finish. Africa women scholars in Hebrew Bible include Madipoane Masenya in South Africa, Dora Mbuwayesango from Zimbabwe (but currently working overseas), Anastasia Malle in Tanzania, and Dorothy Akoto at Trinity College in Ghana. Two other South African women, Sarojini Nadar and Makhosazana are completing their dissertations on the Hebrew Bible. In the New Testament field Okure and me are joined by Elna Mouton, a white South African woman currently teaching in Stellenbosch. Those who are still working on their dissertations include Grace Imathiu from Kenya and Alice Yaffeh from Cameroon. Mary Sylvia C. Nwachukwu of Nigeria recently completed a dissertation on Paul[27]; Sr. M. Bibiana Muoneke, Dr. Margaret

---

[25]Teresa Okure, *The Johannine Approach to Mission: A Contextual Study of John 4:1-4*, (Tübingen: Mohr-Siebeck, 1988).

[26]"Feminist Interpretations in Africa," pp.76-85 in Schüssler Fiorenza, ed. *Searching the Scriptures. Vol. 1.*

[27]*Creation-Covenant Scheme and Justification by Faith: A Canonical Study of the God-Human Drama in the Pentateuch and the Letter to the Romans* (Tesi Gregoriana Serie Teologia, 89; Roma: Gregoriana, 2002).

Umeagudosa and the late Rosemary Edet (also Nigerians!), have published several books and articles. Musimbi Kanyoro, although trained in linguistics has also made a contribution to biblical scholarship.[28] While I have endeavoured here to single out those whose training is in biblical studies, biblical interpretation among African women is not limited to those who studied the Bible as their primary academic discipline. Many other women theologians and non-academic women read and interpret the Bible.

I think what is distinct and promising with the work of African women biblical scholars is not so much that they add gender to both inculturation and Black biblical hermeneutics, but that they are in fact coming out with new ways of reading. Gone are the days when Teresa Okure could say there are no methodological differences between African women and men. African women are making methodological contributions, as I said, not only to African scholarship, but to biblical scholarship in general. Of note here are Madipoane's *Bosadi/* womanhood, Okure's biblical hermeneutics of life; post-apartheid feminist hermeneutics, postcolonial feminist hermeneutics, and other methods such as of storytelling, divination, gender-inclusive and postcolonial biblical translations, cultural hermeneutics[29] and HIV/AIDS biblical hermeneutics. Although these methodological innovations are all represented in the volume *Other Ways of Reading, African Women and the Bible*, the works of each of the above women is worth reading for greater depth. It would be interesting to see how African male scholars will dialogue with the works of African women, and how this will change the face of both inculturation and Black biblical hermeneutics of the Bible. Currently one finds an embarrassing omission.

---

[28] For bibliographical details on the writings of these women see Grant LeMarquand, "A Bibliography of the Bible in Africa" in West and Dube, *The Bible in Africa*, 630-800.

[29] Musimbi Kanyoro, "Cultural Hermeneutics: An African Contribution," pp. 18-28 in Ofelia Ortega, ed. *Women's Visions: Theological Reflection, Celebration, Action* (Geneva: WCC Publications, 1995).

Conclusion

To conclude, I wish to outline a few concerns in the area of African biblical studies. First, there is a great need to train more biblical scholars - while the continent is growing more Christian, its biblical scholars are still too few. This has several implications. To start with, the few available biblical scholars are called on to do many other jobs in the church and society. While this is good, for it often produces socially engaged scholars, in the end scholars can spread themselves too thin to be able to focus on their academic vocation. This has a bearing on their research productivity as scholars. For example, we still need books and commentaries, both for the academy and for communities of faith, to be written by African scholars. So far there are quite a few articles but very few books. Consequently, those of us who are teaching the Bible still depend on books written from the Western context and by Western scholars.

Second, given that training for biblical studies is a long process, which includes many language requirements, it is important that institutions of Africa should have a plan and commit themselves to training a certain number of their promising students over a particular period. It will be important to raise supporting funds for those who wish to undertake training in biblical studies. My training, for example, was facilitated by the University of Botswana which had a staff development programme which identified interested and intelligent students for full training so that they could come back and serve the institution. I believe biblical studies needs such a commitment from educators and theological institutions.

Third, stronger forums for biblical scholars to meet and discuss and share their research are essential. This means forming and strengthening societies or associations of biblical studies as well as increasing the number of journals and their circulation on the continent. There is an insufficient number of journals in biblical studies and the available ones do not circulate effectively. So far, most African scholars seem to meet only in some international meetings of other organisations.[30]

---

[30]There are a number of theological societies that are either regional, national, or denominational, but an 'All-Africa religious studies society' that would regularly bring all scholars together is yet to be realised.

So far the Circle of Concerned African Women Theologians serves as a good model of an academic association.

Fourth, one of the major issues confronting biblical studies in Africa, and theological education as a whole, is the dilemma of publication and distribution. Often one can get a book published by some publisher on the continent, but then the distribution is often so inefficient that most people in Africa do not have or even know of the book. Books published overseas may be unaffordable for most African libraries and lecturers. As the Journey of Hope conference had suggested[31], it would seem that this issue will be best tackled through collaboration of publishers both within and outside of the continent.

Fifth, biblical studies and scholars must be decolonized. Although books by African scholars themselves are now available it is troubling that most of us still make Western/first world books on biblical studies the core required books for our students. We still teach Western ways of reading first, and then deal later with African biblical studies. When African scholars are included in our required list they occupy the periphery. African biblical studies and its lecturers and leaders need to be decolonized.

Sixth, it is an issue of great concern that we are working within poverty stricken nations and corrupt national leadership, which ignores the needs of their people. It is, therefore, essential for African biblical scholars to sharpen skills in liberation hermeneutics that will empower the most marginalized members of our societies to speak and to be heard.

Seventh, African biblical studies will also need to focus on studying how the Bible is interpreted through crafts, songs, art and prayers. We also need to examine how the unopened Bible is used as a symbol of power and protection.

Finally, the HIV/AIDS era has exposed the need for liberating, prophetic, life-centred and compassionate readings of the Bible. Biblical interpretations that have emerged from many faith communities and

---

[31]This was an all Africa conference on theological education which brought together theologians, publishers, and church leaders. It was held in Kempton Park, South Africa, 16-21 of September, 2002.

their leaders concerning HIV/AIDS are noted for associating HIV/AIDS with judgement and punishment for sin, the coming of the end times, or promoting a theology of sexual purity that subjugates life and ignores social oppression. Clearly HIV/AIDS is a context that calls upon all biblical scholars to assist faith leaders and communities to re-read the Bible for life, prophetically and for liberation. In this context of death and discrimination, biblical scholars must ask ourselves, 'Have we adequately responded to the HIV/AIDS epidemic?' If so, what do we have to show, to prove our commitment? Have we called conferences on the Bible and HIV/AIDS? Have we written books on Bible and HIV/AIDS? Have we integrated HIV/AIDS in our courses? The greatest challenge confronting biblical scholars of our day is that we must read the Bible in order to become part of the solution in the fight against HIV/AIDS.[32]

---

[32] Musa W. Dube, "Theological Challenges: Proclaiming the fullness of life in the HIV/AIDS and Globalisation," *International Review of Mission.* 91/363 (2002): 535-49; Dube, "Healing Where There is No Healing: Reading the Miracles of Healing in an AIDS Context," pp. 121-33 in Gray Phillips and Nicole Wilkinson Duran, ed.., *Reading Communities, Reading Scriptures.* (Harrisburg: Trinity Press International, 2002); Dube and Tinyiko S. Maluleke, "HIV/AIDS as the New Site of Struggle: Theological, Biblical & Religious Perspectives," *Missionalia* 29 (2001): 119-24.

CHAPTER FOUR

Learning to Read the Bible in Limuru: Textual and Hermeneutical Reflections of a Non-African Guest

Grant LeMarquand

Introduction

In January of 1987 my wife, Wendy, and our first-born, David, arrived in Kenya where I was to teach New Testament here at St. Paul's United Theological College. We came to this continent and to this country quite uninformed—ignorant, actually, of the riches of Africa. The Western press is able to paint something of a picture of the problems of Africa and of the beauty of African wildlife—but little of the wealth of African culture and tradition or of the reasons why Africa is in such trouble much of the time.

We also came ignorant of Kenya in particular. We had been appointed by the Anglican Church of Canada to go to the Sudan. We began conversations about Sudan in 1983. There had been a decade of peace in Sudan. Although the South was desperately poor, there was hope put in education and development. But the latest phase of civil war began in 1983 and by 1986 the war had heated up to such a degree that the town of Mundri was threatened. Mundri housed a small Anglican theological school called Bishop Gwynne College. We had seen pictures of the college, including pictures of the house in which we would live. We had learned something (not much upon reflection) about life in Southern Sudan and we were anticipating becoming members of the Bishop Gwynne College community. Six weeks before we were to leave for Sudan, we were informed by the mission personnel staff in Canada that it was too dangerous a place to send a young family with a baby. We were asked to go to Kenya to 'wait until Sudan got better.' We are still waiting for Sudan to get better. But now we were in Kenya – ignorant and unprepared.

Frankly, our mission board and the theological college where I had studied in Canada were not of much help in our preparation; neither seemed to know of the existence of African theology, much less African biblical studies. I found myself attempting to teach New Testament (and for some reason!) Systematic Theology to students although I had little understanding of their questions or their context. They were very patient with me and we agreed together that I would tell them what I had learned and that they would contribute questions and issues from the African context so that we could work out how or whether this theology with a Western accent that I was teaching was any help at all.

We shared at least three common commitments, though. The first was a trust in and love for the Lord Jesus Christ that led to a love for one another. Love for Jesus leading to love for the fellowship seems to be an important principle of the Revival Movement. My students at Limuru believed me when I told them that I had a testimony! My wife and I went to fellowship meetings and *Keshas*[1] and worshipped the way the students wanted to worship. In fact some members of the administration were concerned that we were becoming friends of students. The adversarial atmosphere between administration and students was fairly high in the late 80s at St. Paul's and it was considered unseemly (by some) for a member of the teaching staff to befriend students. Thankfully I was ignorant of this as well—at least for a while. These students and their families

---

[1] A *kesha* is a particular East African manifestation of a 'prayer vigil' or all-night prayer meeting involving singing, dancing, preaching and testimonies.

were sisters and brothers in Christ. That was all that mattered. My status as a member of faculty meant little to me.

Our second shared commitment was to the Bible. We, both the students and myself, believed that the Bible spoke God's word and that careful attention to the scriptures would help us personally, would help our families, would help the churches, would help Africa, would help the world. Since I was not a 'systematic theologian' I made a deal with the students who had to listen to me that I would take the syllabus and teach each topic by first looking at what the Bible seemed to say about it. In the meantime I would spend time studying, trying to find out what the 'theologians' had to say. The students were happy. I was relieved. The Bible ended up as our chief text for systematics – and everyone passed the dreaded external exams.

Our third shared commitment was to Africa. I knew little of Africa as I've said, but I had met some Africans in Canada and I had found their faith contagious. I wanted to help build up the church in Africa, but there was also something about African Christianity that I knew that the old, tired churches in the West needed.

And so with these three commitments shared with my students I began my experience of teaching the Bible in Africa. Here are a few things that I have learned about the Bible from Africa since that time.

Learning about the Cross: Galatians 3:13

In the second week of teaching Systematic Theology to the BD II class I was required to begin a section on 'the atonement.' Following my plan I began by giving a lecture on what the Bible said about the cross. Since theology should not be divorced from history, I reasoned, it would be best to begin by talking not about the meaning of the cross, but about the fact of crucifixion. So I began by describing in some detail this Roman method of execution. It was a fairly gruesome lecture, I think, as I recounted the process of torture and humiliation that crucifixion entailed. I also spent some time discussing Greco-Roman and Jewish reactions to this method of execution, from Cicero saying that the word 'cross' should not even be mentioned in polite company,[2] to the Jewish revulsion over crucifixion because it reminded them of Deuteronomy 21:23: "Everyone who is hanged on a tree is under God's curse."

During the break in the class a student approached me and said, "What you said about hanging as a curse is just what my people think." I was intrigued and asked to hear more. He said that among the Bukusu people when a person commits suicide by hanging, they are not buried. The family hires foreigners to take down the body. The body is burned and thrown into the river. The tree is uprooted and burned. No funeral is held. And no child is ever named after that person. This is done because otherwise a curse will come on the land (actually Deuteronomy goes on to say the same thing about a curse on the land). I encouraged that student to continue to think about this and to write his BD project on the pastoral problems involved in preaching the cross to a group of people who think hanging is curse.[3]

And of course this was not the only time that African culture confronted me with the reality of the cross. The singing of hymns and songs rich in sacrificial imagery strike a Western visitor as somehow more 'real' when sung with Christians who have probably seen actual goats and chickens sacrificed in the hope that rain will come or to seal a covenant between quarrelling people groups.

As modern African biblical exegesis began to be published in the latter half of the twentieth century, perhaps the largest single interpretative issue was the relationship between African cultures

---

[2]See Martin Hengel, *Crucifixion in the Ancient World and the Message of the Cross*. (London: SCM, 1977), 42.

[3]See Eliud Wabukala, "The Idea of Hanging on a Tree among the Babukusu People of Kenya and Implications for the Teaching of the Message of the Crucifixion of Jesus Christ." St. Paul's United Theological College, Limuru, Kenya: Unpublished thesis, 1988. Cf. Eliud Wabukala and Grant LeMarquand, "'Cursed be everyone who hangs on a tree': Pastoral Implications of Deuteronomy 21:22-23 and Galatians 3:13 in an African Context" pp. 350-59 in Gerald O. West and Musa W. Dube, eds. *The Bible in Africa: Transactions, Trajectories and Trends* (Leiden: Brill, 2000).

and the cultures of the Bible. African authors wrote learned studies which pointed out that there were similarities between African traditions and traditions found in the scriptures. Much has been done in this area and much more is still possible. From the perspective of a Westerner much of this work is exciting simply because it throws new light on the ancient biblical text.

Learning about Injustice: Matthew 2:13-18

I recall my first Christmas in Africa. It was 1987. My wife Wendy and our baby boy David had been in Kenya for about a year. Cara, our daughter, had been born in November. We were supposed to have gone to teach in a small theological College in Mundri, Sudan but the Anglican Church of Canada wisely discerned that the war in the Sudan was heating up and we were diverted to Kenya. A few months after we arrived in Kenya four of our would-be colleagues in Sudan were kidnapped by the Sudanese Peoples' Liberation Army and disappeared for almost two months in the Sudanese bush. After his release, one of the hostages, the Rev. Marc Nikkel, a mission partner of the Episcopal Church serving in the Sudan, returned to Africa. Unable to return to Sudan he taught with us at St. Paul's for almost a year. We had maintained a strong interest in things Sudanese, so it was a joy to have Marc living next door. A few days before Christmas he gave me a report prepared by some Mennonites who had surveyed the situation in a particular area of Sudan around the town of Rumbek, an area of the Southern Sudan which had recently been devastated. The authors of the report detailed atrocities beyond description. One of the most striking details, however, was the fact that in a vast area of hundreds of square miles they had found no living children: they had been killed, succumbed to starvation, fled as refugees, or carried off as slaves. A few days after reading this report I opened my Bible to read the lesson for the daily office: it was December 28 and this was the lesson:

> Now when they had departed, behold, an angel of the Lord appeared to Joseph in a dream and said, "Rise, take the child and his mother, and flee

to Egypt, and remain there till I tell you; for Herod is about to search for the child, to destroy him." And he rose and took the child and his mother by night, and departed to Egypt, and remained there until the death of Herod. This was to fulfill what the Lord had spoken by the prophet, "Out of Egypt have I called my son." Then Herod, when he saw that he had been tricked by the wise men, was in a furious rage, and he sent and killed all the male children in Bethlehem and in all that region who were two years old or under, according to the time which he had ascertained from the wise men. Then was fulfilled what was spoken by the prophet Jeremiah: "A voice was heard in Ramah, wailing and loud lamentation, Rachel weeping for her children; she refused to be consoled, because they were no more" (Mt 2:13-18).

The stories of Sudan and the massacre of the innocents under Herod are now somehow fused in my mind. Sometimes reading the Bible in a new situation, or with new eyes, reading the Bible in a "mission" context will confront the reader, perhaps even assault the reader, with its message. To be in Africa meant that I was compelled to reflect on Scripture in ways that I had not previously dreamed. I came to Africa ostensibly to teach the Bible to theological college students – but I ended up being taught the Bible in remarkable and often very uncomfortable ways.

Learning about God's Presence: Daniel 3

In the small town of Mundri in the Equatorial region of Southern Sudan, where our family had first intended to go, there is a small Anglican theological institution called Bishop Gwynne College. The school has been abandoned since 1987 when the Sudanese Peoples Liberation Army took control of the compound kidnapping four expatriate members of the college staff and holding them as hostages in a vain attempt to gain the attention of the world to the plight of Southern Sudan.[4] The chapel of that college, which is still intact,[5] is octagonal in shape. On three-quarters of the wall space is a mural.

---

[4] For an account see Mark R. Nikkel, "'Hostages of the Situation in Sudan,' 1987: Christian Missionaries in Wartime" *Anglican and Episcopal History* 71/2 (2002): 187-222.

[5] According to Canon Baringwa of the ECS Dioceses of Lui and Mundri, in Nairobi, June 2002.

The subject of the painting is a biblical scene which is widely considered to be the one of the most frequently mentioned Bible stories in Sudan: Daniel 3, the story of the three men in the fiery furnace. Sudanese often refer to Daniel 3 as a key text. According to Samuel Kayanga, who was a student in Limuru in the late 1980s, there are several Sudanese songs about this story. "Many people in Sudan live their life in a fire situation. It is only by looking back that they can see the hand of God delivering them."[6] In fact stories of miraculous deliverance are fairly common in Sudanese conversation. Bishop Nathaniel Garang, for example, as a way of explaining the story of the three in the furnace, tells a story of bullets tearing up the ground on both his right side and his left side, but leaving him unharmed. The same miraculous deliverance that the Hebrews experienced is also believed to be experienced in Sudan.[7] Similarly Joseph Acuil of Wau Diocese reported to me that in Sudan, "Someone is bitten by a snake, people pray, Jesus heals them. Many songs are composed about that story. They were put in fire, but because they trust in God, God was able to deliver them"[8]

Some Sudanese point out that God does not always deliver. For them, an important part of the story in Daniel is when Shadrach, Meshach and Abednego are asked if God is able to deliver them. Their answer: "God is able...but if not" (Daniel 3: 17-18) has particular significance for Sudanese. They have seen God deliver, but they have also seen suffering and death and know that deliverance does not always come. But they believe that God is with them in the fire nonetheless.

Once again, as a Westerner I found this very challenging. We in the West tend to live lives which are sheltered from the kind of suffering we call 'persecution.' When most people in Europe or North America think of the persecution of Christians they think of those Christians who were thrown to the lions during the Roman Empire. Although this is changing, too few Western Christians are aware

---

[6]Interview in Nairobi, June 2002.
[7]Interview in Nairobi, May 2002.
[8]Interview in Kabare, Kenya, June 2002.

that their sisters and brothers are oppressed for their faith in places like Sudan.

Learning about Discipleship: Matthew 21:1-10

The Thursday afternoon 'Fellowship' meetings at which my wife and I were regular attendees while at St. Paul's were a source of much encouragement. They were sometimes, however, a source of some confusion for non-African visitors. During our first year in Limuru a Church Army officer named Trajan came up from Nairobi to preach on more than one occasion. He was a great preacher. But at one point in one of his sermons he lost me. At what was a dramatic point in a sermon on discipleship he looked at the gathered congregation and asked "and what do you see when you sit on a donkey?" to which (to our astonishment) the entire congregation (except my wife and me) answered back "a cross!".

Of course I understood the biblical allusion. Trajan was referring to what we know of as 'Palm Sunday,' the procession of Jesus into Jerusalem on the back of a donkey.

> Now when they drew near to Jerusalem and came to Bethphage, to the Mount of Olives, then Jesus sent two disciples, saying to them, "Go into the village in front of you, and immediately you will find a donkey tied, and a colt with her. Untie them and bring them to me. If anyone says anything to you, you shall say, 'The Lord needs them,' and he will send them at once." This took place to fulfill what was spoken by the prophet, saying,
>
> "Say to the daughter of Zion,
> 'Behold, your king is coming to you,
> humble, and mounted on a donkey,
> and on a colt, the foal of a beast of burden.'"
>
> The disciples went and did as Jesus had directed them. They brought the donkey and the colt and put on them their cloaks, and he sat on them. Most of the crowd spread their cloaks on the road, and others cut branches from the trees and spread them on the road. And the crowds that went before him and that followed him were shouting, "Hosanna to the Son of David! Blessed is he who comes in the name of the Lord! Hosanna in

the highest!" And when he entered Jerusalem, the whole city was stirred up, saying, "Who is this?"

(Matthew 21:1-10)

The so-called 'triumphal entry' of Jesus into Jerusalem portrays Jesus taking up the role of king. But this is a different kind of reign than the ordinary first century Jewish onlooker would have imagined when hearing or reading the terms 'Son of David', 'Messiah' and 'king'. Jesus is a king but his crown is of made of thorns, his attendants (on the right hand and on the left) are political prisoners, his throne is a cross, his royal robe is his nakedness. Clearly Trajan was correct – when Jesus was sitting on the donkey on his way into Jerusalem surely he foresaw that his doom was to be handed over to sinners and executed. But how did the congregation at the Fellowship meeting know the answer to Trajan's question? A mystery.

A few weeks later another preacher came to the Fellowship meeting, a priest from Mt. Kenya South. And once again, at a particularly important point in the sermon he asked the question, "what do you see when you are sitting on a donkey?" And once again the Fellowship answered "a cross!" This time I had to find out what was going on. Clearly there was some secret knowledge which was being kept from the *Wazungu*. So right after the meeting I went to a place in the compound where I knew there would be a donkey and I had a look. Sure enough, there on the back of the grey animal was a dark line of hair extending the length of the spine and across the donkey's shoulders there was another dark line – the two lines together forming 'a cross'. If I had mounted that donkey and looked down at its back the way Jesus must have done on his way into Jerusalem I would have been looking at a cross. The donkey itself was a visible symbol of what Jesus was to encounter at the end of the Passion Week.

For Trajan and the other preacher the story of Jesus' triumphal entry into Jerusalem was transformed into an instant lesson on discipleship. To follow Jesus is a matter of following him on the road of service. To be a Christian "is not to be served, but to serve" (Mark 10:45).

A contemporary Sudanese Christian song makes the same point, but this time not by alluding to the donkey in the gospel story but by a reference to an African forced, as it were, into a position of discipleship in the Passion story:

> We called and cried before so that you would hear,
> Embrace us intimately for we are your children.
> Let us carry the cross and follow you.
> Let us be like Simon, the man of Cyrene,
> Who followed you to the place of the skull."[9]

Christian discipleship does not lead inexorably to the 'health and wealth' that so many preachers of the so-called 'prosperity gospel' proclaim. Discipleship leads to suffering on behalf of others, following the way of Jesus.

Learning about Allegorical Reading: Acts 27

Not every reading of the Bible is received favourably by those who hear it. And not every reading of the Bible is accurate or wise. As was the custom at St. Paul's, towards the end of every academic term, that one of the Sunday evening Holy Communion Services would be led by a group of students. It had been a particularly tense year. Students and administration had had a number of disagreements and trust was not running at a high level. The preacher, who shall remain nameless, chose as his text a lesson from the Acts of the Apostles, the 27th chapter. He began, as many African sermons do, simply by retelling the story. This is often a helpful way of reinforcing the message and of highlighting particular aspects of a text. The preacher was able to tell the story of Paul's shipwreck in a vivid and compelling way. It would have been good and helpful if it had stayed a 'retelling' in general terms. The sermon began, however, to mutate from a retelling of the text into an allegory. Slowly the congregation

---

[9]The song was written by John Chol Ater and is quoted in Dau, *Suffering and God: A Theological Reflection on the War in Sudan* (Nairobi: Pauline, 2002), 225.

became aware that the ship being referred to in the sermon was no longer a ship, but an institution in peril and in desperate need of rescue. In fact the institution in question was an educational institution whose leaders had forced the ship onto the rocks. And the educational institution was soon revealed as a theological institution – and one very close to us. The story had left the waters of the Mediterranean ocean and become transformed into a lesson about our current crisis at St. Paul's. Even then the preacher could have saved himself but on he went (perhaps throwing himself upon the rocks!) to name the names of the pilot and the navigator of the ship. The student, of course, was expelled the next day.[10]

This incident has often led me to wonder about the value of an allegorical method of reading scripture. The technique is quite popular in many African circles although frowned upon by most teachers in African theological institutions. Most students will no doubt be aware of the possible abuses of the method. St. Augustine's famous allegorical use of the parable of the Good Samaritan is often cited as the wrong way to use the biblical text:

The man (Adam) going down from Jerusalem (the city of heavenly peace) fell among robbers (the devil and his angels) who left him half dead (spiritually dead). The priest (the OT priesthood) did not help, the Levite (the OT prophets) did not help, the Good Samaritan (Christ) helped, binding up wounds (stopping sin), pouring in oil (hope) and wine (exhortation to spiritual work), put him on the beast (the body of Christ), took him to the inn (the church), paid two coins (the commandments to love God and neighbour) to the innkeeper (Paul) until his return (Jesus' resurrection).[11]

Obviously allegory can be abused. Clearly this kind of eisegesis is a danger to be avoided. This is not just because there are so few

---

[10] He was reinstated several months later and was able to graduate with his class and has had a fruitful ministry.

[11] From Augustine, *Quaestiones Evangelionium* II.19, as summarized in R.H. Stein, *An Introduction to the Parables of Jesus* (Philadelphia: Westminster Press, 1981), 46.

controls on this kind of reading, but also because **love** requires treating the 'other' (in this case the text) with respect. In the words of N.T. Wright,

> In love...the lover affirms the reality and the otherness of the beloved. ...When applied to reading texts, this means that the text can be listened to on its own terms, without being reduced to the scale of what the reader can or cannot understand at the moment. ...At this level 'love' will mean 'attention': the readiness to let the other *be* the other, the willingness to grow and change in oneself in relation to the other.[12]

To act in love in regard to the biblical text means that the reader will not abuse the text, will not beat the text into submission or force the text to say something that the reader wants to hear. Love will mean close attention to the original context of the text as well as to the contemporary needs and aspirations of the readers. African exegetes have had much to say about reading the text of the Bible in ways that actually make a difference in the lives of African people.[13] We need also to be sure that it is the biblical text which is being read and not simply our own clever ideas read into a text.

At the same time, the so-called 'original' meaning of the text does not empty the text of its meaning. That Sunday evening sermon did point out that there was a connection between the text in Acts and the situation in St. Paul's at the time. Perhaps we need to rethink allegorical reading and find ways to pursue such readings as long as they do not do violence to the text.

Learning about Honour and Shame: 1 Corinthians 11: 17-34

Shortly after our family arrived in Limuru a church dignitary came to the campus to bless a new building. Naturally a meal was involved. This seemed good to us – the visit of a leader of the church who was

---

[12] *The New Testament and the People of God* (Minneapolis: Fortress, 1992), 64.

[13] See especially the wonderful essay by Teresa Okure, "'I will open my mouth in parables' (Matt 13.35): A Case for a Gospel-Based Biblical Hermeneutic" *New Testament Studies* 46/3 (2000): 445-63.

also one of the leaders of the college should be a time for a celebration feast! I was not quite prepared for this meal, however. In the new cafeteria a high table was set up with a clean, white tablecloth, fresh cut flowers and good china. The administration and the visiting leader sat there. They were served an excellent meal (including a fair bit of meat). The rest of the tables had no table cloths or flowers, but there were plates (not china) and food of a decent quality (although less meat was involved). The faculty and senior staff of the college and their families as well as some other visitors sat there. Outside were the students. Although they had no tables or chairs, they were given food (although they had no meat). The workers of the college were not fed.

The text which came to mind immediately was James 1:2-5 which warns of the dangers of welcoming the rich and powerful and ignoring the needs of the poor. Perhaps even more important is a Pauline text. Whether we are Reformed, Presbyterian, Methodist or Anglican we are familiar with the Pauline version of the words of institution from 1 Corinthians 11:23-26:

> For I received from the Lord what I also delivered to you, that the Lord Jesus on the night when he was betrayed took bread, and when he had given thanks, he broke it, and said, "This is my body which is for you. Do this in remembrance of me." In the same way also he took the cup, after supper, saying, "This cup is the new covenant in my blood. Do this, as often as you drink it, in remembrance of me." For as often as you eat this bread and drink the cup, you proclaim the Lord's death until he comes.

In these four verses Paul reminds the Corinthian church of the tradition which Paul himself had received and which he had passed on to them. Unfortunately most of our lectionaries omit the verses which frame Paul's recording of this bit of traditional material. Paul speaks of the tradition for a pastoral reason: the meals (and it is fairly certain that most early Christian 'eucharists' were real meals, involving much more than simply token amounts of food) in Corinth were not a reflection of the Lord's will for his church. Listen to Paul's warnings:

But in the following instructions I do not commend you, because when you come together it is not for the better but for the worse. For, in the first place, when you come together as a church, I hear that there are divisions among you. And I believe it in part, for there must be factions among you in order that those who are genuine among you may be recognized. When you come together, it is not the Lord's supper that you eat. For in eating, each one goes ahead with his own meal. One goes hungry, another gets drunk. What! Do you not have houses to eat and drink in? Or do you despise the church of God and humiliate those who have nothing? What shall I say to you? Shall I commend you in this? No, I will not...

Whoever, therefore, eats the bread or drinks the cup of the Lord in an unworthy manner will be guilty of profaning the body and blood of the Lord. Let a person examine himself, then, and so eat of the bread and drink of the cup. For anyone who eats and drinks without discerning the body eats and drinks judgment on himself. That is why many of you are weak and ill, and some have died. But if we judged ourselves truly, we would not be judged. But when we are judged by the Lord, we are disciplined so that we may not be condemned along with the world. So then, my brothers, when you come together to eat, wait for one another—if anyone is hungry, let him eat at home—so that when you come together it will not be for judgment.

These two paragraphs form brackets around the familiar recounting of the story of the Last Supper. In the first paragraph outlines the problem: there are divisions in the congregation which appear to be divisions of class or wealth. Some are eating and drinking too much; others are going hungry. Some are being well treated; others are 'despised' and 'humiliated.' A bit of Greco-Roman background will help fill in the background. In Paul's day celebratory meals were often held by organizations called *collegia*. People joined these organizations for a variety of reasons which need not detain us here but the important thing to note is that they joined at a variety of levels. Some members hosted the meetings or were the 'patrons' of the gathering—since they paid the bills they and their friends were treated the best, being given lavish amounts of food while reclining at table. A second rung of members would eat in the same room, but in an outer circle at the feet of the guests of honour. Others would eat outside in the courtyard. Evidently the Corinthian 'Lord's Supper' (note that Paul says that their behaviour shows that it is not the Lord's Supper which they are eating!) had taken on the characteristics of the pagan Greco-Roman society – they are making distinctions among themselves based on class and wealth. As a result, Paul says in the closing paragraph, they are profaning the meal and endangering themselves. They are under judgement.[14]

Perhaps the kind of meal I witnessed in Limuru when our church leader came to visit was simply the copy of a pattern of meal behaviour learned during British colonial times. It certainly does not reflect the meal practices of Jesus who welcomed the poor and the sinners at his gatherings.[15] As is true in every culture, not everything that I witnessed in the African church reflected the mind of Christ.

Learning about the Church: Revelation 7

In May of 1998 I was privileged to accompany a group of Canadian theological students to Kenya where they spent over a month in parishes around the country seeing how ministry is done in this context. On the last Sunday that we were in the country we were invited to attend a Nairobi congregation of the Holy Ghost Church of East Africa. This congregation met behind a set of flats in Nairobi. They were quite poor, but they had purchased a piece of land next to the local garbage heap and they had begun to build a church. In the meantime they met outside. As the Bishop got into his robe I noticed that the people in my group were going to be the only ones at worship that morning that did not have white robes. The congregation had already arrived and was singing, and each one of them had his or her

---

[14] On this text and its background see especially, Suzanne Watts Henderson. "'If Anyone Hungers...': An Integrated Reading of 1 Cor 11:17-34" *New Testament Studies* 48/2 (2002): 195-208.

[15] See, for example, Luke 15:1-2; A good discussion of the whole issue of Jesus' table fellowship can be found in Marcus Borg, *Conflict, Holiness and Politics in the Teachings of Jesus* (New York and Toronto: Edwin Mellen Press, 1984; now reprinted by Trinity Press International, 1998).

own robe. Of course as an Anglican priest I found this somewhat ironic since I was usually the only one *with* a robe. The Bishop turned to me and said, "you will be expected to give a word." So, I was the preacher. This seemed to give me little time to prepare, although actually I ended up with a couple of hours of preparation since the service took a bit of time! As the worship progressed and I began to implore God to give me something to say I found myself pondering this group of white-robed Africans in front of me and to wonder about their lives. "Who are these people, dressed in white robes," I thought. It dawned on me that there is a biblical text that asks precisely the same question! That text became the text of my sermon that morning and I have subsequently had the opportunity to meditate on the passage at greater length. Here it is:

> After this I looked, and behold, a great multitude that no one could number, from every nation, from all tribes and peoples and languages, standing before the throne and before the Lamb, clothed in white robes, with palm branches in their hands, and crying out with a loud voice, "Salvation belongs to our God who sits on the throne, and to the Lamb!" And all the angels were standing around the throne and around the elders and the four living creatures, and they fell on their faces before the throne and worshiped God, saying, "Amen! Blessing and glory and wisdom and thanksgiving and honor and power and might be to our God forever and ever! Amen."
>
> Then one of the elders addressed me, saying, "Who are these, clothed in white robes, and from where they have come?" I said to him, "Sir, you know." And he said to me, "These are the ones coming out of the great tribulation. They have washed their robes and made them white in the blood of the Lamb.
>
> "Therefore they are before the throne of God,
>   and serve him day and night in his temple;
>   and he who sits on the throne will shelter them with his presence.
> They shall hunger no more, neither thirst anymore;
>   the sun shall not strike them, nor any scorching heat.
> For the Lamb in the midst of the throne will be their shepherd,
>   and he will guide them to springs of living water,
> and God will wipe away every tear from their eyes."
>
> *(Rev 7:9-17)*

Several things should be noted about this "great multitude". The passage itself, of course, helps us to understand what question should be asked of the text. The author of the book, who is identified as "John" is asked by one of the elders, "Who are these?" (v.13). John recognizes that the elder is probably more of an authority on these matters and throws the question back at him. The text in fact identifies this multitude in several ways.

First of all, they cannot be numbered. Actually, they had (somewhat confusingly!) already been numbered in verse 1 of the chapter: they are the 144,000. This interpretation of this number has caused problems for centuries with various groups claiming to be members of this select number. We must remember that almost everything in the Apocalypse is symbolic, and this number should certainly be treated as symbolic. If 1000 is a number which means simply 'a large group' and 144 is recognized as 12 x 12, then 144,000 is probably a way of saying 'the complete people of God.' (Remember that 12 is the number of the tribes of Israel and the number of the apostles.) 'The large multitude that no one can number' is simply a different way of viewing the same group. There is no need to worry about whether one is part of the exact number – the number is simply a symbolic way of saying 'all of God's people.'

Second, they are those who have come out of 'the great tribulation.' This is probably a reference to the political and religious situation of persecution during the time the book was written. As I worshipped with the Holy Ghost Church of East Africa that morning I was reminded that they, that we, are in a world of suffering and pain and evil. Their world and mine is place were political corruption, AIDS, war, and a variety of other demons seem to set the daily agenda. But the text also says that this is (no matter how long it may seem from our perspective) a temporary situation. This text promises that there will come a time when there will be no suffering: no hunger, no thirst, no tears (vv.16-17).

Third, this is a great 'washed' multitude. They are, the elder says, 'washed in the blood of the Lamb.' The image probably strikes most of us in the sanitized Western world as somewhat grotesque. It is, however, simply one part of a long line of biblical passages which link purity and forgiveness of sins to sacrifice. In the book of Revelation Jesus is 'the lamb that was slain' (see 5:6) but is now risen. The image links the Christian tradition back to its Jewish roots in the temple tradition where animal sacrifice connected the worshipper to God. It is continued in our Eucharistic liturgies every time we echo the words of John the Baptist when we say or sing the *Agnus Dei* ('O Lamb of God who takes away the sin of the world, have mercy on us,' see John 1:29). The Revival Movement continues to remind us that the church only exists because of the blood of Jesus. This multitude is that great throng which has found 'salvation' (v.10) through their allegiance to the crucified one, through their faith in the lamb of God, Jesus, who in the words of another New Testament writer 'loved them and gave himself for them' (Galatians 2:20). They have turned their lives away from other allegiances, towards the God who in the cross has turned to them.

Fourth, they are 'from every nation, tribe, people, and language' (v.9). They are a worldwide people, a global gathering. It must be noted that they do not become 'homogenized' by joining this multitude. Cultural distinctiveness is not lost but, rather, all that is good in their particularity is redeemed. In Christ there is no longer Jew or Greek, African or *Mzungu*.

Fifth, the great multitude of human beings is only one part of a greater crowd around the throne. The angels are there and so are the 'four living creatures.' This group was first mentioned in Revelation 4 and seems to represent all of the animal life of the created world (domestic and wild animals, birds and human beings: see 4:6-7). We are not alone in our world – and, it seems that God, who 'hates nothing that has been made' (Collect for Ash Wednesday), has a plan not only for human beings but for all of creation. (The Revelation is not alone in this, of course: see Psalm 96:11-13, Jonah 4:11, Luke 19:40.) Some in Africa are beginning to remind the world of the intricate connection between all of life and that to do violence to the environment, to the earth, to the animals, will ultimately result in violence to human beings as well.

Sixth, the vision tells us that the multitude, together with the creatures and the angels are at worship. Their ultimate purpose, it seems, is doxological. Redeemed humanity adds its voice to 'all in heaven and earth' who are gathered around the throne of God in praise (vv.10-12).

Finally, this great multitude is protected by God's presence. The Greek word in Revelation 7:15 is an interesting one. In the NIV we read that God will "spread his tent over them." The NRSV say that God will "shelter them." The Hebrew word *shekinah* (tent) forms the root of the verb here. God will 'en-tent' them, or perhaps we should say he will 'tabernacle' them. The idea seems to be that God, whose presence was made known to the people of Israel through the coming of the *shekinah* (God's glory) to the Holy of Holies, will one day shield and protect God's people from every harm by enfolding them in the divine presence.

The vision of the Revelation is a vision of renewal and redemption which recognizes that the world is in desperate need of being 'saved.' The Bible is clear that the world as we know it is not the way God wants it; therefore much of the Bible is the story of God's rescue of the world, and God's plan to remake the world. It is the story of God's plan to bring all things together, 'to unite all things, in Christ' (Ephesians 1:10).

Being with that congregation of the Holy Ghost Church in East Africa once again opened me to seeing things in the biblical text that I had not seen before.

Conclusion

A few years ago I met a former professor of mine at an academic conference. I had been in Africa teaching and had returned to my native Canada to study. He asked me what I was working on. "African biblical scholarship," I replied. He looked a bit puzzled, scratched his head and then suggested, "There isn't enough material, is there?" This was not a professor who was out of touch with biblical scholarship. He was, in fact, very interested in new modes and methods of attempting to understand biblical texts. Neither was he an unkind man. Like the disciples of John the Baptist in Ephesus who didn't know that there was a Holy Spirit until Paul asked them (Acts 19:1-7) he simply did not know that there was an 'African biblical scholarship.'

Disturbed by my professor's response I immediately set out to demonstrate the existence of my field of interest! In a few days I mailed him a bibliography of some 15 pages. Of course much of the material I knew of was either published in Africa or was in the form of unpublished dissertations. Perhaps my former teacher could be excused for not knowing. That was over a decade ago. With the abundance of recent publications by African biblical scholars and about African biblical scholarship, some of this material published in the 'West', there is no longer any reason to claim that, 'there isn't enough material.' To paraphrase the Apostle, 'they are without excuse, for what can be known [about the reading of the Bible in Africa] is plain for all to see.'[16]

In many ways African culture and African experience can help the church around the world to understand the Bible. But how can the rich biblical insights which Africa can provide become a part of the genetic code of our theological colleges? I know of few African theological institutions that teach courses on 'Reading the Bible in Africa.' I have simply stumbled across most of the first things that I have been privileged to learn about the Bible from Africa and Africans. My hope is that institutions like St. Paul's can be more intentional about this process of biblical reflection in the light of African culture and experience.

---

[16]That bibliography has grown considerably from the original 15 pages. See now Grant LeMarquand, "A Bibliography of the Bible in Africa," pp.633-800 in West and Dube, *The Bible in Africa*.

CHAPTER FIVE

Ecumenism and Theological Education in Africa

Nyambura J. Njoroge

Introduction: Holistic Character

I return to St Paul's United Theological College exactly twenty-five years since I registered as a theological student. Since I graduated in 1980, I have enjoyed fulltime church ministry at the local and global level. My ministry has not been without moments of dark days of disillusionment and anger when I have seriously contemplated leaving not only the ministry but the church all together. It has been through such moments of deep frustrations and despair, however, that I have heard the 'still small voice' that reminds us that there is a difference between the institutional church, structured and moulded by people, and the church of Christ, the body of Christ, which St. Paul, the great theologian and missionary struggled to know and to serve (1 Cor 12).

I am pleased to be back and to have this opportunity to test some of the ideas that I have harvested through my own struggle of attempting to be a faithful follower of Jesus. This consultation gives us the space for cross-fertilization of ideas. I rejoice that I am part of this occasion of celebrating a century of service by this college. The topic assigned to me—ecumenical theological education - is one that I wrestle with daily in my responsibilities at the World

Council of Churches as I communicate with many theological institutions globally.

Creating appropriate curricula for ecumenical theological education in Africa is a critical and challenging task in this day and age as we are faced with endless death-dealing activities in the world and ongoing disunity in the church. The responsibility of creating appropriate curricula calls for research, critical social analysis, dialogue, advocacy and action because we yearn for a theological education and ministerial formation whose products are relevant, effective, transforming and which give realistic hope to people in death-stricken circumstances. In other words, a theological curriculum must take seriously the historical, socioeconomic and religio-cultural milieu of the people it is meant to benefit in the light of the gospel. Above all, it must be contextual, ecumenical and viable. We need to remember at the outset that we live in a globalized context. What happens in Hong Kong, Beijing, Washington, London, Harare, Caracas, Abuja, Baghdad, and Nairobi has direct impact in our lives. Whatever happens in Kenya is not all determined locally. There are many players in our lives. We must always take our global reality seriously as we create curricular programmes in theological institutions. After all, we belong to a catholic and universal church. Most importantly, because of the nature of the gospel any curriculum must have a holistic character.

> [Theological education] is grounded in worship, and combines and interrelates spirituality, academic excellence, mission and evangelism, justice and peace, pastoral sensitivity and competence and the formation of character. For it brings together education of:
> - the ear to hear God's word and the cry of God's people;
> - the heart to heed and respond to the suffering;
> - the tongue to speak to both the weary and the arrogant;
> - the hands to work with the lowly;
> - the mind to reflect on the good news of the gospel;
> - the will to respond to God's call;

the spirit to wait on God in prayer, to struggle and wrestle with God, to be silent in penitence and humility and to intercede for the church and the world;
the body to be the temple of the Holy Spirit[1]

Why Ecumenical?

From the beginnings of the church at Pentecost (Acts 2) when people from many nations gathered in Jerusalem, the church has known that through the power of the Holy Spirit they had been made into an international, multicultural, and multilingual community. Yet, the followers of Christ seem to have failed to grasp "the breadth and length and depth and height of the love of Christ that surpasses knowledge" (Eph 3:18-19). The writer of Ephesians understood clearly that the root of the problem was a lack of unity in the love of Christ, and prayed earnestly for his fellow Christians, to lead a life worthy of the calling to which you have been called, with all humility and gentleness, with patience, bearing one another in love, making every effort to maintain the unity of the Spirit in the bond of peace. There is one body and one spirit, just as you were called to the one hope of your calling, one Lord, one faith, one baptism, one God and Father of all, who is above all and through all and in all" (4:1-6).

Similarly, Paul spoke against divisions among the early Christians in Corinth and urged them to be God's servants, working together building on the foundation, Jesus Christ (1 Cor 1-4). Paul's question to the Corinthians: "Has Christ been divided?" is still with us today as we continue to take pride in our cherished denominational cocoons and narrow ecclesiasticism. Being ecumenical has to do with the way we should conduct our lives together as people created in God's image, sharing the same faith and hope in Christ and taking care of the whole inhabited earth, despite our diversity or, perhaps, because of it.

---

[1] John S. Pobee, ed. *Towards Viable Theological Education: Ecumenical Imperative, Catalyst of Renewal* (Geneva, WCC Publications, 1997), 1.

The intentional nurturing of the visible unity of the church is fundamental. The visible unity of the church is a high calling that sounds simple but over the last two thousand years has proved most difficult to achieve. The call to unity demands that we practice and live out our faith in God by breaking the barriers that divide us and threaten the well-being of humanity and God's world. We are invited to embrace the gift of unity in Christ and to work towards the abolition of injustice and inequality that exists among us, taking our cue from the mission statement of Jesus (Lk 4:18-19).[2] Being ecumenical is to fulfil the mission of Jesus which he taught his followers.[3] It means participating in God's mission in Christ for the sake of God's kingdom.

How do we create curricular programmes that will help theological educators and students grasp the meaning of God's mission for us today in a continent that is inflicted by so many forces of evil?

The Nature and Architects of the Curriculum

Let me from the outset declare that my interest in this discussion is not to discount and discredit what already exists in theological institutions in this country and in Africa as a whole. Rather it is to engage in a process that will affirm what has been effective and to discard what is outdated or has proved to be irrelevant for the well-being of our people. Obviously we cannot ignore or forget that for centuries Africa has suffered under ideologies of slavery, racism, colonialism, and religious and cultural imperialism often aided by the missionary enterprise itself. As if that is not enough, Africa entered the 21st century under the yoke of globalization, HIV/AIDS pandemic[4]

---

[2] "The Spirit of the Lord is on me, because he has anointed me to preach good news to the poor. He has sent me to proclaim freedom for the prisoners and recovery of sight for the blind, to release the oppressed, to proclaim the year of the Lord's favour."

[3] See especially John 13, 17, 20, 21; Mt 28; Lk 24.

[4] See Musa Dube, "Theological Challenges: Proclaiming the Fullness of Life in the HIV/AIDS & Global Economic Era," *International Review of Mission* 91/363 (2002): 535-49.

(and many other killer diseases), endemic poverty, violations of human rights, and a culture of violence, corruption, poor governance—let alone the patriarchy and sexism in the church and society.

Furthermore, ecumenism in Africa is fragile and a new wave of denominationalism is complicating the situation. We must, therefore, critically evaluate whether we have severed ourselves from these ideologies that adversely erode our dignity, security, and well-being if we are to assess critically whether our theological curricula adequately addresses today's challenges. Therefore the process of creating appropriate curricular programmes for ecumenical theological education must include a critical evaluation of what exists in all areas of study currently offered. Only then can we make informed decisions concerning what should be added or dropped from any curriculum.

As well as the content of the curriculum, theological educators must be equipped in research, teaching, and communication methodologies that will enable a ministerial formation that promotes critical theological thinking. It is a curriculum that begins by exploring the causes of pain and suffering in the lives of our people and seeks to identify what has brought fullness of life to people in the midst of destruction and death. Such a curriculum takes seriously what Paulo Freire has called the pedagogy of the oppressed and education for critical consciousness.[5] Above all it must be biblically, theologically, and spiritually consistent with God's mission following the life and ministry of Jesus. Our programmes must promote the practice of evangelism and mission in unity of faith in Jesus Christ. The primary architects of this curriculum are theological educators, church leaders, and students. The time is gone when students can be considered empty vessels receiving knowledge from the seasoned teachers, what Freire called the 'banking' method. Even kindergarten and Sunday school children have something to offer if we care to

---

[5]Paulo Freire, *Education for Critical Consciousness* (New York: Continuum, 1973); idem, *Pedagogy of the Oppressed* (New York: Continuum, 1990).

listen and observe their expressions, moods and body language. For instance, if a child comes to Sunday school hungry or from a home where parents spent the night abusing alcohol and fighting, an observant teacher will know something is wrong. Similarly, theological educators must be open to hearing the needs of their students.

Any project of curriculum revision will only work if church leaders are patient, intentional, and committed to a process of transformation, which may include interruptions and surprises. Although we may map out the goals and objectives of what we wish to achieve, like a river a process can always encounter sharp rocks causing it to meander and to create waterfalls, lakes and tributaries. The life and ministry of Jesus was full of interruptions and surprises as people reached out to him for healing, for themselves or their family members. Flexibility, courage, boldness and humility must accompany the process of creating appropriate curricula. A contextual, ecumenical, and viable theological curriculum will change as the context changes.

Other players must also take their place at the discussion table. The primary architects must take into account the demography of this country and the continent to ensure that each generation and different categories of people are heard and their needs and struggles taken into account. The demography of the churches must also be taken into account. Let me be more specific.

In Kenya, according to the 1999 census, the population was nearly 29 million. Of this number, 43% were children 0-14 years, and 54% were 15-64 years and the final 3% were 64 years and over. It is obvious that more than 50 percent of Kenyan population are children 0-18 years.[6] In the church, we all know that we have a preponderance of women and we would certainly not be wrong to say that the majority of our members are relatively young, between 0-40 years. Yet we also know that the majority of those in leadership

---

[6]According to UNICEF. The population census is from http://kenya.compeople/people_006.htm retrieved on 5/3/2003.

are from the older generation. So there is always a huge age gap between the membership and the leadership as well as a gender imbalance since the leadership is male-dominated. All these factors are important to take into account if indeed the curriculum will be relevant. Theological curricula should be concerned about the well-being of the person from the cradle to the grave.

The architects of curricula in theological institutions must listen to and dialogue with children who flood our churches in Sunday school and with their mothers in the worship services. Special attention must be given to the pastoral needs of orphans, children with disabilities, and girl-children — the most vulnerable among children. It is also vital that in war situations, boy-children must be protected from being recruited as child soldiers. The youth must also play a critical role in the articulation of their frustrations and dreams in the church and society today. Youth fellowships are a good place for theological students and educators to be doing research and developing curriculum.

Certainly, women are fundamental in this enterprise. Women come in many different categories, principally as the primary care-takers and nurturers of children (even when they are not biological mothers), home makers, and breadwinners. Some are widows, others divorcees, or those who have never married. In most of the churches women have strong, dynamic and well organized associations, which actually do a lot of theologizing, fund raising, and charitable work that is foundational for the church. Womanist sociologist Cheryl Townsend Gilkes has argued that women form a group that has known exclusion and invisibility and yet without them the story of the church would be very different.[7]

Men, although a relatively small group in the demography of the churches, play a significant role because they tend to occupy positions of authority and power in the church and society. They

---

[7] *"If It Wasn't For The Women...": Black Women's Experience and Womanist Culture in Church and Community* (Maryknoll: Orbis, 2001), 4.

tend to be the policy and decision makers. They are the leaders and managers of church institutions and almost exclusively determine the direction of the churches' life. Paying critical attention to leadership models and patterns in the churches as well as in Sunday school, brigade, youth, men, and women's fellowship is critical for the development of theological curricula.

Finally, in any community there are groups that are often forgotten; they too must be given a chance to tell their own stories as we shape and fashion a holistic curriculum: people with disabilities (mental and physical), the elderly, the poor, refugees, and internally displaced persons.

The Contexts of Theological Education:
The Socio-Historical Location

A necessary part of developing a theological programme is to know the context in which the students who graduate will do their ministry. Part of that context is historical. Every people has a story. Therefore it will be necessary to identify the socio-historical setting of the people being taught and of those who will receive our graduates' ministry. Of course, Christianity has been with us in Africa for two thousand years, so we will need to understand our present context in the light of this long African history. Neither can we neglect the universal and global nature of the church and the impact it has on the local situation.

Theological students must also learn to name their particular social location as they begin to identify the different aspects of their lives that will form the fabric of their ministry. Activities like keeping a journal, recording what we remember of our childhood, reading newspapers, and Bible study and reflection can all be fruitful ways of helping students to identify and analyze their social location. In my own research I have found that Kenyan newspapers often capture the heartbeat of the society and if we care to listen, we can make a difference in peoples' lives.

Critical socio-historical analysis is foundational even for specialized subjects such as biblical studies. Since the Bible is central in the lives of Christians in Kenya, tracing the history of the Bible in Kenya and how it has been translated and used is critical. Learning how ordinary Christians in different socioeconomic classes articulate the Bible's message should be a necessary part of our theological curriculum.

The purpose of this social analysis by students is to help shape a list of issues that emerge out of our own life experiences. With an awareness of these issues students can begin a more intensive bibliographical research for documentation that will enable a critical evaluation of these issues. Students and lecturers must pay particular attention to theological literature written by Africans. This will help to identify issues that are in need of further reflection. Hopefully, any curriculum revision will give special attention to issues which emerge from such interaction between social location, historical awareness and bibliographical research.

The Contexts of Theological Education: the religio-cultural milieu
Similarly, the integrity of a theological curriculum will depend on a clear perception of the religio-cultural milieu of our peoples. This is particularly important because religion and culture are dynamic aspects of our lives. Any curriculum revision must highlight the primary beliefs and practices that make us Africans and Kenyans. What values and beliefs are known to promote unity and/or disunity among us, for instance?

Over the years Kenyans have interacted with the outside world, especially, in the last one hundred years or so, in the context of religious imperialism and colonial domination. Consequently, many Christians are now at a loss when it comes to understanding African ways of life and the importance of some of our religious rituals and ceremonies. The church in Africa will not be effective if we do not have an in-depth engagement with the African religious worldview. How often do Christians in Africa revert to traditional ways of healing when all else has failed? On the other hand, some practices like female genital mutilation, dowry, and wife inheritance are harmful and demeaning to the dignity of girl-children and women and can only be eradicated through a continuous process of education. The church has a critical role to play in eliminating cultural and religious practices that are life-threatening and dehumanizing. With the same vigour the church must embrace and affirm African religious and cultural values that are life-giving and liberating. Therefore religio-cultural hermeneutics will be a crucial component in formulating appropriate curricula for theological education.

Such study will inevitably lead us to aspects of our corporate life that must be confronted. This process of critical scrutiny will lead us to identify systems, structures, institutions, and ideologies that marginalize, oppress, exploit, and devalue people. We should be alert, therefore, to manifestations of injustice in our societies.

Patriarchy, Sexism, Hierarchy, Clericalism, and Elitism

The above list names systems and structures that are deeply entrenched in our societies and churches but have been neglected or denied, but yet have lasting damage in peoples' lives. The ever-growing global women's movement has emphatically named patriarchy, sexism, hierarchy, and religious elitism and clericalism as fundamental in the exclusion and exploitation of many in the world. Feminism has much to offer us as we reshape appropriate ecumenical theological curriculum.

In Africa there are several women's organizations which rally behind the eradication of these social injustices. In the area of education there is the Forum for African Women Educationist (FAWE); in law there is International Federation of Women Lawyers (FIDA-Kenya); in religion and theology there is the Circle of Concerned African Women Theologians ('the Circle').

For the benefit of those unaware, the Circle aims at a faith-based exploration and critical analysis of the many facets of African women's spirituality. It attempts to create theology and ethics in conversation with the complex realities of African women's lives. These theologians recognize the imagination and initiative that African women have utilized in developing practical religious responses to their lives. In this process, African women theologians are engaged in critical analysis which takes lived experience seriously and which clearly names patriarchy, sexism, hierarchy, religious elitism, and clericalism as major hindrances of the well-being of all people, especially children, the poor and women. In other words, African women theologians together with men seek to create health within African churches societies and to oppose manifestations of injustice.

Theological institutions in Africa stand to benefit if they take seriously what women (and especially the Circle) are saying together with the men who have carefully heeded these voices and have constructively engaged in dialogue. Obviously the majority of women in Africa (and the world over) are still trapped in oppressive structures and there is much work to be done. But the days are gone when African male scholars could argue that "issues of sexism [and patriarchy]...belong to a minority of disgruntled, leisure-saturated, middle class women of the capitalist West. The few Third world women who speak that language are just allowing themselves to be co-opted."[8]

Hence there is an urgent need for a theological curriculum that is intentional about the need to dismantle beliefs and practices that shape and sustain social injustice. In this discussion, religious elitism and clericalism must be given attention since they contribute to the exclusion and marginalization of the majority in the churches (children, women and the poor) and permit the abuse of power in the church. An analysis of power dynamics must be a tool in our theological reflection. A careful reading of the gospels demonstrates that Jesus' life and mission was committed to challenging the patriarchy, sexism, hierarchy, elitism, and clericalism of the day. Africa will be better off if we study the life and ministry of Jesus in this light.

---

[8]Mercy Amba Oduyoye, "Reflections from Third World Woman's Experience: Women's Experience and Liberation Theologies" in *Irruption of the Third World: Challenge to Theology* (eds. Virginia Fabella, and Sergio Torres; Maryknoll: Orbis, 1983), 249.

A study of the structures of injustice will inevitability lead to a critical examination of the family, gender-based violence, and the management and leadership of the institutional church. It should also include the way we communicate the gospel asking who has been excluded from the gospel promises. Because of escalating violence, especially domestic violence against children and women, theological institutions must be prepared to provide pastoral theology which grapples with this reality.

In my view, given the dysfunctional reality of our family life, no area of theology has been so underdeveloped in this country as pastoral theology. On the subjects of polygamous relationships, single-parent homes (run mostly by women), and the ever-growing reality of absent fathers, the church has been largely silent. One only need listen to stories told by girls who have been sexually abused by step-fathers or the stories of abandoned children in which only the mother is blamed (since few seem to ask where the father is). As I was writing this paper, I came across the story of a two-year old girl suing the attorney general in Kenya for a discriminatory law that exonerates fathers from parental responsibilities for children born out of wedlock.[9]

What is needed here is thorough study of the relationship between the rich and poor, female and male, young and old, leaders and followers, literate and non-literate, ordained and non-ordained. Areas such as the taboo subject of human sexuality, sex education, and theology of the body need to be explored. Misinterpretation and misuse of the scriptures has not helped. Violence exists even within the church and requires the attention of sound theological ethical scrutiny of the family, the church, and society. These entrenched social injustices and systematic sins should be subjected to feminist critical theories of liberation as theological students are introduced to ecumenical theological education.

---

[9]*Daily Nation,* Friday, May 16, 2003.

Slave Trade and Slavery

Because of its historical background St. Paul's College needs no convincing that a critical study of the impact of the slave trade and slavery on the African people is critical. This dark history of the African peoples was hidden from us by missionary and colonial education and we the "survivors" must investigate how it has affected our way of life and faith and our ongoing relationship with the countries that participated in this hideous crime against humanity. This part of the curriculum should not overlook the fact that there was also the Arab slave trade as much as we dig into slave trade carried out by Europeans and Euro-Americans.[10] Our curriculum should encourage trips to the East coast of Africa including, the Zanzibar market place, for Christians to glimpse this ugly history in which Christianity played a critical role in both practicing the slave trade and in its abolition. The story would be incomplete without critical engagement with Africans in diaspora in the Americas (South, Central and North America) and elsewhere whose ancestors were subjected to slavery. It would also be helpful for our students to listen to the voices of Sudanese Christians who are still victims of this crime against humanity.

Exchange programmes between Africans and Africans in diaspora should be encouraged. Such trips should also consider visits to the West coast of Africa to the slave trade castles there. Christians, especially theological educators, should not live and work in ignorance of their history. There are many lessons to learn from this story and appropriate theological curriculum in Africa must reveal this ugly past so that we do not continue to repeat it. In Africa, it is important to investigate what kind of faith sustained the families

---

[10][See John Alembillah Azumah, *The Legacy of Arab-Islam in Africa: A Quest for Inter-religious Dialogue* (Oxford: One World, 2001), especially chapter 4: "Muslim Slavery and Black Africa"; cf. the series of books published in Nairobi by Paulines Africa entitled *Faith in Sudan*, edited by Andrew Wheeler and William Anderson (a one-time tutor at St. Paul's Limuru), and the frequent reference to the still current traffic in slaves in that country – Ed.]

and communities torn apart by slavery. Africans can benefit from the research by African-American scholars which has focused on the experience and faith of their enslaved ancestors who embraced but transformed the Christian religion of the white man, the slave traders and owners.[11]

Divide and Rule: Missionary Evangelism and the Colonial Era

In my view, the period of colonial and missionary activity is a subject that deserves much attention as we create theological programmes that will grapple with the true nature of the Church in Africa. Most of the churches today continue to depend on theologies that developed during the missionary enterprise and colonial era. We not only tend to reduce the gospel to "saving of lost souls", we have not gone far enough to decolonize our minds from an inferiority complex. We still tend to treat white people and their ways as superior.

One legacy of the missionary enterprise and colonial era was to divide and rule. The impact of this policy is still seen today. 'Divide and rule' is still alive, for example, in the way we do evangelism and mission to the extent that some Christians have no knowledge of the ecumenical calling of the gospel. We are not only divided according to denominational labels, we also claim to be 'evangelical', 'Pentecostal', 'charismatic', 'spiritual', or 'ecumenical' churches. Rather than develop local ecumenical relationships we prefer to link bilaterally with Euro-American churches and, recently, South Korean churches. Many of these churches encourage denominationalism. A good case in point is the mushrooming of Christian denominational universities in this country and elsewhere in Africa that are supported with money from the Western churches and from South Korea.

Part of the reason ecumenism is fragile in Africa is because theological education and African theology have given little attention to this legacy of divide and rule. We have lived with a colonized

---

[12]Dwight N. Hopkins, *Down, Up, and Over: Slave Religion and Black Theology* (Minneapolis: Fortress, 2000).

mind. Most of the existing curricula in Africa are trapped in Eurocentric theology, leaving many pastors, church leaders, and theological educators unable to tackle the problems of the day, among them divisions in our churches and lack of unity between denominations. Our curriculum revision, therefore, should analyse the beginnings of attempted ecumenical engagement by the mission churches and the reasons for its failure. It is necessary to study why ecumenism in Africa is in crisis after a century of consultations, seminars, dialogues, assemblies, and statements, and the creation of councils of churches that are interested in development projects but almost totally neglect matters of unity, faith, and theology.

Although missionary evangelism and colonialism were very different projects their intricate collaboration demands attention and research. In their own ways, both promoted and exercised imperialism. It is worth engaging in the developing postcolonial theories, including African feminist postcolonial biblical hermeneutics spearheaded by Musa Dube.[12] Theologians must pay more attention to the narrative theology that is found in the African Instituted churches and to other Christian initiatives by Africans that have attempted to decolonize theology. Storytelling, music, and drama must become central methodologies in the process of involving people from all walks of life as we attempt to theologize and formulate life-affirming and life-giving theologies and ethics.[13] We have a long way to go in the quest to decolonize our theology and our minds. Another aspect often overlooked as we focus on the western

---

[12]Dube, Musa. ed., *Other Ways of Reading: African Women and the Bible* (Geneva: WCC Publications, 2001); eadem, *Postcolonial Feminist Interpretation of the Bible* (St. Louis: Chalice Press, 2000).

[13][See, for example, the use of drama in biblical study by Musimbi R.A. Kanyoro in her *Introducing Feminist Cultural Hermeneutics: An African Perspective* (Introductions to Feminist Theology; Cleveland: Pilgrim, 2002); and the indigenous theology in the hymns of the Jieng (Dinka) people of the Sudan collected and translated by the late Marc Nikkel (a one-time tutor at St. Paul's Limuru, in his *Dinka Christianity: The Origins and Development of Christianity among the Dinka of Sudan with Special Reference to the songs of Dinka Christians* (Faith in Sudan, 11; Nairobi: Paulines, 2001) – Ed.]

missionary enterprise is its interaction or lack of interaction with the Orthodox churches in Ethiopia and Egypt that predate this period by many centuries. More research in this area is needed.

Tribalism and Racism

It is no secret that tribalism and racism have found a home in the church. As in sexism, God-given, beautiful differences have been turned into mechanisms of dividing and tearing people apart to the extent that Kenya and Africa as a whole continues to suffer from ethnic conflict, war, racial oppression, and discrimination. The continent has not been spared from genocide even in countries that claim large numbers of Christians.

The church in Africa has the daunting task of breaking down barriers of tribal and racial discrimination. Our theological curricula must not shy away from ongoing injustice and violence promoted by tribalism and racism. It is no secret that some churches in Africa have split because tribal differences have been used to fuel hatred and division. Tribalism and racism breed a culture of mistrust and betrayal in both the society and the churches. In this regard, pastoral theology must lead to self-awareness and recognition that tribalism and racism are sins that call for repentance, forgiveness, reconciliation, and healing of broken relationships. Tribal and racial discrimination must be dismantled if the promise of Pentecost is to be realized in our lives.

Poverty and Ecological Destruction

When I revisit my childhood (in Ihiga-ini village, Nginda location, Maragwa district, Central Province) and remember my early days in parish ministry at the Presbyterian Church of East Africa (PCEA) Bahati Martyrs Parish in Nairobi, I am amazed at the enormity of poverty among our people. After a few months in Bahati parish, I was forced to ask: "Why are we so poor?" My encounter with poverty in the slums of Nairobi taught me how little I knew of my history and how inadequate St. Paul's curriculum was in helping me to come to terms with this reality. Poverty affects the whole person, and whole families and communities. Poverty is the root cause of many injustices and much violence. Poverty should become a central concern of every theological institution on this continent. After all, the mission of Jesus first and foremost had a preferential option for the poor (Mt 25).

Again pastoral theology must recognize that poverty and the accompanying degradation of the environment should be given a central place in our theological programmes, since these realities affect our people at every level. Extreme poverty and ecological destruction create fertile grounds for disease to flourish, for malnutrition and starvation, and ultimately for misery and death. Biblical scholars also must wake up to the occasion to help in the shaping of a curriculum that facilitates a critical understanding of economics, ecology, and ecumenism. The biblical concepts of peace and wholeness (*shalom*) and the year of jubilee must be integrated into our theological agenda.

Our pastoral and liturgical practice need also to take seriously the day to day suffering of the people and to help the church to recognize the agency of the poor as a central factor in contesting poverty. The poor must be mentored to confront political systems that allow poverty to prevail in our continent despite the plentiful natural resources in Africa.

Offering Life-Giving Theological Education

What we have attempted in this paper is to offer a vision of life-giving theological education. An appropriate curriculum for ecumenical theological education will be both deconstructive and constructive and will employ a variety of disciplinary tools. Both field and bibliographical research and study are necessary in the process of creating such a curriculum which will offer life-giving theological education. The experience and perspective of real people are critical if we are to create a life-affirming and life-giving theology and ethics.

It is particularly critical that theologians in Africa study the Bible and African religion and cultures since these are so central in the life of Christians. Despite the fact that the Bible, African religion and cultures have been used to dehumanize individuals and groups of people over the centuries, they are still life-affirming and life-giving and have the potential to shape our lives as Christians. However, given the deep roots of patriarchy and sexism, our curricula must use feminist and liberationist theories and models as we develop each area of study. In other words, gender studies, feminist theology, and liberation hermeneutics must become integral to our ecumenical theological education if we are to contribute to the fostering of justice, peace, dignity, freedom, and responsibility in Africa. This means that African theology and biblical studies must focus on overcoming violence, poverty, hunger, disease, corruption, abusive leadership, and ecological devastation that continue to cause untold suffering and senseless death.

Finally, it has become obvious in my remarks that the architects of any theological curriculum must believe in change and transformation by the power of the Holy Spirit. Space must be given to baptized members of the church, including children, in this process. Appropriate curriculum for ecumenical theological education must be fashioned by all baptized members of the church under the guidance of trained leaders and theologians.

St. Paul's as a Centre of Excellence in Ecumenical Theological Education in Africa

Let me conclude by highlighting my dreams for St. Paul's college as it prepares for its next grand celebration at the 125th birthday.

Africa deserves and needs well-trained theological teachers and leaders, so let me highlight some practical areas that will make this college a centre of excellence in ecumenical theological education for Africa. Given the long list of areas in need of study, and the high expectations we should have of our students, I suggest a programme of five years for a Bachelor of Divinity (three years of course work and two years of practical work), two years for a Masters degree, and four to six years for doctoral studies. The college could offer options for specialisation of ministry, for instance, on children, youth, women, men and people with disability, refugees, and so on. The following suggestions are divided into three areas: finances and physical facilities; areas of study; and alliances and relationships between theological educators, students and church leaders.

Finances and Physical Facilities
A sustainable financial base must be developed through well-organized income generating strategies. This will ensure a well compensated African staff, lecturers and professors, with a well-established promotion track. The college should recruit a proportionate number of lecturers and professors from other continents to enrich the diversity.

The college will need a well-equipped library with computer and media facilities that take into account African traditional ways of communication as well as radio, TV, video, DVD, and whatever information communication technology has to offer. Publishing facilities including a website should be developed. Translation and interpretation facilities, and speech and tape recording facilities are needed.

The college will need buildings and grounds that are accessible for people with disabilities, and alternative ways of learning for those with particular disabilities.

Areas of Study
Research, teaching and preaching methodologies are needed which incorporate inter-disciplinary approaches and the intentional mainstreaming of feminist and liberationist critical theory into all disciplines.

Writing and editorial skills of teachers and students need to be developed.

Study of culturally appropriate worship, liturgy, music, art, and drama should be encouraged in which African creativity and humanity is taken seriously.

Studies in pastoral subjects need to include health and healing ministry for individuals, families, and congregations with a mandatory emphasis on human sexuality, theology of the body, female-male relationships, and sex education. These should integrate HIV/AIDS training.

Theological ethics, ecclesiology, missiology, ecumenical theology, and women's theologies should give prominence to African scholarship without neglecting scholarship rooted in other continents. African religio-cultural studies and biblical hermeneutics should be encouraged without neglecting studies from other cultures and continents.

The historical study of the church in which ecumenism, the women's movement, and liberation movements are emphasized should be an intentional part of any curriculum.

The study of African Traditional Religion, Islam, Judaism, Hinduism, Buddhism, the Baha'i faith, and other faith communities should not be neglected.

Studies which nurture a culture of peace, reconciliation, and justice and encourage the dismantling of a culture of violence should be implemented. This should include critical study of continental and international human and peoples' rights charters, conventions, and declarations.

Biblically and theologically-based practical skills should be taught which equip the student to fight against poverty, starvation, corruption, bad governance, and ecological devastation. This should be a field-based programme that is community-oriented and promotes hands-on work and team ministry.

Building Alliances

Exchange programmes should be encouraged in which visiting theological educators (including Africans in diaspora) enrich the college in various disciplines. This kind of programme should replace the recruitment of missionaries that has a tendency of promoting dependency and paternalism.

The college should develop programmes which attempt to provide career guidance and development for students and continuing education and alumnae relations for graduates.

An office within the college should be devoted to promoting unity and close collaboration with other theological institutions through viable theological associations — nationally, regionally and globally. Such networks should cater for students, lecturers, and church leaders.

Concluding Remarks

These thought-provoking words are from the global consultation on the Ecumenical Response to the Challenge of HIV/AIDS in Africa, held in Nairobi, 25-28th November 2001.

The church is an influential and powerful institution, with the potential to bring about change. The intention is that its activities become more effective, efficient and sustainable as a result of greater coordination, better networking, strengthened communication, and also improved mechanisms for working together, building on each other's experience and success, and avoiding unnecessary duplication of effort.

But the challenge to the churches is felt at a deeper level than this. As the pandemic has unfolded, *it has exposed fault lines that reach to the heart of our theology, our ethics, our liturgy and our practice of ministry.* Today, churches are being obliged to acknowledge that we have—however unwittingly—contributed both actively and passively to the spread of virus. Our difficulty in addressing issues of sex and sexuality has often made it painful for us to engage, in any honest and realistic way, with issues of sex education and HIV prevention. Our tendency to exclude others, our interpretation of the scriptures and our theology of sin have all combined to promote the stigmatization, exclusion and suffering of people with HIV/AID. Given the extreme urgency of the situation, and the conviction that the churches do have a distinctive role to play in the response to the epidemic, *what is needed is a rethinking of our mission, and the transformation of our structures and ways of working.*[14]

Theological education and ministerial formation are powerful and influential processes that can bring change and transformation in the life of the people and communities. It is therefore important that theological institutions rethink their mission and the creation of curricular programmes that will address issues that have lasting effect on our faith and who we are as a people created in God's image. Appropriate theological curriculum must address the "fault lines that reach to the heart of our theology, our ethics, our liturgy and our practice of ministry".

---

[14]*Plan of Action: the Ecumenical Response to HIV/AIDS in Africa* (Geneva: WCC Publications, 2002), 4.

CHAPTER SIX

HIV/AIDS and Other Challenges to Theological Education in the New Millennium

Musa W. Dube

Even long before the scourge of HIV/AIDS, dare I say that creating new theological thinking is long overdue? For so long, many churches in Africa have been living with imported theology, which does not speak to the fears and hopes of the people...
    I am here begging for a theology that will help us ask critical questions about our inactivity or wrongdoing; a theology that will help the child, youth, woman and man in the pew and streets to cultivate a dialogue that will lead to life-giving action in the midst of suffering, misery and death... I am begging for a theology that will provoke us to come together, to argue it out when things go wrong, with or without academic theologians. We need a theology that will creatively help us to retell our story of colonization, cultural and religious imperialism, people's resistance and struggle for land and freedom (*uhuru*, in Swahili) to the point where we say no to injustice, exploitation, globalization and senseless death.[1]

Introduction

I wish to congratulate the alumni, members and staff of this institution, on this occasion of the centennial celebration of St. Paul's United Theological College. I am sure that historians of this theological institution can inform us that you are not only one of

---
[1]Nyambura J. Njoroge, "Come now, let us reason together," *Missionalia* 29/3 (2001): 254.

the oldest institutions of the Kenyan church but of the African continent as well. I hope that you will take this occasion to document, not only the history of your institution, but also a short biographical history of your graduates. We need to know the graduates of this institution and what they have done for their churches, societies, and the world as a whole. One thing I have been told is that when the college was founded its aim was to respond to issues of development and social justice in an area of freed-slave settlement. As you reflect on your vision for mission in the 21st century, you need to keep this history in view, to understand your past, your strengths and weaknesses in order to sharpen this vision. You will indeed need to have an understanding of your world - how it is changing and how you can best position yourself to serve God's changing world. But in particular, I think it will be absolutely important to remember and uphold the role of being guardians of social justice in your theological education.

For my part, the task I have in this celebration and consultation is to highlight the role of theological education by focusing on HIV/AIDS and other challenges in the new millennium. "Theological education has been defined as the task to motivate, equip, and enable the people of God to develop their gifts and give their lives in meaningful service."[2] The easy part of my contribution is that HIV/AIDS automatically includes all other challenges. The difficult part is that HIV/AIDS, as an epidemic that functions within other social epidemics and as an epidemic that affects all aspects of our lives, impacts everything. To speak about the challenges of HIV/AIDS in any thorough way is daunting. At the same time, the task might be lightened by the fact that we are all aware of the devastating impact of HIV/AIDS - the question we must address is how it affects and informs theological education. In this paper I intend to select and

---

[2]Ofelia Ortega, "Theological Education," in *Dictionary of Feminist Theologies* (eds., Letty Russell & Shannon J. Clarkson; Louisville: Westminster John Knox Press, 1996), 282-283.

highlight some of the major aspects of HIV/AIDS and the ways in which they challenge theological education.

Defining Theology

Since I am by training a biblical scholar and only a theologian by practice, it is important for me to give my own working definition of theology and theological education. This is particularly so because two weeks ago I was in a workshop in which a professor spoke about HIV/AIDS and theology and people disagreed with his definition. If I give you my working definition, you will at least judge my words within their own framework.

In my understanding, theology is a reflection on the Divine Being within a particular context, people, time, and framework of belief. It is a search for the divine will and revelation within the lives of a people in their given circumstances. When we define theology from a Christian point of view, we may say it is the interpretation of biblical scriptures for contemporary meaning. It follows that there will/should be many theologies depending on who is doing the reflecting, since we all live in particular contexts, circumstances, and frameworks of faith in God.

Thus, in our age we have seen the rise of theologies with various names such as liberation theology, African theology, black theology, women's theology, feminist theology, Asian theology, contemporary theology, Catholic and Protestant theology, as well as theologies that do not identify themselves. All these different names denote that theology arises from particular people, reflecting within a particular context, within a certain set of circumstances and terms of belief. For example, when we speak of African theology we are referring to a theology that arises from Sub-Saharan Africa, and is linked to the struggle for liberation and independence. This theology regards African cultures and biblical tradition as its most important theological resources. African theology assumes that God has been revealed in African cultures and thus the latter serve as an important base for the propagation of the Gospel of Christ. Asian theology in all its varieties, seeks to address the various social circumstances that confront Asian people such as poverty and suffering and religious pluralism. Latin American theology arises in the geographical area that co-exists with superpowers in a situation of dire poverty. Latin American theology is thus a theology of liberation that begins with the assumption that God takes sides with the poor against all the social structures and circumstances that have reduced them to ungodly oppression.

If theology is a contextual and particular reflection, it follows that theology is not neutral or static. It can arise from upper or lower classes, dominant and oppressed groups, men or women. Theology can assume official and unofficial status. If it also depends on particular terms of reference or frameworks of belief in God, it follows that theology can be liberating or oppressing, depending on the terms of reference used by a particular group to reflect on their context and their circumstances. Regretfully, theological institutions have sided with official, dominant, upper class theology, a theology that does not help the most marginalized members of our societies to assert what they believe is God's will for them in their particular circumstances. When this happens, the prophetic voice, the voice of social transformation is lost in our theological formation. Theological education becomes another servant of the *status quo* rather than the voice of liberation. Happily, in the last thirty years many marginalized voices have been raised, calling for a theology that springs from village prayers and songs[3] or from ordinary readers.[4]

My Theological Framework

The question immediately arises as to whether a particular theology is legitimate. I believe this will largely depend on the frame of reference that we hold and the relationships that we believe are

---

[3] Mercy Amba Oduyoye, *Hearing and Knowing: Theological Reflections on Christianity in Africa* (Maryknoll: Orbis, 1986); Henry Okullu, *Church and Politics in East Africa* (Nairobi: Uzima Press, 1974).

[4] Gerald West and Musa W. Dube, eds. *Semeia 73: "Reading With"* (Atlanta: Scholars Press, 1996).

sanctioned by God. Our frame of reference informs the ethics of our belief in the Divine Being and what passes as God's will for creation, humanity and the relationships within. That is, what passes as legitimate or let me say, godly, theology will largely depend on what we believe holds true as God's will for humanity and for creation as a whole in this world. My own theological framework is largely informed by the fact that I subscribe very much to the following beliefs; namely, that creation as a whole was created by God and it was created good, hence all life is sacred; that all people, regardless of their color, gender, class, race, religion, ethnicity, health status, age, or sexual orientation, were created in God's image and are loved by the same, and given human dignity and access to earthly resources; that the Divine hand created all things to be interconnected and in balance; that when some people are denied their human dignity, God's will is disregarded; that when balance, the goodness, the image of God is violated in creation, evil results; that human beings are made in God's image to become co-creators with God, given the task of ensuring that the goodness of the earth and its balance remains to and for all and to God; that the church is particularly positioned to be the guardian of God's will in the world; that God's revelation continues to be manifested to us through the Holy Spirit and the prophets that arise among us. Clearly, this framework does not subscribe to perspectives which, for whatever reason, hold that certain groups of people - on the basis of their ethnicity, health status, gender, race, age, class, or sexual orientation - should be subjugated, oppressed or denied their God-given human dignity. In this framework, salvation is liberation from spiritual, physical, economic, cultural and political oppression and from exploitative structures and institutions. In this framework, social structures and institutions that sanction oppression and exploitation do not represent God's will, and must be counteracted by those of us who accept the role of God's stewards in caring for the earth.

Theological Education

My theological framework shapes my understanding of theological education and its role. I believe that theological education should be a servant of God's will for God's world and God's people. Theology thus aims to shape faith communities to be the voice that speaks God's will and seeks the establishment of God's will for creation as a whole. It follows that theological education does not have a choice but to be socially engaged and socially educated. Theological education should not just be the voice of the voiceless (in which theology is considered to be the province of trained academic theologians and the clergy) but theology should empower the powerless to speak for themselves and to insist on their God-given human dignity. Theological education must enable the laity to be God's servants and co-creators in the world, by being the stewards of God's will in our communities. This, I believe, is essential for us to recapture as we seek to sharpen our vision for mission in the 21st century and as we search for ways forward for ecumenical theological education. That is, we seek a theological education that seeks to empower all subjects to know God's will, to seek it, and to speak it in our world. If you agree with me on some of these views, in particular on my frame of reference, what shape would our theological education take? What shape does it have now and how does it need to change?

We have often turned our theological institutions and their programmes into icons of power, prestige, patriarchy, hierarchy, and elitism. We measure the quality of each institution and programme according to the amount of official, upper class, standards or sometimes church theology that a particular institution can showcase. Thus when we assess institutions for accreditation we look for particular academic standards. For an institution to be considered a strong place of theological education, its library must stock certain Greek philosophers and German scholars, and the student reading lists and course outlines must reflect the use of particular theological authorities. We expect the lecturers to be graduates of particular universities and departments that have upheld these standards. We tend to expect theological colleges to reproduce certain concretized theologies and perpetuate them. In other words, our standards are not measured by just how much the particular institution, its lecturers and research are socially engaged and how their programmes seek to be midwives of God's justice in the world and for all creation. I am not saying there is something wrong with holding on to very concrete traditional standards. But if we have come to a point where these standards stifle the very heart and role of theological education then we should rethink those standards. We must review our theological education so that it shapes our faith communities into dynamic prophetic voices that constantly bring our societies and institutions to the light of God's justice.

The question of relevant theological education is even more pressing here in Africa, where our theological education is not only threatened by the role of preserving concretized academic theological standards, it is also historically colonized. Many theological programmes are transported from the West to Africa through historically colonial relationships, through training scholars in the West, through paternalistic sponsorship, through accreditation, sometimes, through unimaginative African scholars who do not want to take the responsibility of constantly re-viewing and re-writing their programmes to make them answerable to our communities. One finds that in many African institutions, the theological formation of students is based on western theology, that is, a theology that was meant to deal with pressing issues of the western world, which nonetheless has no immediate, obvious, or direct relevance for the African context. Further, this theology is cast in thought forms and languages that do not immediately communicate to African students. Such formation has unfortunately given rise to a socially divorced theological education, an educational consciousness that hardly has anything to say about the presence, activity, and will of God in our particular contexts. Such theological formation has often produced stillborn church leaders and scholars, whose theological voice is non-existent. Their theological vision is dead by the time they march in their graduation robes.[5] Such faith leaders cannot help the communities that they lead to insist that God's justice roll through our streets. With such theological education, what hope can we find in our faith communities? Theological education is central to social formation and to understanding the mission of the church in the world. So we must constantly seek to make theological education relevant to its contexts.

Many years ago, John Mbiti satirically presented a picture of the weakness of African theological education. Mbiti told a story of a newly returned PhD graduate student who was called upon to save his sister from spirit possession. Instead of focusing on the demands of his context, he went to the wonderful theological book of Bultmann, who said such a phenomenon has been demythologized. The graduate student then said the sister must be taken to the hospital. Unfortunately the hospital was many miles away! With all his theological education he could not help his sister. The theological formation of this student was shown to be impotent.[6] As the new millennium begins, it remains to be seen just how much African theological education has moved to design theological education that sparks God's light amongst all God's people within their various contexts and in creation as a whole. Now in the 21st century, as we reflect on a vision for mission and seek for ways forward in ecumenical theological education, I believe it is imperative for this institution to centre its quest around the question 'How can our theological programmes become midwives of social justice in the society and the world, by grooming faith communities that understand their role?'

I can almost hear the bang of some protesting hearts! Some are saying, 'What! Are you saying we should discard established theological standards that have been built over the centuries? What would be the mark of quality for theological education and

---

[5]Dube and West, *Reading With*, 7-17.

[6]Re-told by Maluleke in "The Challenge of HIV/AIDS for Theological Education in Africa: Towards an HIV/AIDS Sensitive Curriculum" *Missionalia* 29/3 (2001): 126-27.

formation?' Well, this is what we are called to re-imagine in this Consultation. For me it is not the standards that matter, but the impact of our theological education on the social formation of our faith communities. Some may be saying, 'You graduated from western institutions and you still have a voice.' I will tell you my own history of theological training shortly.

I think it is also clear that if theological education is to assist the social formation of the church, then we cannot limit ourselves to teaching only prospective religious leaders or academic theologians. Rather, theological education must be extended to the laity, to the faith communities. Our theological institutions must make space for faith communities to be theological subjects. Similarly, lay training institutions and programmes should be strengthened to equip faith communities to live out their faith. And the churches themselves need to raise their 'Sunday school' theology up to relevant levels. This really calls us to become faith communities that value theological education as a necessity for all, as an instrument of social transformation which is constantly seeking the presence of God in our world. In my Africa-wide travels, where I train theological educators and faith communities about theological thinking in the HIV/AIDS era, I have heard people saying, 'A theology of HIV/AIDS is really needed' or, 'Yes, yes! This is the theological question that I have been having questions about. You tackled it very well.' One has the feeling that when our faith communities confront theological questions concerning issues in their societies, they wait for their religious leaders or some trained theologians to tackle the issue. If they hear these issues tackled in ways that are insufficient or not addressed they keep quiet. They do not feel empowered to articulate the relevant theology themselves, even when they harbour legitimate questions in their hearts. They are not (or they do not feel) theologically empowered to become speaking subjects. As theological educators we should not only believe that the laity should be theologically trained, we should also make concrete plans for this implementation.

My Story of Theological Education

Turning to the story of my theological training, I did my first degree in the University of Botswana, where I did a double major in Environmental Science and Theology. For my second degree, I went to the prestigious University of Durham in the U.K. For my third degree I went to Vanderbilt University in the U.S.A. One thing I found common to both of my prestigious graduate schools is that I did not find one course on African religions and African theology, nor did I ever find one textbook written by an African as a required book. I was really struck by this. Even in my first degree in Botswana, I had had to grapple with such famous theological thinkers as Paul Tillich, Rudolf Bultmann, the Niebuhrs, and Karl Barth in addition to reading John Mbiti, John Pobee, Desmond Tutu and Itumeleng Mosala (clearly they were all male!). I was so surprised how theological institutions of the West could so completely ignore us when we could not ignore them. While studying in Durham, a beautiful college town on a peninsula of land surrounded by meandering river, I sat one afternoon on a bench beside the river. The grass and the trees were heavenly green. I gave a moment of thought to my studies. In particular I said to myself, "If my father was to ask me what I am studying, what would I tell him?" I found that what I was studying was excellent but was not communicable, in the sense that it was totally another world, one whose relevance could hardly be seen within my own context.

When I got to Vanderbilt, I found the same exclusion of anything African. I spoke to one of my professors and said, "This school is racist and discriminatory. Why is that African Religions, theologies and authors are not studied? I think I want to stage a one-person demonstration for this is evident racism." My professor said to me, "Go ahead and demonstrate. Maybe you will bring the necessary changes." Then he said to me, "As for biblical studies, if you give me names of African authors, I will be glad to include them in my required and recommended reading list." While the latter seems an amicable response, we have to ask ourselves, what is wrong with a world system where after fifty years of African biblical studies, their works are still unknown (or should I say unread) in the western world, when we have been reading western theologians since God knows when.[7] Be that as it may, someone must tell me why *African theological programmes and institutions feel that we need western theological works and scholars when the West does not feel the same need about us? Why do we keep to their theological standards if it stifles our theological spark?* These questions beg to be answered. Some of you are probably asking how I moved from being a stillborn graduate student to becoming a speaking voice. Before I share that I must say that I feel like I am trying to resurrect myself from the valley of dry bones. First, I occupied my theological studies with resistance, suspicion, and with constant questioning of what it means that I am an African Motswana woman who is studying the Bible in the West.[8] Second, I found ways of learning from the periphery. For my Master's thesis I wrote on "Mary as Our Ancestor: An African Woman's Search for Identity."[9] I did a research project on African biblical hermeneutics and found that several works on Christology had been done - but from an African male perspective. Jesus had been read as the Ancestor, Big Brother, Elder brother, Proto-ancestor, Chief, King.[10] Not only was I alienated by white male biblical interpretation, but the African works themselves were quite male. As an African woman I was doubly alienated. Thus I made attempts to construct an African feminist Christology on *Mary as our Ancestor.* For my PhD at Vanderbilt I asked for two independent studies, one

---

[7] Cf. Musa Dube, "Villagizing, Globalizing and Biblical Studies," in *Reading the Bible in the Global Village: Cape Town* (Justin Ukpong, et al; Atlanta; SBL, 2002), 41-63.

[8] See West and Dube, *Reading With*; Musa Dube, "Go Therefore and Make Disciples of All Nations," (Matt 28:19a): A Postcolonial Perspective on Biblical Criticism and Pedagogy," in *Teaching the Bible: The Discourses and Politics of Biblical Pedagogy* (ed. F.F. Segovia and Mary Ann Tolbert; Maryknoll: Orbis, 1998), 224-243.

[9] M.A. thesis, University of Durham, 1990.

[10] Elizabeth Amoah, "Christologies, African," in *Dictionary of Third World Theologies,* ed., Virginia Fabella and R.S. Sugirtharajah (Maryknoll: Orbis, 2000), 41-42.

on Postcolonial theories and another on the portrait of African women in the African novel. In the end, I combined these to write a dissertation now published as *Postcolonial Feminist Interpretation of the Bible*.[11] Indeed, many Africans who have studied in the West can tell their own stories of how they had to learn from the periphery or had to come back and re-educate themselves. Yet not all are lucky enough to design independent studies that help them to refocus on their backgrounds, nor do all have sufficient space and time to reconstruct our theological thinking once we return. But why should African students spend the bulk of their graduate education learning a theological discourse that is alien to their contexts and only get self-taught when they seek to be relevant for their context? This kills a great part of our theological imagination, especially considering that most African scholars, once they are back in the field, are really overworked.

Further questions need to be asked. If we have institutions such as yours in Limuru, a hundred years old, why do we still need to send our students overseas only to come back theologically muted? Why are we not providing appropriate theological education ourselves? And when we provide education here, why do we have to provide foreign theological education? Why do we have our programmes accredited from outside? Finally, western theological institutions cannot be completely exonerated. If the western institutions realize that the center of Christianity is shifting towards the south; if they realize that our world is becoming more pluralist everyday and if they care to provide ecumenical theological education, why is it that African religions, theologies, and authors (indeed Two-Thirds World theologies generally) hardly feature in their programmes? In short, it is not only the African continent that needs to reassess theological education, a worldwide rethinking is needed. We all need to ask how our theological programmes serve to equip our graduates, our communities of faith, and our societies to be

---

[11]St. Louis: Chalice Press, 2000.

guardians of God's goodness on earth. With that let me return to the question of HIV/AIDS and its challenge to theological education.

The Context of HIV/AIDS & Theological Education

In this day of HIV/AIDS, we are in a context that produces particular circumstances. Since theology is a reflection on God's activity and will for creation in all circumstances, it follows that there is already a theology of HIV/AIDS. The moment we ask what God is saying to us through HIV/AIDS, what God's will is concerning this disease, whether God loves us, whether God cares, and where God's healing is in this HIV/AIDS era, then a theology of HIV/AIDS has begun. We have begun to reflect on a particular context and to seek God's will for God's own people in their particular circumstances of HIV/AIDS.

The statistics of HIV/AIDS infection are staggering: 40 million have been infected; 22 million have died in twenty-two years and 14 million children have been orphaned.[12] And as we speak people are being infected. The statistics hide the truth. They do not tell us how many billions of people are gripped by HIV/AIDS stigma, which manifests itself as fear, hopelessness, lack of belief in the future, indifference towards the suffering, and isolation and rejection of those who are HIV/AIDS positive.

As a new epidemic, HIV/AIDS produces a particular context on three fronts. First, the fact that HIV/AIDS is a global catastrophe means that it calls for the response of all of us, wherever we are. HIV/AIDS is not (as some have come to mistakenly think) an African disease. It is a global epidemic. In that sense, it offers us a chance to develop and strengthen our ecumenical theology and response. Second, HIV/AIDS is an epidemic within other social epidemics such as poverty, gender inequality, abuse of children, racism, ethnic conflict, war, international injustice, and discrimination on the basis of sexual orientation. Given that HIV/AIDS functions within other social epidemics, it is the most marginalized members of the world

---

[12]UNAIDS 2001:1; UNAIDS 2002:8.

who are the most vulnerable to infection and lack of quality care. The worst part about HIV/AIDS is that it makes the marginalized even more marginalized. The poor become poorer, children become more disempowered, widows become dispossessed and thrown out of their homes. Third, HIV/AIDS affects all aspects of our lives: the spiritual, mental, political, cultural, social, economic, and psychological. It affects everything and everyone. It questions the very fabric of our existence and calls for rethinking and research on what we have always taken for granted.

These three aspects have a multitude of implications for a theological education which is socially engaged and which seeks to enable religious leaders and communities of faith to be partners with God in keeping all creation within God's intention and will. It goes without saying that if HIV/AIDS is a global catastrophe then, globally, theological institutions should have by now integrated HIV/AIDS in their programmes. It has been twenty-two years since this epidemic invaded our world; how many of our theological programmes have responded to this global context by developing such courses as 'Reading the Bible in the HIV/AIDS Era', 'Doing Theology in the HIV/AIDS Context', 'Christian Mission and HIV/AIDS', 'Ethics and HIV/AIDS', 'African Religions and HIV/AIDS', 'Islam and HIV/AIDS', 'Human Sexuality and HIV/AIDS', or 'Liberation Theology in the HIV/AIDS Era'. It would be interesting to carry out a worldwide survey of theological institutions to assess how they have programmatically responded to HIV/AIDS. This would be telling in so far as it would measure the relevance of our theological education to our contexts and time.

Second, the fact that HIV/AIDS is an epidemic within other social epidemics is a critical issue for how we formulate our theological content and the intention of our theological education. If HIV/AIDS works with poverty, gender inequality, violence against women, war, national corruption, international injustice, child abuse, human rights violations, stigma, racism, war, ethnic conflict and cleansing, and discrimination on the basis of sexual orientation, we can only be theologically answerable if we have an understanding of these social epidemics and if we are able critically to assess their origin, causes, and how they can be stemmed. Theological education will be able to stand up to the challenge if it gives students and communities of faith concrete tools for social analysis. Our theological programmes will have to have a frame of reference that enables our students to reflect on the question of what God's will is concerning these social evils. Unless our theological education brings our students and our faith communities to see these social evils as violating God's will and creation; unless it underlines that all life is sacred; unless we underline that healing is God's will for all, then how can our students become theological leaders who seek to be partners with God in caring for the earth in the HIV/AIDS era? Theological education must be social formation; it must provide a vision for mission that underlines that all life is sacred.

Indeed, the initial theological response to HIV/AIDS has demonstrated our theological poverty in many ways. First, there was silence and indifference. Then there was an association of HIV/AIDS with immorality and God's punishment upon the sinful. When the churches finally decided to be actively involved, they insisted on abstinence and faithfulness as the only answer to the fight against HIV/AIDS. The condom is still outlawed as encouraging promiscuity. While A (abstinence) and B (be faithful) seems ideal, the truth is that this perspective overlooks that HIV/AIDS is an epidemic within other social epidemics. While it would seem that every individual could prevent HIV/AIDS by applying A or B, unjust social circumstances and institutions make it impossible for many individuals to apply these ideals. An effective fight against HIV/AIDS must, therefore, not only focus on the individual, but must equally address the social injustices that fuel HIV/AIDS since an individual's choices are determined by their social location and the institutions in which they live. For example, both poverty and gender inequalities render A and B strategies ineffective. Many poor, unemployed and unmarried mothers or evicted and dispossessed widows, who nonetheless have children to feed, have to choose between dying of starvation in two weeks or engaging in sex work and dying ten years later of HIV/AIDS. While I will agree that the condom, like A & B, is not one hundred percent safe, I have found it troubling that churches are unwilling to admit that it is another usable tool. One could well say that while the world said ABC, faith communities were saying ABD: abstain, be faithful, or die. There is here a theological perspective that has dangerously subjugated the imperative to preserve life to the ideal of sexual purity. Christian faith communities were overlooking a central theological base, namely that all life is sacred. This reflects a dire theological poverty and immaturity. As I have argued elsewhere,

In our fight against HIV/AIDS, we must develop a well-grounded theology of respect for life. Our prophetic theology must be grounded and propelled by a theology of respect for life. It must be based on the conviction that God does not wish anyone to be infected by HIV/AIDS—regardless of whether that person was failing to abstain or to be faithful. We need, therefore, to continue saying, abstain, be faithful, but whenever you have sex, condomise.[13]

I believe theological education has a great task to address here, namely, that HIV/AIDS is not only an issue of individual immorality, but rather, it is also very much a disease of social injustice. The two must be seen and tackled together. Theological education needs to assist in bringing our faith leaders and communities to realize that our mission in the HIV/AIDS era is to develop and implement a prophetic theology of life in the fight against HIV/AIDS, one that is able to address the individual and the social circumstances around her or him.

It is at least fifty years since the United Nation Charter of Human Rights was passed and many other charters and declarations have challenged us to have a better respect for life; declarations for women's rights, children's rights, protection of the environment, and culture have been signed. The world itself is trying to respect life. Most of our theological programmes, however, still need to reflect

---

[13]Musa Dube, "Preaching to the Converted: Unsettling the Christian Church," *Ministerial Formation* 93 (2001): 38-50.

on this international context of seeking to respect life and to build on it. Here we will do well to heed the voice of Sr. Teresa Okure, who insists that the phrase 'a biblical interpreter' refers to "anybody who reads the biblical text in order to discover life" and that "any interpretation that fails to do this... becomes suspect and should be regarded as inauthentic," since it would have failed to "be in tune with universal intention of God to liberate, save, give and sustain life."[14] We need a life-centered theology for our communities and for our world. The fact that the response of faith communities has emphasized only individual responsibility or lack of responsibility to the exclusion of evil, unjust social structures and institutions has been quite telling. It reveals that faith leaders do not have the skills of social analysis to be able to discern how social structures and institutions affect individual decisions. This is both a statement and challenge to our theological education to raise up faith leaders and communities that are prophetic, that are able to see social injustice and to challenge it. We cannot afford to offer theological education that does not seek social justice.

Turning to the issue of gender justice, it is at least forty years since modern feminist theology began. Yet many of our theological programmes treat it as a novelty; they leave it to a few women in the staff or completely ignore it. Often even the women in theological institutions struggle to introduce gender studies; they are ridiculed, marginalized, and sometimes threatened. In the HIV/AIDS training that I hold for theological educators, I always talk about gender and HIV/AIDS. In these workshops some heads of departments have openly told me to stop this 'gender nonsense.' In some evaluations people have written that this was an excellent workshop, but almost spoiled with 'our gender nonsense.' This resistance from theological leaders and educators means that our students who become religious leaders graduate with no understanding of what gender inequalities

---

[14]Teresa Okure, "Reading From This Place: Some Prospects and Problems," in *Reading From This Place, Volume 2*, ed., Fernando Segovia and Mary Ann Tolbert (Minneapolis: Fortress Press, 1995), 55, 57.

are and how religious leaders are to work with the cultural, social, economic, political, and spiritual institutions of our world.

In this HIV/AIDS era, however, gender inequalities are second only to poverty in being a major driving force behind the spread of HIV/AIDS. Many economically, culturally, politically, and religiously powerless women find that abstaining, being faithful, or having a condom or femidom shields will not save them from HIV/AIDS infection. Many men who know about the dangers of HIV/AIDS still refuse to give up the culture of multiple partners and refuse to share power with their women partners. Further, they refuse to use condoms, for in so doing they would betray their manhood, which encourages them to be brave and take risks. At the end of the day no one wins. Only HIV/AIDS wins. Any theologically responsible education, which wants to contribute to the struggle against HIV/AIDS and which subscribes to the theological economy that says we are all made in God's image, must address gender inequality and provide theological education which helps us to establish gender justice. Subjects such as gender and theology; gender and HIV/AIDS; gender, the Bible and HIV/AIDS; gender and African religions, all must be a compulsory part of the curriculum. Gender must be mainstreamed across all subjects, for we are always gendered men and women. All forms of knowledge must acknowledge this in research, writing and teaching. Failure to do this is failure to prepare our students for leadership in society. Worse, failure to do this is to become guardians of social evil rather than agents who work to curb the spread of HIV/AIDS.

When it comes to the issue of children, this is perhaps one area where most of our theological programmes are glaringly lacking.[15] Being some of the most powerless members of our societies, children hardly have any theological voice. Our institutions have not yet fully

---

[15]T.S. Maluleke and Sarojini Nadar, ed., *Special Issue: Overcoming Violence Against Women and Children: Journal of Theology for Southern Africa* 112 (2002); Musa Dube, "Fighting and Crying With God: Children and HIV/AIDS in Botswana," *Journal of Theology for Southern Africa* 114 (2002): 31-42.

found a way of allowing them to speak and be heard. HIV/AIDS has once more highlighted the plight of children as powerless citizens of our world communities. Children face an uncertain future as their parents die, as they are dispossessed by neighbours and relatives, as they are stigmatized at school and at home and as they are subjected to child labour. Given the myth that virgins can cleanse one of HIV/AIDS, rape has escalated. Orphans are increasing. Most of our governments have not yet responded by putting into place legal instruments that will protect children. Our theological education needs to develop a theological perspective that allows our faith communities to become guardians of children's rights as well as allowing children to speak and be heard.[16]

Here in Africa, most of us are doing theology in corrupt nations and under repressive leadership, where populations are condemned to exploitation and poverty. HIV/AIDS research and documentation indicates that poverty is the number one underlying cause of the spread of HIV/AIDS. How much has our theological education done to equip students and communities of faith to be prophetic voices in the society? What can our theological education do? We need to concern ourselves with what theological education can do to equip faith communities with a prophetic theology of life against national corruption and poverty. National corruption is not only limited to Two-Thirds World countries; it also applies to First World Countries. Indeed the poverty of the former is linked to unjust international trade policies which have locked many of our countries into huge debts and perpetual poverty. In this HIV/AIDS era we know that, poverty is the chief contributing cause of the epidemic. This, as well as the reluctance to let Two-Thirds World countries produce affordable HIV/AIDS drugs, has seen many die unnecessarily of HIV/AIDS. What should be the perspective of theological education and training concerning the resources of the earth and access to them? If we believe that the earth and everything in it belongs to the Lord then, I believe, our theological education should empower our faith

---

[16]Dube, "Fighting and Crying With God," 31-33.

leaders and communities to be prophetic and programmatically to undertake to fight poverty and national and international injustice.

In addition to all these social evils, HIV/AIDS has spawned a second epidemic, perhaps a more deadly one: the HIV/AIDS stigma. Fear of an incurable disease, fear of death after long suffering, misunderstanding about HIV/AIDS transmission, the association of HIV/AIDS with sexuality and misinterpretation of the causes of HIV/AIDS, and indifference to suffering have all contributed to this second and even more deadly disease of HIV/AIDS stigma. It is deadly because it hinders both prevention of HIV/AIDS and the provision of quality care. It is deadly because every human being is a social being. When rejected the social, psychological, and spiritual health of a person is also affected, thus leading people to die long before the virus could kill them. Our theological education needs to help our students and communities of faith to develop a theology of compassion, compassion as the capacity to suffer with, to enter the pain of the other, not just to be in solidarity with the suffering, but to translate our compassion into the energy needed to transform the conditions of people. Those of us who are in the Christian faith need to recapture the compassion of Christ, who asked the believers to see his face in the face of all who suffer (Mat 25: 31-46).[17]

Before I turn to other challenges, the fact that HIV/AIDS is an epidemic within other social epidemics underlines the reality that for our theological programmes to enable our students to be effective leaders in the society, they must be given tools that enable them to understand society and social evils. Our theological programmes must also emphasize that social evils, together with HIV/AIDS, violate God's creation. Therefore our mission in the 21st century is to speak out and search for new models of a better world. Instead of engaging in theological theories and content that are divorced from our social context, we will need theological programmes that are largely informed by a framework that holds that God's salvation is

---

[17]Cf. Musa Dube, "Theological Challenges: Proclaiming the Fullness of Life in the HIV/AIDS and Global Economic Era," *International Review of Mission* 91/363 (2002): 536-40.

the liberation of all humankind and creation as well as one that holds that faith communities should be trained to be midwives of God's will on earth.

Other Challenges

Other challenges that confront us as theological educators of Africa and elsewhere are globalization, increasing violence in the form of civil wars, ethnic conflicts, religious differences, violence against children and increasing violence against women. Globalization has been defined as the "compression of the world,"[18] "the creation of a single international financial or capital market,"[19] "the absorption of all countries and systems into one,"[20] or the process whereby the "search for more profits became the search for cheap labor."[21] The problem with globalization has been graphically described for us by the Asian Theological Conference, which holds that in globalization, Money with a capital M was promoted as the storehouse of value, rather than a medium for exchange. ... Every relationship in which people were involved and stayed outside the purview of the markets, such as education, health care and religious practices were also brought into the reality of market. Market now has control over the

---

[8]Roland Robertson, "Globalization and the Future of Traditional Religion," in *God and Globalization Volume 1: Religion and Powers of Common Life,* ed,. Stackhouse Max L. & Peter Paris (Harrisburg: Trinity Press International 2000), 53-54.

[9]Christopher Lind, *Something is Wrong Somewhere: Globalization, Community and the Moral Economy of the Farm Crisis* (Halifax: Fernwood Publishing, 1995), 31.

[20]Peter Tolloch, "Globalization: Blessing or Curse? Buzz-word or Swear-word," in *Sustainability and Globalization.* ed., Julion de Santa Ana (Geneva: WCC Publications, 1995), 101.

[21]Mohau Pheko, "Privatization, Trade Liberation and Women's Socio-economic Rights: Exploring Policy Alternatives," in *Africa: Gender, Globalization and Resistance,* ed., Yassine Fall (New York: AAword, 2000), 90.

social, economic, political and cultural relationships of the people. All other social forces, including the state, which regulated people's needs, have ceased to operate...therefore, people are turned into labor or prostitutes, nature as land or raw materials or golf parks and culture as souvenirs ... in tourist market. Moreover, the organizing philosophy of the market ecclesia... is social exclusion: Those who have no commoditable money or commoditable commodities (including skills) were excluded from the market and left as expendables.[22]

In short, while globalization seeks for trade liberalization, "which would allow goods and services and money to move easily across the borders"[23] and while it is noted for producing massive profits, these profits are concentrated in the hands of a very few individuals, while its policies and impact exclude and exploit the majority. In the age of HIV/AIDS, globalization - which increases mobility, separates families, creates job insecurities, increases poverty, and weakens social services - cannot help but spread the infection rate and deny people quality care. In the economy of God's will for creation, the impact of globalization is highly problematic and needs our theological attention. Again, we must ask ourselves how many of us have meaningfully begun to dialogue with globalization as an issue that must inform our theological education.[24] Turning to violence, of late we have become aware that our world is becoming even more violent or using violence as a solution to attempt to solve problems. What immediately comes to our minds is 9/11, the subsequent so-called war on terrorism, the unending Palestine-Israel conflict, and the ethnic and civil wars of Africa. In these past

---

[22] Asian Theological Conference 2000: 218-219.
[23] Pheko, "Privatization, Trade Liberation and Women's Socio-economic Rights," 90.
[24] Justin Ukpong, "Reading the Bible in a Global Village: Issues and Challenges From African Readings," *Reading the Bible in the Global Village: Cape Town*, ed., Justin Ukpong, et al. (Atlanta: SBL, 2002), 9-40; Musa Dube, "Villagizing, Globalizing and Biblical Studies," 46-63.

weeks we have seen a string of bombings. I even had to avoid using British Airways to come to this Consultation, because they had shut down flights to Nairobi for fear of a possible terrorist bombing. Those of us who are here will remember the horror of the Rwandan Genocide in 1994 and on-going massacres in Burundi and how Christians participated in such crimes against humanity and God. I think that these events are really a theological indictment of all of us who are involved in Christian theological education as social formation. Reports from Rwanda-Burundi indicate that more Christians are turning to Islam, having lost confidence in the relevance of the Christian faith for their well-being. Indeed, given the number of civil wars that characterize the African continent, we run a danger of accepting violence as a permanent part of our lives.

But maybe these are simply the most evident symptoms of a violent world. Underlying these public events we have violence against women and children which happens in the streets and in homes. Women and children are beaten and raped and we do not feel safe to walk freely without looking behind our back. Is this God's will for us? Are there other ways of dealing with our differences rather than turning to violence? In their *Special Issue: Overcoming Violence Against Women and Children*, Tinyiko S. Maluleke and Sarojini Nadar hold that, violence is "a deadly covenant cultivated and reinforced in attitudes, teachings, practices and rituals that tear human societies apart. ...Above all, this is a covenant of silence - silence about violence, especially violence against women."[25]

Maluleke and Nadar continue to say,

> In our experience women victims of violence in society are up against a social covenant with violence against them. For example, in cases of domestic abuse the battle is not only against the abuser, but also against a host of other conspirators, people who have entered into a covenant of violence with the abuser himself. Such participants in the unwritten covenant with violence and silence often include pastors, church elders,

---

[25]Maluleke and Nadar, *Overcoming Violence Against Women and Children: Journal of Theology for Southern Africa* 112 (2002): 7.

siblings and parents. Their participation in the covenant often manifests in the advice and counsel they give to the woman victim: telling her that it is her fault that she is beaten; advising her that 'the Bible says' that she must be submissive; telling her that marriage is *like that*.[26]

Living as they do in violent contexts, African theologians are grappling with violence both at national and continental levels. In her article, "Come Let Us Reason Together," Nyambura Njoroge writes that "Kenya has increasingly become a violent nation" and continues to say, "this has become so bad to be almost a civil war," and that "most of the people in Kenya are indifferent, apathetic, complacent, disillusioned, hopeless and in despair. Violence and poverty have deeply destroyed people's self-confidence and dignity."[27] Njoroge thus calls for "a spirituality and ethic of resistance, of not giving up and of transformation."[28] As she explains, "This ethic and spirituality drive people to confront leadership crises and the structural sins of imperialism, globalization, patriarchy, hierarchy, sexism, and other social sins that leads the majority of people into a life of misery, agony and suffering."[29] Similarly, in his article, "Mission and Social Formation: Searching for an Alternative to King Leopold's Ghost", Emmanuel Katangole examines the colonial effects of violence on the psyche of African people. Here Katangole echoes Mercy A. Oduyoye, who holds that, "throughout many locations in the Third World, the violence and exploitation of colonialism was undertaken in many cases with the complicity of the church."[30] Katangole's question is: "Can Christianity save Africans from the politics of dispossession, violence and powerlessness?"[31] Katangole calls for social imagination, holding that

> the call to discipleship is not just a call to believe certain things about God, Christ and the World, which beliefs might have social implications. It is a call for Christians to be socially formed in a distinctive way. But

---

[26]Maluleke and Nadar, *Overcoming Violence Against Women and Children*, 7.
[27]Nyambura Njoroge, "Come Let Us Reason Together," 234.
[28]Njoroge, "Come Let Us Reason," 255.
[29]Njoroge, "Come Let Us Reason," 255.

this formation is not an extra to what it means to be Christians. It is the core of the call to discipleship. For without being so socially formed, Christians would not even know what it means to have the convictions they have, let alone to claim those convictions as true.[32]

One thing is certain. In the HIV/AIDS era, violence hampers prevention and the provision of quality care. Safer sex cannot be negotiated in homes where wives are subjected to physical violence. Abstinence does not work in war zones, where rape is used as a weapon between the warring powers. Faithfulness becomes a myth, when families are uprooted and separated by war and poverty. Indeed, funds that could be used for serving and saving lives are diverted to war, thereby neglecting health and educational services. Women and children who live in violent circumstances cannot be saved from HIV/AIDS by abstaining, nor can they insist on the use of condoms. In this Decade to Overcome Violence, our theological education needs to integrate into our programmes ways and means of solving or living with or celebrating our differences without resorting to violence. In particular, we need theological programmes that will stand in solidarity with all marginalized groups, particularly women and children.

Conclusion

I congratulate you again for your one hundred years of theological education, and even more importantly for taking this time to evaluate your role in the search for a theological education that enables religious communities to live out their mission in the world. We happen to be reflecting in this particular context, the context of the global HIV/AIDS epidemic, an epidemic within other social evils. The advantages of responding to this epidemic theologically is that

---

[30]Mercy Amba Oduyoye, "Violence," *Dictionary of Third World Theologies*, 235.

[31]Katangole, "Mission and Social Formation: Searching for an Alternative to King Leopold's Ghost," *African Theology Today* (ed. Emmanuel Katangole; Scranton: University of Scranton Press, 2002), 139.

[32]Katangole, "Mission and Social Formation," 139.

it calls us to address all other social evils, thereby forcing us to offer theological education that is socially engaged and that seeks the salvation of God as liberation for the whole creation. For this task, I am sure that we would all do well to start by revisiting our vision for mission as we seek for ways to move forward. This is a fitting role for an institution that began as a school for freed slaves with the aim of meeting development and social justice needs. I wish you another fruitful one hundred years of theological education as you struggle to be partners with God.

CHAPTER SEVEN

The Challenges Posed by HIV/AIDS: A Way Forward for Educators

Maryann N. Mwangi

Introduction

It is almost two decades since the eruption of HIV/AIDS in the world. The decades of struggling to prevent its spread have proven to be very complex and demoralizing. This is an epidemic that has left everybody in a situation of disbelief as the spread of the disease continues to challenge every part of the globe. According to some statistics, there are seventeen thousand new infections every day, totaling to about six million new infections every year. The most affected are the sexually active in the age bracket of 15-49 years. The numbers of the affected are more in Africa than anywhere else in the world. The following statistical observation is very revealing in this regard:

> According to a UNAIDS report, over twenty-five million people in Africa are infected with HIV or are living with AIDS. Approximately 70% of newly infected people live in Africa. In addition, 83% of the world's AIDS deaths have occurred in this continent. The report goes on:

> Most global reports indicate there to be 34.3 million adults and children living with HIV/AIDS. Of these, 24.5 million reside in Sub-Saharan Africa. To date, 134 countries reported injection drug use, of which 144 also reported HIV infection among injection drug users. Several of these

countries reporting injection drug use and HIV infection drug users for the first time, were located in Africa.[1]

AIDS deaths have left behind many orphans. It is said that AIDS has orphaned about 8.2 million children around the world by the end of 2000. Each year, AIDS deaths create 1.6 million new orphans, of which over 90% of them are found in Africa.

With these devastating figures of the infected, affected and HIV/AIDS related deaths, theological educators are being called upon to respond. Theological reflection needs to be brought to bear in such a way that the churches and education systems will learn to adapt to the major political, economic and social changes and scientific discoveries that have taken place in a world affected by AIDS. A concerted effort is needed from all quarters in the fight against this pandemic.

HIV/AIDS' devastating impact also necessitates intensive education and research programmes in pursuit of the most effective strategies and methods of preventative care, mitigation and a possible cure. Learning in this area needs to be used to reshape our theological curriculum. Real life experience and research have demonstrated that HIV/AIDS affects and permeates every aspect of our lives, social, economic, political, and religious. Our theological colleges are not immune from the need to respond.

It is also clear that HIV/AIDS cannot simply be blamed on a lack of individual morality, for many innocent children are born with HIV/AIDS. Some people are infected as they take care of the sick. Unfaithful spouses infect faithful partners and innocent girls and women are infected through rape. Many poor women have to choose between dying of hunger and raising some money through selling sex thus becoming commercial sex workers. Many economically poor governments and nations are unable to provide services for their infected and affected populations. Politically unstable conditions

---

[1] UNAIDS "Local Responses Satellite Meeting, 9th July 2002: Durban Conference" <www.unaidsorg>.

and war in many countries create socially displaced people, and make it difficult, if not impossible to reach the people with the message of HIV/AIDS' prevention and care. In sum, HIV/AIDS has demonstrated that its fertile soil is social injustice.[2]

The Reality of the War on HIV/AIDS

These realities affect both human and national development in Africa. Consequently, educators, researchers, government and non-governmental agencies need to emphasize the value of sex education and its impact in the spread of HIV/AIDS. For this reason, educators, including theological educators, should include in their curriculum reflection on issues of poverty, injustice, violence against women, political instability, and inadequate medical care as factors which fuel the spread of HIV/AIDS.

The world needs to declare war against this epidemic, which impedes development. Millions have already died through it. So we must now say "no" to its further claim on human lives. Our children must be taught and informed about responsible sexual behaviour and they must also be openly educated about the deadliness of this disease. With proper strategy, information and right commitment in terms of resources it is possible to turn the tide against HIV/AIDS. And by faith we could also say, 'when God is on our side and when we are ready to act responsibly, we will surely win this war.' This disease is deadly but, with the determination of David in the Old Testament, who killed Goliath with a sling, we will be able to overcome it.

The churches are influential and powerful institutions, with the potential to bring about change here in Africa that is currently the region worst affected by HIV/AIDS. The churches engaged early with HIV/AIDS, and many have excellent care, education and counselling programs. In spite of this involvement by the churches and other religious organizations in most parts of Africa, the situation

---

[2]"Special Report: Methods of Integrating HIV/AIDS in Theological Programs" *Training of Trainers Workshops, 26th – 31st August 2001, Johannesburg, South Africa.*

has continued to deteriorate in many places. We are now in a state of emergency that threatens development, social cohesion, political stability, food security, and life expectancy. This situation imposes a devastating economic burden, and the situation on the continent needs urgent and exceptional national, regional, and international action.

As the pandemic unfolds, it has exposed fault lines that reach to the heart of our theology, ethics, and liturgy as well as to the churches' pastoral ministry. Theologians have the challenge of developing a curriculum that draws on the depth of biblical and church teaching about human sexuality and which is realistic in meeting the challenges of a modern world that is becoming increasingly more and more secular. There is need for sex education to be taught in schools, colleges and churches. There is also an urgent need to train the clergy in psychosocial counselling which would assist the infected and affected to live positively. The curriculum should sensitise people concerning the risks of unsafe sex as well as discourage such dangerous traditional beliefs as so-called 'sexual cleansing' and widow inheritance.[3] Training should also encourage voluntary testing at all levels.

The Situation in Kenya

This disease was first reported in Kenya in 1984. The National AIDS/ STDs Control Programme (NASCOP) estimates that 2.2 million people in this country have developed AIDS since the epidemic started and over 1.5 million have died. Consequently, the churches cannot maintain what appears to be an unrealistic approach to a pandemic that has already killed over a million Kenyans.

No theological or religious organization can ignore the number of people who are dying. It is estimated that over seven hundred people die of AIDS in Kenya every day. Although this is what is

---

[3]Many African communities belief that a widow of a deceased is ritually unclean until a specially designated man performs sexual intercourse with her. Such a practice as well as 'inheriting' or marrying off the widow to a relative, (mainly brother of the deceased) often becomes an avenue for the spread of HIV/AIDS.

reported, there are, no doubt, many cases, which go unnoticed. Since medical cure has not yet been discovered, educating the masses towards a change in attitude and behaviour, and to a deeper reflection on the meaning of our Christian faith will help stem the tide. Ignorance and lack of information has been identified as a major source of its spread. More research is needed as to why this part of Africa is so deeply affected in spite of the fact that there are so many Christians. Theological educators and pastors will need to find new ways to communicate in their teaching since discussion of sex still remains a taboo subject in both family and the church. Those who argue that sexual education increases risky behaviour among the young do so without any scientific data. Social scientists have shown that education on HIV/AIDS does not result in increased sexual activity, but rather, leads to its decrease. Sex education creates awareness, skills, and knowledge that enable people to become sexually responsible and accountable about themselves and others in the community. Sex education has been known to succeed in helping youth to delay their sexual debut. According to a Christian Aid report entitled "Young people, HIV and the Churches" (page 1) by Mary Garvey, *Sexual Health and Education* must mean frank, open, supportive education that promotes abstinence as the best way to prevent HIV, faithfulness and safer sex practices including information about access to condoms, and provides young people with the skills they need to communicate about sex, say 'no' or negotiate safer sex. *Promiscuity* is understood to mean earlier sexual debut and increase in sexual activity and number of sexual partners.

Education can transform and change human beings. Awareness should become one of the main tools used in checking the spread of HIV/AIDS. Such awareness also demands that Christians re-affirm their faith in Christ, the one who has conquered death by his love. HIV/AIDS is a call of our time to reach out in Christ's compassion and love to those who suffer. We need to reach out to the victims of this deadly disease so that we are able to identify with the Christ who has died, has risen, and will come again in glory.

In Africa, informal education is as important as formal education. Pastors and educators will need to use music, song, dance, plays, and skits as ways of educating and creating awareness. Comedy, puppetry, proverbs, and riddles can also be effective. Although the subject matter is life threatening and not funny, light moments that carry an important and serious message can be an effective way to reach those infected and affected by this disease.

Stigmatization and Discrimination

The use of appropriate language, language that is inclusive rather than exclusive, is important. This is because both women and men with AIDS suffer in the same ways and require the same amount of respect and attention. We cannot speak of "them" and "us" when it comes to HIV/AIDS. The pain and fear of this disease has touched us all, but people living with HIV/AIDS are our greatest resource. We must no longer speak of "victims" in terms that diminish the courage, dignity, and gifts of people living with HIV/AIDS. It is necessary to work with all people regardless of their status, religion, colour or gender.

One cannot talk about the need to address the problem of HIV/AIDS without making an attempt to eradicate the stigma and discrimination associated with it. Stigmatisation, discrimination, and denial have posed a major challenge to efforts seeking to combat HIV/AIDS and to protect those infected. In most countries for instance, those affected and infected with HIV/AIDS are at times isolated and treated with contempt such that they are not even considered for job opportunities in their communities.

'Stigma' can be defined as an attitude that significantly discredits a person with a particular attribute. Stigma functions as a mechanism of social control in the sense that it marginalizes, excludes, and exercises power over individuals with attributes viewed as not worthy. For example, a stigma is often associated with a social group such as commercial-sex workers, homosexuals, drug users, and migrants.

HIV/AIDS stigmatisation added to already existing stigma may in many cases reinforce already existing social inequalities.

'Discrimination' refers to the actual action or the negative treatment of those who are already stigmatized.[4] Rather than discriminate against various groups, we must work towards acceptance. As observed in a World Council of Churches document:

> All cultures have both positive and negative aspects of culture that promote healing and wholeness, and not shirk from challenging others, which violates the dignity of any person, or promote or allow death. There is a lot of work ahead and lessons to learn from our reflections of culture and the way in which it intersects with Christian ethics.[5]

Since culture is a way of life, we must emphasise cultural values that uphold moral and upright living. As with any other disease, HIV/AIDS has affected our very way of life; it has challenged our ethical behaviour and questioned our Christian living. For AIDS to be minimized and eradicated there will have to be a change of heart, a form of conversion that will emphasize the moral values found in our African Culture.

> There is a dire need to approach HIV/AIDS with an open mind. The churches' tendency to exclude others, our interpretation of the scriptures and our theology of sin has all combined to promote the stigmatisation, exclusion and suffering of people with HIV or AIDS. This has undermined the effectiveness of care, education and prevention efforts and inflicted additional suffering on those already affected by the HIV. Given the extreme urgency of the response of the epidemic, there is need to rethinking the genesis, value and direction of our mission, and the transformation of our structures and ways of our working.[6]

All forms of education should include ways of overcoming stigma and discrimination so that society will learn to respect the rights and dignity of people living with HIV/AIDS and condemn acts that stigmatize people in this situation. Since we are all made in the image

---

[4]*Norwegian Church Aid: HIV/AIDS and workers' Rights, understanding the Issues 2002.*

[5]World Council of Churches, *Plan of Action: The Ecumenical Response to HIV/AIDS in Africa,* (Geneva: WCC, 2002) 6.

[6]*Plan of Action,* 6

of God, those who discriminate and stigmatize those infected and affected by this disease sin against God's clear command: "love one another as I have loved you." (John 13:34)

Success has been seen in countries such as Uganda, Senegal, and Thailand. These countries have increased education and care at community level, through strong political and religious leadership. Vigorous and targeted campaigning at all levels, and a willingness to fight the stigma and prejudice often associated with HIV/AIDS, have made these countries a source of hope.[7]

In East Africa, Uganda has been leading the way in the fight against the spread of HIV. Some Ugandans have gone public about their status. Most are no longer afraid to say that they are HIV positive. Because of publicity and education, the rising levels of infection that was there in the eighties have gradually declined. Both the religious and political leadership have campaigned vigorously by creating awareness and removing stigma.

Bishop Samuel Ssekkadde of the Anglican Diocese of Namirembe is exemplary. While in Berlin in May 2003 to attend a conference organized by the Ecumenical Advocacy Alliance, Bishop Ssekkadda related vivid stories of the experience of people living with HIV/AIDS in Uganda. He informed us that one day one of his pastors, Canon Gideon Byamugisha, informed him that he was 'positive.' The bishop asked him, 'positive with what?' He told him that he was HIV positive. They talked and the bishop embraced him and encouraged him to continue in his ministry without fear.

The bishop decided not to condemn. He asked Gideon not to hide his status, but to go public. He did not chase him out of the church as has happened in many cases. He has truly demonstrated that the church should act as the body of Christ. Gideon revealed the reality that AIDS is in the church. Since Gideon went public about his status ten years ago, he has remained healthy and his bishop has become his 'social father' and still assists him to acquire medicines,

---

[7]*Christian Aid Policy Briefing: Towards a Christian Aid Policy on HIV/AIDS*, 2.

which he needs. When many would have given up, Bishop Ssekkadde has seen new life in Gideon whose confession is nothing else but a beacon of hope for the Ugandans in particular and Africa at large. They have even formed an organization called African Network of Religious Leaders Living/Affected by AIDS (ANERELA)

Today Canon Byamugisha is known worldwide because of his willingness to go public about his status. Much of this progress is due to support and acceptance that he received from his bishop. His outright acceptance about his situation has made him a famous person. He has had the opportunity to address powerful groups such as the United States Senate, and World Bank officials. And although he is not himself a bishop, he was invited to address the Anglican Primates meeting held in Canterbury.

Canon Byamugisha's story contrasts with a true story entitled 'Don't tell the neighbours...' told of Pastor Luke who tested positive. He informed his bishop who advised him not to go public with the information, as he was a disgrace to the church. Luke's first wife died, and he was asked to remarry so that people would not become suspicious. He refused to re-marry, as he would have knowingly put an innocent life in danger just to save the church from embarrassment. How many people in a similar situation could have stood their ground, as did Pastor Luke?[8]

Sex Education and Ethics

According to African tradition there is a time and place to address matters pertaining to sexuality. For example, in Kikuyu tradition, sex education was taught to the newly circumcised or initiates. Both boys and girls were put into seclusion for nine days and were taught and educated on the matters sexuality, sexual ethics and moral values. Soon after this period their 'sponsors' would escort them back to the community where the same values would be practised. Sex education was taken seriously, and senior members of extended family like

---

[8]Gillian Paterson, "Church, AIDS & Stigma" *Ecumenical Advocacy Alliance Discussion Paper 002* (Geneva: Ecumenical Advocay Alliance), 3

uncles and aunts were expected to provide appropriate guidance. After this initiation period, it was not easy to talk casually about sex. Only peers could do so, and never among the elders. Sex was not a causal subject and, in some Africa cultures, it was taboo to mention certain words linked to sexuality. Unlike today in which we see sex treated as routine by the young, in the past, Kikuyu initiates would have to wait until they marry to engage in sex.[9]

In the modern world, extended family members often live far away and a gap has evolved in which our youth are learning more and more about their sexuality through the media, peers, and often permissive social influences. In most cases what the youth learn is a sensationalized and romanticized version of sexuality. Modern parents find it difficult to talk to their children about sex. The time has come for us to go back to our traditional advisors and sponsors in matters relating to sex and sexuality. This would be proper and a good challenge to parents in communicating openly and honestly with their children before it is too late.

In Kenya the Government attempted to introduce sex education in schools but some parents and religious bodies fiercely fought against it. The schools were trying to fill a gap left behind by a fast changing society. Parents and religious people argued that the children would become promiscuous if exposed to this kind of knowledge. Although the educators tried to change the term "sex education" to a "family life education" parents and religious leaders did not believe that a change of name meant a change of content, and to date the discussion is still going on.

But education and the creation of awareness is not enough. On a recent programme shown on Kenyan's "Family TV" Dr. Frank Njenga, a psychiatrist interviewed a young woman and a man who had tested positive. He asked the young woman, who was well educated, whether she had ever been exposed to HIV/AIDS information. He found it strange that with all of the HIV/AIDS

---

[9]See Jomo Kenyatta, *Facing Mount Kenya*, (Nairobi: Heinemann Kenya, 1978 [Originally published 1938]).

information going up on billboards, radio, TV, literature, and from many other sources, that she had still lived a lifestyle, which had resulted in her contracting HIV. She answered that she had heard the message even before guest speakers had been invited to her school to speak on family life education. Her peers and herself made fun of the acronym AIDS and did not take the information seriously. They proceeded to live their lives unaffected by the seriousness of the situation. She had multiple sex partners and she could not say from whom she had contracted the virus.

The above shows that educators should not just aim at creating awareness of issues related to AIDS and other sexually transmitted diseases (STDs) but equally aim at a change in attitude and behaviour. This is because the HIV risk is the product of social, cultural, economic, and interpersonal forces that affect us all. Our behaviour has been shaped by a multitude of factors including our cultures, religious beliefs, social categories, exposure to other cultures and experiences, which may put us at risk of contracting HIV infection.

Myths abound which require correction. Myths like 'if you have sex once, you cannot become pregnant or infected' could have been rectified if people had the right information. Another myth recorded from an interview conducted among secondary school students was 'you cannot get pregnant or infected if you have sex standing up' (the poor children are ignorant about the reality of sexual intercourse and the biological process). Education would have helped solve many problems that young people get into if they had had the right knowledge. The church is also undergoing the same challenge:

> Today, churches are being obliged to acknowledge that we have however unwitting – contributed both actively and passively to the spread of virus... Our difficulty is addressing issues of sex and sexuality has often made it painful for us to engage, in any honest and realistic way, with issues of sex education and HIV prevention.[10]

Churches, parents, and educators need to develop common tools and messages so as to advance a unified approach, as we are all

---

[10]*Plan of Action*, 4.

interested parties, fighting for the same goal. Theological educators, for example, will need to encourage students to become reflective practitioners who can demonstrate the ability to engage in theological reflection that enhances HIV/AIDS prevention and care of the infected. Both educators and their students will need to live exemplary lives that would encourage others to practice moral and upright lives. Theologians and pastors must strive to give people accurate and factual information so that they can make informed choices with regard to their lives.

Global partnerships are needed in this struggle. However it will be important for those in the West who are writing about AIDS to consult theologians based in the southern hemisphere. At times, scholars from other continents have claimed to be authorities on what has been happening in Africa, and yet they have had limited knowledge about HIV/AIDS that has been destroying our people. International consultation is an important factor when dealing with the AIDS pandemic in Africa.

Conclusion

A curriculum should be designed for use by theological colleges to impart both pastoral and counselling skills to pastors in training. These skills will empower the churches to respond effectively to the challenges posed by HIV/AIDS.

The curriculum should be designed to assist instructors, teachers, lecturers and professors in institutions, which prepare clergy for ministry, to mainstream HIV/AIDS into their training programs in order to produce church leaders and a church which is better equipped to serve in this age. HIV/AIDS Education should also give learners the capacity to develop church based community programmes to address HIV/AIDS prevention and care. Theologians need to develop programmes that will help sensitise people to the risks of unsafe sex, which was once discouraged by traditional culture. Some traditional practices such as female genital mutilation should be discouraged as they further fuel HIV/AIDS infection.

It has also shown that prevention works as long as there is openness and dialogue which in turn leads to willingness to accommodate all the scientifically proven HIV prevention strategies: Abstinence, voluntary testing and counselling, mutual faithfulness in marriage and the use of condoms.[11]

Research has shown that there is a close link between HIV/AIDS and social injustice, poverty, culture and gender inequality. Poverty undermines the lives of many young people and denies them living in dignity. This issue needs to be fully addressed and methods of alleviating poverty must be incorporated into our theological curriculum. Due to poverty, people have often turned to participation in immoral behaviour, including selling sex, use of dangerous drugs and other substance abuse. Lack of employment has also contributed to the spread of HIV/AIDS epidemic. The poor are the vulnerable when it comes to HIV infection and dying of AIDS. It is not enough to create awareness, as there is little that can be done with the information, if the community lacks a meaningful source of livelihood.

Education can break the wall of silence by openly encouraging discussion of HIV/AIDS in pre-marriage counselling, youth group discussions, faith based publications and research, radio programmes, education at religious health facilities and in training programmes lay leaders. Our teaching should also seek to remove the stigma and discrimination attached to HIV/AIDS and to help people understand that AIDS is a disease and that the affected need to be treated with compassion rather than contempt.

Proper education should further strive to remove such myths that AIDS is the result of a curse or witchcraft. HIV/AIDS education can also correct the perception that those who get infected are suffering a punishment from God and they deserve it. AIDS can affect anybody as is evidenced by those affected stretching though the rank and file of the rich and famous, professionals, the clergy, educated, modern and traditional. Effective education and creating awareness should aim to equip people with the knowledge and skills

---

[11] These principles are often called the 'ABC's of HIV/AIDS education: Abstain before marriage, Be faithful in marriage, and use a Condom if necessary.

necessary to address HIV/AIDS issues in their personal and professional lives and to create a climate of openness and sensitivity to enable this to happen.

Resources will need to be made available in training institutions such as Bible colleges, theological colleges and universities if we are going to be able to address adequately the complex issues surrounding HIV/AIDS. St. Paul's United Theological College, in partnership with MAP international, has for the last 3 years introduced into its curriculum a unit called "Christian response to HIV/AIDS: Knowledge for intervention." This unit is aimed at enlightening the Bachelor of Divinity students with the required knowledge for their pastoral work and counselling. Efforts are also being made to introduce the same unit to St. Paul's nine constituent colleges. It is hoped that with this kind of approach pastors will be able to handle and counsel HIV/AIDS cases.

St. Paul's has launched a post-graduate diploma leading to a masters in HIV/AIDS in partnership with MAP International and the Oxford Centre for Mission Studies (OCMS) with the aim of enabling practitioners working in the field of HIV/AIDS intervention to become critically reflective, theologically informed, and professionally grounded research developers. This would enable the students to formulate their own contextual policy, theological position, and skills and practice as appropriate. Any such course will need to be holistic, examining all of the various dimensions of the AIDS issue. St. Paul's course will include: Global, regional and local dimensions; Human sexuality; Social sciences; Pastoral care and practice; Theological and spiritual dimension; Ethical and legal dimensions; and Strategic dimensions. Themes such as poverty, gender, stigma and discrimination will be addressed.

Since this is a practical course, the students will each have a base group of twenty people that they will work with who are infected or affected. This will ensure that this course is not just another academic exercise. It will be a course that will be responding to the needs of the community. Students will be expected to acquire knowledge and internalize it in their professional work.

In addition, effort, space, and finances should be set aside to integrate HIV/AIDS education into concerned institutions to help the churches and their leadership to assume a prophetic and healing ministry in the HIV/AIDS era. If pastors are well trained and informed, the issue of HIV/AIDS could become minimal and manageable. But failure to prepare the church to serve God's people in this most trying moment of human history is tantamount to failing Christ in his ministry of healing.

HIV/AIDS education can empower people to take charge of their lives and to take responsibility for their actions. Transformation and conversion of heart in our lives will enable us as we tackle stigmatisation, discrimination, and self-denial. Like Jesus Christ, we are called to live a productive and challenging ministry, a new form of ministry that involves a paradigm change in the way we think about the values that underpin our faith. This will be painful. We follow a Jesus who followed this way of love and was crucified and died as a result. But death and suffering was not the end because he rose from the dead and has given us the joy of abundant life now and hope for the future!

CHAPTER EIGHT

Beyond "Victim Theology": Reconstructing Theological Education in an Era of HIV/AIDS in Africa

Peter Mageto

Introduction

When future generations of African scholars conduct their historical research on the theological, moral and political life of African leadership in the final decade of the 21st century, how shall they judge our performance regarding AIDS in sub-Saharan Africa? Shall our inaction - especially the inaction of African theological educators - withstand the judgment of history? What verdict will our descendants render upon their ancestors who stood silently as a generation of African children was reduced to an underclass by this viral 'genocide'? No doubt, they will find that a few lonely voices spoke out, but will they not ask whether *we as theological educators could not have done more?*

I am reminded that there are at least two other viruses which are enabling HIV to spread among the most vulnerable in society. The first is a virus which makes colonized peoples believe they are inferior. The second is a virus of global economic injustice.[1] For the purpose of this paper, I propose that there is a third virus, "victim

---

[1] Kevin Kelly, "Conclusion: A Moral Theologian Faces the New Millennium in a Time of AIDS," in *Catholic Ethicists on HIV/AIDS Prevention* (ed. James F. Keenan; New York/London: Continuum, 2000), 324-32.

theology", which utilizes the sources of theology but fails to account adequately for the relationship between God and humanity. This paper proposes to examine this third virus through three lenses, three different 'taboos'—sex, disease and death—in order to address the question raised by Tinyiko Maluleke: "How can theological education in Africa be conducted in a 'business-as-usual' manner when thousands and millions of Africans are dying of AIDS?"[2]

The challenge posed by new diseases around the globe can be summarized in the words of William McNeil:

> It is obvious that human (and nonhuman) diseases are evolving with unusual rapidity simply because changes in our behavior facilitate cross-fertilization of different strains of germs like never before, while an unending flow of new medicines (and pesticides) also present infectious organisms with rigorous, changing challenges to their survival.[3]

With regard to HIV/AIDS, part of the problem is church teaching implemented by leaders who make people feel bad for being human and sexual at the same time. Teaching in a dualistic fashion that 'flesh' and 'spirit' are locked in a battle; the church has often treated human sexuality as a bane of human existence rather than as a gift from God. The direct association of sin with disease has been at home in some theological circles for a long time. The simplistic association of good health with righteous living has condemned many who find themselves in a state of sickness and suffering. The often-repeated assertion that there is a direct connection between death and sin, and especially "sexual" sin, is a matter that theological educators cannot avoid in the era of HIV/AIDS.

Beyond "Victim Theology": Sex, Disease and Death

I define "victim theology" as that so-called Christian teaching (since it uses biblical, theological and ethical language) that blinds its hearers

---

[2] Tinyiko S. Maluleke, "The Challenge of HIV/AIDS for Theological Education in Africa: Towards an HIV/AIDS Sensitive Curriculum," *Missionalia* 29/2 (2001): 138.

[3] William H. McNeil, *Plagues and Peoples* (New York: Anchor Books, 1977), 15.

to the hardship of this life, by focusing exclusively on the life to come, while shielding people from the reality and demands of the present life. Victim theology serves as a kind of sedative which insulates but does not cure the illness. Indeed, victim theology provides a set of rules and rituals to be observed, and hope in promises to be fulfilled in the next world. Almost five decades ago John Mbiti said that the church "finds itself in the situation of trying to exist without a theology."[4] It is my contention that it is not that the church had no theology, but that, in the era of HIV/AIDS, the church has been found to have a faulty theology, detached and unrelated to real life.

Victim theology is revealed in statements such as 'HIV/AIDS is a judgment of God for immoral living.'[5] This common sentiment fails to account for the children who are born with HIV/AIDS infection, or those infected through blood transfusions or for the fact that many of the people who fall into such "risk groups" have either been forced into their lifestyles by the awful reality of having to choose between poverty and development, food and medicine, health and school fees. Indeed as Musa Dube asks: "Is God against these groups of people?"[6] The way Christians answer this question in many instances has created and enhanced victim theology. Victim theology blames the victims, adding stigma and discrimination to the suffering caused by the disease. Victim theology ignores the fact that many who are infected with HIV/AIDS have been sinned against. In order to theologize faithfully in an era of HIV/AIDS, we must reconstruct and understand what theology is all about: What does it

---

[4] John S. Mbiti, *African Religions and Philosophy* (Nairobi: East African Educational Publishers, 1969), 232.

[5] Cf. Richard and Rosalind Chirimuuta, *AIDS, Africa and Racism*. (London: Free Association Books, 1989); Mirko D. Grmek, *History of AIDS: Emergence and Origin of a Modern Pandemic* (trans. Russell C. Maulitz and Jacalyn Duffin; Princeton, NJ: Princeton University Press, 1990).

[6] Cf. Musa Dube, "Preaching to the Converted: Unsettling the Christian Church" *Ministerial Formation* 93 (2001): 41, where she calls upon the church and its leadership to repent of theological mediocrity.

mean to do theology faithfully? I submit that to theologize is to venture with others in an existential practice by expressing and celebrating the presence of God, who loves and saves in Jesus Christ. Thus, persons and communities are drawn to risk a new future.[7] This new future that points to the purpose and meaning of life, centered in the creator God and exemplified in the life, death, resurrection and glorification of Jesus Christ as made known to us in the Bible.

The church has had to deal with epidemics before. For example, five centuries separate the appearance of AIDS and syphilis, but both epidemics have been labeled 'God's judgment,' and both epidemics appeared mysteriously, leading to disputes over their origin and treatment. The course of these diseases through the population produced terror but little change in sexual behavior. The social response included blaming and excluding the affected, denial, retribution and charlatans with 'cures.'[8] In the case of syphilis, women were treated as vessels of evil, and their treatment was neglected. The presence of such epidemics in the history of mankind reveals that we have learned little about how to respond to sexually transmitted diseases.

Part of the problem is our fear, especially in Africa, of talking about sexuality and sexual conduct. The subject is so delicate and forbidding that even adults are uncomfortable discussing the topic

---

[7]Gary D. Bouma, "Faith, Scripture and Community in the Development of an AIDS-Relevant Theology," *AIDS - The Church as Enemy and Friend: Ambiguities in the Church's Response to AIDS*. (ed. Alan H. Cadwallader; North Blackburn, Australia: Collins Dove, 1992), 143-61.

[8]Cf. F. M. Mburu, "The Social Production of Health in Kenya," in *The Social Basis of Health and Healing in Africa* (eds. Steven Feierman and John M. Janzen; Berkeley / Los Angeles/ London: University of California Press, 1992), 409-25; Sheldon Watts, *Epidemics and History: Disease, Power and Imperialism*. (New Haven/ London: Yale University Press, 1997); Terence O. Ranger, "Godly Medicine: The Ambiguities of Medical Mission in Southeastern Tanzania, 1900-1945," in Feierman and Janzen, 256-84. It is also important to note how a caring Christian response to epidemics has aided the church's mission, as detailed by Rodney Stark, *The Rise of Christianity*. (Princeton: Princeton University Press, 1996).

among themselves or with their children. It is unfortunate that even among theological educators, many are often unwilling to pronounce the word 'sex' or mention the names for 'sexual organs' in their own native languages. How can we discuss the prevention of HIV/AIDS, if we do not have the courage to use the necessary language? I argue that the heresy of Gnosticism that has permeated many of the sexual attitudes of the Christian church is responsible for a great deal of the fear of sexuality in our culture.

HIV/AIDS offers an opportunity for Christian theology in Africa to engage with questions of sex, disease and death that have troubled all peoples. Theological educators must come to terms with the fact that many of our traditions and theological formations have not been able to provide an adequate theological response to these issues. African theologians must not sit on the periphery and await their counterparts from the Northern hemisphere to suggest a theological response that caters to the present crisis. African theologians must come to terms with the reality that HIV/AIDS is here with us, and that the churches and her theologians must engage this crisis and turn it into a *kairos*.

Sex

In many traditional societies sexual activity was confined mostly within the family for the purpose of procreation and functioned as a symbol of the stability of relations between the sexes and the generations. In recent years, however, sex has been 'freed' from its traditional social context within the family. Sexual activity has become more a matter of individualistic choice. Sexual acts are now practiced without shared responsibility for its consequences. As Christians we need to re-claim a more holistic understanding of sexuality beyond simply the biological act and realize that "the biological aspect is thoroughly integrated in the *humanum*; and the

---

[9] Helmut Thielicke, *The Ethics of Sex* (Trans. John W. Doberstein; New York, Evanston, London: Harper and Row Publishers, 1964), 19.

humanum lives and moves and has its being in the *divinum*."⁹ Sex cannot be separated from community living or from God, the creator. In the Old Testament, we find little evidence of denigration of the body. Men and women are commonly portrayed as having sexual lives. The Song of Songs, for example, is replete with explicit sexual imagery. Neither does the Old Testament shield its readers from the dark side of sexuality. The Old Testament actually appears to permit the sexual violation of women taken as booty in war (Deut 21:10-14, Num 31), although the text also warns that this violation can result in a plague coming among the people (Judges 21:15-23). We are sometimes left wondering whether God actually approved of the genocide and violation that appears in parts of the Old Testament, or whether God, as John Calvin suggested, 'accommodated' such human wickedness as part of the historical process of spiritual development.[10]

In order to understand the movement from the Hebrew culture which affirmed human sexuality to popular Christianity's persistent discomfort with sex and pleasure, we have to be aware of three interwoven threads: the dualistic cosmology of Plato (i.e. the soul and mind are at war with the body); the stoic philosophy of early Greco-Roman culture (i.e., nothing should be done for the sake of pleasure); and the Persian Gnostic tradition (i.e., that demons created the world, sex and the body in which the soul is trapped and the only key to salvation is to free the spirit from the bondage of the body by denying the flesh). It is from these backgrounds that many early Christians came to view the body as problematic and ultimately as a

---

[10]For various Christian responses to these questions see now C.S. Cowles, Eugene H. Merrill, Daniel L. Gard, & Tremper Longman III, *Show Them No Mercy: 4 Views on God and Canaanite Genocide* (Grand Rapids: Zondervan, 2003); cf. Kelly Brown Douglas, *Sexuality and the Black Church: A Womanist Perspective*. (Maryknoll: Orbis, 1999); Lisa Sowle Cahil, *Sex, Gender and Christian Ethics*. (Cambridge: Cambridge University Press, 1996); Renita Weems, *Battered Love: Marriage, Sex and Violence in the Hebrew Prophets*. (Minneapolis: Fortress Press, 1995).

disposable container for the eternal treasure it contained. The body was 'the prison of the soul.'[11] These views have contributed to the deeply ambivalent Christian attitudes toward both health and sex.

In the New Testament, on the other hand, we find Jesus associating with real people who had real sexual lives. He allows himself to be confronted by a woman in a manner that would have rendered him ritually unclean (Mk 5: 25-34), and by another 'sinful woman' who anointed him with oil (Mk 14:1-11). It shocked the culture around him that he stood up for a woman's right to learn spiritually (Lk 10:38-42). Even when Jesus was confronted with the question of divorce he affirmed the male-female sexual relationship as part of God's created order.

Many people have found the writings of Paul more ambiguous and some have argued that they seem to owe much to the Hellenistic mindset of the Greek world in which Paul wrote. When Paul's writings are read out of context, they can appear to be ascetic and patriarchal.[12] It is the theologian's responsibility to investigate the scriptures and elucidate Paul's intentions in passages that have been used to misrepresent Paul negatively.

The post-New Testament church soon became tied to the ethos of the Greco-Roman culture which wanted to escape the body, suffering, the endless cycle of birth and death, and, of course, sex. Turning away from sex, some Christians argued, could free a person in preparation for the promised heaven.

It is clear that the thrust of the teaching of the Old Testament and New Testament have a positive and healthy view of sexuality. Many church traditions, however, have not handed down this positive teaching. The planting of the church in many different cultures has been obsessed with the supposed paganism situated in the sexuality of the recipients of the gospel. The traditional lifestyles of many

---

[11]Peter Lewis Allen, *The Wages of Sin: Sex and Disease, Past and Present* (Chicago, London: The University of Chicago Press, 2000).

[12]See passages in Pauline writings related to modest sexuality: Rom. 1:24-27, 1 Cor 7:1-20, 25-40, Eph 5:21-33, 1 Tim 2:11-14.

peoples have been construed as evil. Missionaries often insisted on a complete break from the new converts' old culture.

The early church Fathers were heavily influenced by Greek, Roman, and Persian teachings and traditions. Pushing St. Paul's personal preference for sexual abstinence to the limit, they lashed out against all sex. For example, Tertullian (c. A.D. 150-230) was so repulsed by sex that he publicly renounced his own sexual relationship with his wife and taught that sexual intercourse drives out the Holy Spirit. Women, he declared, are "the devil's door: through them stain creeps into men's hearts and minds and works his wiles for their spiritual destruction."[13] Origen (c. A.D.185-254), became so unsettled by his own sexuality that it is said he castrated himself, becoming a literal eunuch.[14] Jerome, (c. A.D. 331-420) set his seal of approval on the opinion that human sexuality was fundamentally detestable. The ascetic morals of the fourth century made celibacy an ideal and espoused suffering for the sake of greater spirituality. Heaven became thought of as a bodiless and, therefore, sexless place. Sadly, the church through the centuries has perpetuated this myth.

Augustine (A.D. 354-430), the leading African theologian of the fourth century, embraced the faith but his sexual views were affected by the ascetic temperament of the times, and perhaps by a desire to compensate for the libertarian sexuality of his youth. Augustine's concerns came to exemplify what gradually became an official component of European Christianity. Augustine's view of sexuality was negative. To participate in sexual acts left a person guilty and shame-ridden. Augustine argued that the Fall of the first human couple was the loss of rational control over the body,

---

[13] Jon Davies, "Sex These Days, Sex Those Days: Will it Ever End? in *Sex These Days: Essays on Theology, Sexuality and Society*. (ed. Jon Davies and Gerald Loughlin; Sheffield: Sheffield Academic Press, 1997), 18-34.

[14] Ibid.

[15] Rachel Osmer, "The Carnality of Grace: Sexuality, Spirituality and Pastoral Ministry," in *Embracing the Chaos: Theological Responses to AIDS* (ed. James Woodward; London: SPCK, 1990) 60. This argument is also embraced and supported by Lisa. S. Cahill, *Sex, Gender and Christian Ethics*. (Cambridge: Cambridge University Press, 1996).

particularly over the phallus. Thus, for Augustine, the sex act is sinful and transmits original sin to every child that is born of the flesh.[15]

Thomas Aquinas (1225-1274) combined Aristotelian philosophy and Christian theology to respond to the question of sex and spirituality. For Aquinas, since God could not have made anything that was evil, sex must be good. But Aquinas also believed that sex was intended only for procreation and that non-procreative sex violated the natural law and was therefore sinful. Thus, Aquinas even went so far as to argue that prostitutes were a necessary evil, permitted by God in order to prevent male lust from going totally out of control.

Martin Luther (1483-1546), alerted by Scripture, argued that Christianity had been seriously blown off course. During the time of the Reformation, for which Luther was a catalyst, many men and women placed their lives in peril to repel the tide of untruth that had confused the entire message of salvation through Jesus Christ. The major impact of the Reformation on sexuality was indirect: with the demand for and accomplishment of spiritual and political freedom came a demand for a change in sexual norms. It was clear to Protestant leaders like Luther, Calvin, Knox and Zwingli that freedom *of* conscience was in no way freedom *from* conscience. Celibacy, however, was deemed to be an unnecessary requirement for the clergy. Following the example of Luther, Protestant clergy abandoned celibacy, regarding it as unnatural. Calvin encouraged the use of civil law to regulate human behavior in the attempt to suppress immorality and frivolity. Indeed, the position taken by the reformers affirmed sexuality within the realms of marriage and safeguarded the holy institution from debauchery.

Coming closer to home, African sexuality has been an object of stereotyping and false imaging. This stereotyping has influenced the way the prevalence of HIV/AIDS is explained on the African continent. Within the patriarchal set-up of many African societies, and with sex as a taboo subject, many Africans do not have the language to face the reality of sex and sexuality demanded in this era. Generally speaking, the Europeans believed that the African person was someone whose humanity had not reached the desirable stage exemplified in western culture. Some thought of Africans as unable to control their own bodies in sexual matters.[16] Hence, both in the Catholic Church and the Protestant missions, boys and girls were kept at the formation centres for long periods of time to shield them from the 'primitive' home influence which was generally believed not to be conducive to chastity. Some Europeans believed, and some still believe, that African polygamy can be explained by the exceptionally powerful sexual appetites of African peoples. The reality, of course, is that problems related to sexuality are not confined to Africans, but are a concern for all human beings.

Disease

Nothing in human thought appears more inevitable than the idea of supernatural intervention in producing and curing disease. The causes of disease are so intricate that they are learned only after careful scientific investigation. When the cause of a disease is unknown there is often a tendency to attribute what is not understood to a will like their own, and so diseases have often been attributed to the wrath of a good being or to the malice of an evil being. This idea underlies the connection of priestly classes with the healing arts in various cultures. This is the reason why the Old Testament often attributes such diseases as the leprosy of Miriam and Uzziah, the boils of Job, the dysentery of Jehoram, the withered hand of Jeroboam, the fatal illness of Asa, and many other ills, to the wrath of God or the malice of Satan. In the New Testament we find examples such as the woman "bound by Satan", the rebuke of the fever, the casting

---

[16]See how some of the early missionaries and colonialists constructed the African body so as to achieve the goals of planting Christianity and doing commerce in the following writings: Natasha Erlank, Julia C. Wells and Wendy Uban-Mead, *Sex and Mission: Toward a New 'Menschentum'* (Le Fait Missionaire, 2001); Beth Maina Ahlberg, "Is there a Distinct African Sexuality? A Critical Response to Caldwell," *Africa* 64/2 (1994): 220-41; Megan Vaughan, *Curing their Ills: Colonial Power and African Illness* (Stamford: Stanford University Press, 1991); Alexander Butchart, *The Anatomy of Power: European Constructions of the African Body* (London/ New York: Zed Books, 1998).

out off the devil which was dumb, the healing of the person whom "the devil often times casts into the fire" and various other episodes.

With the expansion of Christianity, a great new chain of events was set in motion, which modified this understanding most profoundly. The thought, aspiration, example, ideals, and spirit of Jesus of Nazareth poured into the world promoting self-sacrifice on behalf of the sick. It is under this notion of self-sacrifice, that missionaries championed the well-being of African peoples in the 18th and 19th centuries, though this mission was to some degree tainted with western colonial imperialism. This is well illustrated by the fact that Protestant missionaries portrayed Africans as immoral whose immorality led to disease and death. This image has not yet been corrected and is still found in some discussions of HIV/AIDS.[17]

The response to disease within an African setting reveals a theology that developed out of sacred literature (though read with some local nuances). Physical disease is seen as a result of the wrath of God or the malice of Satan, or a combination of the two. It is unfortunate that within some church circles the desire for the miraculous acts, as the only way of dealing with illness, has grown luxuriantly. The challenging theological point is that there has been a direct association of sin with disease (at times when it is not necessary), a viewpoint which creates more victims.

---

[17]It is becoming clear that the perpetuation of the same ideas about disease in Africa that were current in the colonial and medical missions in the 18th and 19th centuries, are being utilized in the HIV/AIDS crisis. For such an approach, consider: Stephen Neill, *Colonialism and Christian Missions* (New York/ Toronto/ London/ Sydney: McGraw-Hill Publishing Company, 1966); Michael Gelfand, *The Sick African: A Clinical Study* (Third edition; Cape Town/, Wynberg/Johannesburg: Juta and Company, 1957); Megan Vaughan, "Health and Hegemony: Representation of Disease and the Creation of the Colonial Subject in Nyasaland," in *Contesting Colonial Hegemony: State and Society in Africa and India, 1858 Until Independence* (eds. Shula Marks and Dagmar Engels; London: British Academic Press, 1994), 173-201; W. Meredith Long, *Health, Healing and God's Kingdom: New Pathways to Christian Health Ministry in Africa* (Regnum Book International, 2000); Marc-Harry Dawson, "Socio-Economic Change and Disease: Smallpox in Colonial Kenya, 1880-1920" in Feierman and Janzen, 90-103.

However important it is to underscore the fact that some sinful lifestyles lead to deadly consequences, our theology should not take the judgment seat and condemn and exclude the sinners, let alone those who are sinned against. Rather, we should embrace all who suffer in order to show them the way, the truth and the life in Jesus. While there are many biblical connections between sin and disease, the same Bible encourages us to look beyond this situation and see the deliverance God brings to us through Jesus Christ. The responsibility of theology is not to create and exclude guilty offenders, but to help the guilty toward confession, repentance and reformation. Blaming the victim after a disease has been contracted will not help. Rather, any AIDS ministry must be willing to embrace love, justice, mercy and compassion. Since AIDS is showing us how private acts create public consequences, messages of warning and redirection of lives toward the loving God who embraces all despite their sinful status, will transform Christian speech and action from a victim-blaming approach into a caring and healing approach.

Death

Death calls for an explanation, as the human story attests. Why does death happen? What does it mean? Where does it lead to? In an era of HIV/AIDS when death is so common, the questions compel theological educators to offer concrete and contextual responses. Theologians often overlook their context by embracing popular Christian practices which portray death as the gateway to either a disembodied heaven or very literal and physical hell.

In Genesis 2 God said: "When you eat of it (the tree of the knowledge of good and evil) you will surely die" (vs. 17.) However, Adam and Eve did not experience physical dying until many years later. Although physical death was not the immediate consequence of disobedience, I suggest that the death which God threatened is the separation from God which sin inevitably brings, and which is sometimes called 'spiritual death.' The dying which follows sinfulness is, first of all, a spiritual dying. This is also consistent with New Testament teachings in Jesus' conversation with Martha upon the physical dying of Lazarus (John 11:21-27) in which Jesus says, "I am the resurrection and the life. He who believes in me will live, even though he dies; and whoever lives and believes in me will never die" (John 11:25, 26). Obviously Jesus does not promise that believers will never experience physical dying. Jesus promises complete deliverance from the guilt and curse resulting from our sinfulness, but belief in Jesus does not release us from physical dying. Thus, human dying is a consequence of the fall of humanity, but it has also been taken up into God's plan and defeated through the death, resurrection and ascension of Jesus Christ.

Often, however, Christians have taught that 'the world to come' means that 'life in the world' will ultimately be left behind. This teaching does not resonate well with what the Bible proclaims as the resurrection of the body. We do not look for a disembodied heaven, but for a new earth. What we anticipate as Christians is that one day God will re-make his creation. We look not for an ethereal heaven, but for a new earth, a fully embodied, physical, resurrection life.

Unfortunately, some early Christians abandoned this biblical perspective teaching that believers should joyfully welcome disaster and disease. They believed that physical suffering led to spiritual maturity, and that bodily afflictions were designed by God to weaken the ties of the Christian to the lures of this world. Hence, Christians viewed sickness as something to be accepted and welcomed as a divine corrective, as a reminder of spiritual priorities, especially that the life to come is of more importance than the present life.

Contemporary Christianity in Africa is still heavily oriented to this vision of a disembodied heavenly world to come. This makes it hard for theological educators and the church to offer a response which seeks to preserve and enhance life in this world. I can certainly envisage people saying 'people are dying – but at least we can offer them eternal salvation through faith in Christ before they die.' This kind of pastoral care is certainly one part of the care which should be offered to the dying – but it is obviously inadequate for three reasons: (1) because we believe in the goodness of embodied life in this world, (2) because we believe that death is an evil, and (3) because we believe in a bodily resurrection. We need to present a more biblical hope – that God loves his creation and that we look forward to a fully redeemed creation and a fully embodied resurrection life.

Reconstructing Theological Education

Disease

How shall we develop a theology that reflects the experience of the African people in their relationship with God in an era of HIV/AIDS? How do we restructure an African ecclesiology that will see the church as the servant of the sick, the suffering, and the downtrodden who are voiceless because of their gender, economic or societal status? How does theology fit into the current crisis of disease, discrimination and death? Theological education should offer a Christian basis for recreating the African social, political, economic and religious reality from a scriptural perspective.

We must ask, then, what role and voice theological educators should have when it comes to medical research. For a good number of years, money has been spent on studying the origin of AIDS. Africans have sometimes been blamed and sometimes used as objects of study and speculation. One example is research being conducted in Kenya on male circumcision as a strategy for controlling the spread of HIV. Has any African theologian concerned himself or herself with discovering who the principle researchers are in this field, what ethics being used in such research, and what role religion, faith, culture and money play in that research? Above all, who has the power to negotiate and direct this kind of research? Are the culture, dignity and integrity of those Kenyans involved in the research being compromised? What is the role of the church in research?

Sex

In the Hebrew and New Testament writings, God was not sexually described or defined. The Bible does, however, make God the origin of human sexuality. In Genesis 1:27 when God created humanity, we are told "male and female he created them, in the image of God he created them". Human beings were created and given to one another for love and companionship. This gift of sexual loving is recognized as mirroring God's love for Israel (Hosea, Isaiah) and as a sacrament or sign of Christ's love for the church, the community of his disciples (Eph 5). A Christian view of sexuality has no place for the idea that "sex is dirty." Paul reminds us, however, that our bodies are temples of the Holy Spirit, and therefore, whatever we do with them has to lead to the glorification of God (1 Cor 6:15-20).

A biblical theology of sexuality summons us to have the courage and confidence to formulate and teach a positive sexual ethic, which is both truly human and truly Christian, and which emphasizes life-giving and self-giving love. This will only be possible in a true church of Jesus Christ that seeks equality, freedom and faithful relations between people. And in an African setting, the churches have a responsibility to denounce teaching which exploits Africans or denied them their true humanity.

We have also to admit that there are some African traditional cultures which have exacerbated the problem: conceptions of male virility; patriarchal dominance and female dependency; ascribing calamities to witchcraft and prescribing inappropriate cures by diviners and healers; and taboos concerning sex education. These cultural practices must be exposed before a biblically reconstructed theology of sexuality.

Theological educators will have to understand sexuality as God's life-giving and life-fulfilling gift and recognize sexuality as an essential part of our humanity. Such a theology will celebrate the goodness of creation, including our bodies and our sexuality and listen and respond to the suffering caused by violence against women, the HIV/AIDS pandemic, and the commercial exploitation of sexuality. It is a theology that will empower people to celebrate their sexuality with holiness and integrity.

A reconstructed theological education will reaffirm a commitment to biblical standards of sexuality: that it was created by God (Gen 1:27) for mutual care and support (Gen 2:23-35) and for procreation (Gen 4:1); that sexuality is confined to marriage between a man and a woman who are both adults (Prov 5:15-20);

and that both members of the marriage union are responsible agents (1 Cor 7:3-5). Such a view of marriage lays a firm foundation for a society. Those who are not married are called to remain celibate for God's service, as a true witness of God's own holy creation. Theological education must call upon all faithful Christians to uphold biblical standards of human sexuality against all onslaughts. Indeed, in an era of HIV/AIDS, theological education must address the ways in which gender relations can be healed within an African context.

Reconstructing theological education in an era of HIV/AIDS will contend with the hegemony of masculine definitions of sexual behavior. This is a problem not only for women to contend with, but for the whole society to confront in order to establish communities that celebrate the goodness of God's creation, in which each human being is seen to bear the image of God.[18] In African societies, theological education will have to come to terms with the fact that, at present, sexual acts primarily occur under the control of men, and that women feel far-removed and have little or no control over their own sexuality. This hegemony of power must come to an end through biblical teaching that reaffirms the sanctity and dignity of all people. In other words Christianity must engage the subject of sexuality in order to inform and form the lives of all our adherents in the core teachings of the Bible.

Death

The Bible sets us up for an agonizing dilemma. We will have to contend with such questions as: 'Is death a judgment on our sin, and salvation beyond death, a reward for righteousness?' 'Why do the good die young and the apparently righteous suffer?' 'Why do the evil prosper?' A reconstructed theological education will have to engage these questions in an era of HIV/AIDS.

Theological educators must struggle with biblical passages which create a dilemma in relation to death. A theology that skips these passages by pretending that they are not part of the sacred text

---

[18]Baylies and Bujra, "The Struggle Continues," 179.

will be a disaster for the Christian churches. For example, the Deuteronomic covenant had promised that faith would be rewarded by the blessings of home, health, longevity, and prosperity (Deut 28:1ff). When Job's tormentors confront him with this traditional theodicy and imply that Job's suffering must be evidence of God's wrath, Job queries: "Why do the wicked live, reach old age, and grow mighty in power" (Job 21:6).

Paul, steeped in these Hebrew scriptures, forged what would become the Christian eschatology of death in Romans 5: sin and death, drawn into the world by the fall of Adam, have now taken hold of the whole creation. But the new Adam has come, has suffered the punishment for sin, dying the death that we deserved. Thence, the inevitable cycle of sin, guilt, and death has now been conquered by Jesus Christ who has won new life for all those who believe.

Reconstructed theological education will underscore the importance of the death, resurrection and glorification of Jesus Christ. Indeed, death and life have been redefined in the cross, resurrection and glorification of Jesus (Rom 8, 1 Cor 15). Unless African theological education prepares its adherents to welcome and embrace this perspective, the sorrows and suffering that AIDS causes, may not be understood.

Toward a Right Side-Up Theology of AIDS

AIDS provides an opportunity for the church to be what it was intended to be - a witnessing and healing community. Thus, a right side-up theology of AIDS calls upon theological educators interested in the mission of the church to make the church a place where people can share their woundedness, their vulnerability and their search for healing. The church can only retain its identity and mission if its ministers and leaders are grounded in a theology that takes its purpose and context seriously.

I would like to propose a right side-up Trinitarian theology of AIDS. The Trinity presents us with a "WE" relationship, which replaces a victim theology that is founded on the notion of "THEIR" disease. Unless, a view of AIDS emanates from the fact that we are all created in the image of God, and that we live in relationships, then theology serves no purpose. Calls for chastity, abstinence, faithfulness and condom use need to be evaluated according to the experiences of the people and in the light of scripture. It is the responsibility of theological educators to evaluate what proposals may be applicable to the context. Theological educators will need to evaluate African rites of passage to see if they can be useful in shaping the lives of adults-to-be towards responsible sexual and marital behaviour. The good from traditional marriage customs must be incorporated into theological curricula and into materials made available for Bible study discussions in congregations, thus taking the African reality seriously.

A right side-up theology of AIDS demands that discrimination and stigmatization of those infected or affected by HIV/AIDS must be brought to an end. A theology that first and foremost embraces all people as God's creatures must emerge. Indeed, theological educators must help the church to repentance since, in the past churches have participated in the sins of hatred and stigmatization. A right side-up theology of AIDS confronts the forces of evil that exclude people by victimization and discrimination and seeks justice and mercy for the vulnerable in society, both for those inside and for those outside of the church.

A right side-up theology of AIDS demands a common stand from theological educators against the practices and doctrines that have dehumanized African peoples. It will confront church leaders with the reality of the place of condom use, as well as abstinence and faithfulness. A right side-up theology stems from 'below' where the people are living in the daily reality of struggle, strife, pain, suffering and distress in the streets of our cities, the shanty slums annexed to our posh sub-urban areas, our prisons, and our places of industry. Theology must not begin at the 'top', in the international boardrooms of London, Geneva, New York, Washington, Nairobi or Johannesburg, or in the denominational headquarters and the Cathedrals. Unless a reconstructed theology sits with, listens with and theologizes with people where they are, our theology will have no relevant impact on the lives of the people who need it most.

Above all, a reconstructed theology must confront what has been called 'Patriarchal sin'. The inequality that has existed between men and women in societies, families and churches are part of the major reasons that HIV/AIDS is spreading. In order to change the HIV/AIDS epidemiological wave, the church must be summoned to repent from patriarchal attitudes and to struggle to propound a theology that affirms that men and women are both made in God's image and that all are equal before God (Gen. 1:27).[19]

Conclusion

As theological educators and church leaders, we cannot afford to remain spectators when the people entrusted to us are being devoured by HIV/AIDS epidemic. The challenge of building a reconstructed theological education enlightened by biblical teaching and by our social location is possible, if we begin by repenting of our victim theology. Unless victim theology is replaced by a truly biblical theology, theological education in the 21st century will be a disaster for God's suffering people.

Let me close where I started. In the years to come, our descendants will look back and wonder what their ancestors (church theologians) did when the HIV/AIDS pandemic was debilitating the lives of our peoples. Indeed, the church of Jesus Christ (and her theologians!) will stand judged if they do not help the church to recover the theological basis of its pastoral response to AIDS in a way that can extend compassion, promote justice, and offer support, nurture and hope. May this Consultation enable us to renounce victim theology through a reconstructed theological education!

---

[19] Musa W. Dube, "Preaching to the Converted," 43.

CHAPTER NINE

Christian Theological Education in the Context of the Religiously Pluralistic Continent of Africa

Johnson A. Mbillah

Introduction

It is a privilege to be invited to participate in the Centenary Celebration of St Paul's United Theological College, and to be given the opportunity to provide a reflection on Christian theological education in the context of the religiously pluralistic continent of Africa. Religious pluralism, it has to be said, is not the preserve of the African continent but a worldwide phenomenon. Many theologians have grappled with this issue for some time now and they will, no doubt, continue to do so. In spite of the phenomenon being worldwide it is perhaps worth emphasising that for most regions of Europe, for example, religious pluralism is relatively new. In the African situation, however, religious pluralism has from time immemorial been part and parcel of the African worldview and belief system. African Religion or African Traditional Religion or African Traditional Religions,[1] as different writers feel appropriate to describe the African belief systems and practices, are inherently pluralistic.

---

[1] There is currently a debate going on among scholars of the history and phenomenology of religion as to what would be the most appropriate way of describing religion in Africa.

The pluralistic nature of the African belief system, coupled with the fact that such a system has no proselytising ambitions and therefore tends to be very tolerant and hospitable to other belief systems, "has led to the proliferation of religions in the continent to an extent that it can be said with little or no reservation that almost if not all religious systems in the world exist in the continent in one form or another."[2] This situation has further elaborated and expanded the religiously pluralistic nature of the continent, and thereby enabled vigorous missionary religions such as Christianity and Islam statistically to dominate the religious environment.

In our reflection on Christian theological education in the context of this religiously pluralistic continent we propose to outline the main themes of Christian theology in any given environment, provide a brief outline of Christian theologies on religious pluralism, and argue that Christian theological education in Africa cannot ignore the debate on religious pluralism and what that means for the Christian faith in Africa. We shall argue that such a theology must be rooted in the African Christian religious experience, most of which is very much rooted in African spirituality.

Main Features of Theology

Theology (or 'God-talk') is understood to be the attempt of adherents of a faith such as Christianity to present their statements of belief consistently, and to assign to such statements their specific place within the context of every worldly relation such as nature, history, and culture, for example.

The main themes of theology have always been God, humankind, the world, salvation, and eschatology (or the study of last things). These themes are indispensable components of any theological education anywhere. However, in terms of the period, the context, as well as the environment in which these themes have

---

[2]J. A. Mbillah, "Christian-Muslim Relations in Africa: Historical Perspectives and Current Realities" in Arnold C. Temple & Johnson A. Mbillah (eds.), *Christianity and People's of Other Faith Communities'* (Nairobi: AACC Africa Challenge Series, 2001), 32.

to be studied, there ought to be areas of emphasis so as make theology relevant to a given society. It is one of these areas of emphasis (religious pluralism) that we wish to put forward as a theological imperative for African theological educators in the 21st century. We shall do this by first and foremost, reminding ourselves of the two main themes of theology, which are God and humankind.

God

The question of God in theological discourse, as far as African theological institutions are concerned, was (and perhaps still is in some theological institutions) largely inherited from the West. For example, most if not all African theological institutions still spend a lot of time discussing the arguments for the existence of God.[3] Much as these arguments are of intellectual and philosophical worth, they are of less existential worth in the African context since, for the African, the existence of God is not contested.[4] God's existence is so intrinsic or innate that parents do not need to educate their children of His existence. The well known and perhaps over cited proverb of the Akan of Ghana, which states: *Obi nkyere abofra Oyame* ('No one teaches a child that God exists') demonstrates this.

Human Beings

On the second important theme of theology (humanity), the core thought is that theological reflections should have bearing on everyday life issues. This means that there is always the constant need of a balance between what is sometimes described as 'verticalism' and 'horizontalism' in theology. By verticalism we mean that type of theology that concentrates on humanity's relationship with God and relegates to the background, humanity's relationship with fellow

---

[3] We are referring here to the Design (or Teleological Argument), the Causal Argument, and the Ontological Argument, and so on.

[4] It has to be said that Africans who claim to be atheists ought also to claim that their atheism is not innate but acquired from sources outside their African roots.

human beings, otherwise referred to as horizontalism. We therefore have to structure our theological education in such a way that when we speak of God and the question of religious truth we also have to speak of the meaning of human existence. In practical terms this calls for a reflective connection between theological orthodoxy (or 'right belief') and theological orthopraxy ('right action').

Reflection on these two themes in the light of religious pluralism suggests that a theology of God and right belief is as important theological anthropology: a theology of humanities' relationship with God and with their fellow human beings. To attend to these appropriately requires a radical shift from giving primary attention to inherited theological formulations on the existence of God, for example, to the more practical and existential questions of Christian theological truth claims about God as creator, sustainer, and redeemer of the universe. Such claims of truth about God should then be discussed alongside claims of truth made by other religions with the view of discerning where the various religions meet and part. This should then be followed by practical questions concerning the Christian attitude towards people of other faiths with whom Christians rub shoulders in all aspects of human endeavours. To put it bluntly, what we are calling for here is that African theological educators need to produce a Christian theology of religious plurality rooted in the African religious experience. Such a theology should not be isolationist in character but seen in the light of other theologies of religious pluralism with a strong element of what African theology can contribute to the worldwide debate.

In the light of this, and in the light of the need to focus on why and how African Christian theological institutions should take up a theology of religious pluralism as a subject in the theological formation of future African theologians and church leaders, we shall give an outline of the main theologies of religious pluralism that are current, and then offer a suggestion of where, in our opinion, African theological institutions should begin their exploration of what it means to live in a religiously pluralistic society.

Different Strands on the Debate on Religious Pluralism

There are three main views on the nature of religious pluralism. These are: the Exclusivist Model, the Inclusivist Model, and, the Pluralist Model.[5]

Before we provide briefs on these three models it is perhaps fair to begin with the age-old argument propounded by pioneers of Historical Relativism who saw all religions as particular manifestations of the one and only absolute being. For these pioneers since the derivation of religions is from that one absolute being there is no absolute religion.[6] This view, which later was developed (whether consciously or unconsciously) by Arnold Toynbee, argues that all religions are essentially the same and therefore constitute different paths leading to the same essence – to God.[7]

This would suggest that for the adherent or adherents of any religion to hold a view that any religion is intrinsically better than another, is discarded as arrogant and narrow-minded. In this light, it only makes religious sense to say that 'for Christians' Christianity is the best religion and 'for Muslims' Islam is the best religion rather than giving the impression that ones own religion is the best of all.[8] These early statements on religious pluralism engendered further debate and eventually found some amount of sympathy with the pluralist model, which we shall discuss below. With this background in mind we now proceed to present the three main theological perspectives on religious pluralism.

---

[5] Cf. David Bosch, *Transforming Mission: Paradigm Shifts in Theology of Mission.* (Maryknoll: Orbis, 1991), 474- 88 ("Mission as Witness to People of Other Living Faiths").

[6] J. L. Adam "Ernst Troeltsch as an Analyst of Religion", *Journal of the Scientific Study of Religion,* 1, (1961-62): 98-108.

[7] For further reading of this strand see L. S. Betty "The Radical Pluralism of Arnold Toynbee" – Its implications for Religion," *Journal for Ecumenical Studies,* 9 (1972): 819-40.

[8] For further elaboration on this see Paul H. Santmire, "Ernst Troeltsch: Modern Historical Thought and the Challenge to Individual Religions," in N. J. Englewood Cliff, *Critical Issues in Modern Religion* (Prentice–Hall, 1973), 365-99.

The Exclusivist Model

The exclusivist model of a Christian theology of pluralism, often found in conservative evangelical, Roman Catholic and Eastern Orthodox circles, begins with revelation and then moves to salvation. In the past century the chief spokesmen for this position were Emil Brunner, Karl Barth, and Hendrik Kraemer who held the view that human beings by themselves cannot seek God and find him, neither can they know God by their own quest to know him. Similarly, self-effort cannot lead human beings to achieve salvation. Only God can make God known and only God can provide salvation.[9] In this light, they argued, we have to accept God's self-revelation in Jesus Christ and let him save us.

Biblical justification for exclusivist is derived from the Christian belief that Jesus is the absolute revelation of God and that there is no salvation anywhere except through him. "For there is no other name under heaven given by which human beings can be saved except in Jesus Christ." (Acts 4:12) This theology, which in Missiology is referred to as Christocentric, consolidates its biblical imperative by quoting the words of Jesus: "I am the way and the truth and the life; no one comes to the father but by me" (John 14:6).

This theology has unquestionably been the position of the Church for a very long time. In Catholic ecclesiology this theology existed in a particular form in the axiom *'Extra Ecclesiam nulla salus'* (Outside the Church no Salvation).[10]

Inclusivist Model

The inclusivist model, often found in mainline Protestant churches, differs with the exclusivist model in the sense that it has a more a

---

[9]Karl Barth, "The Revelation of God as the Abolition of Religion" in *Church Dogmatics*, 1.2 (Edinburgh: Clark, 1956), 280-361.

[10]Pope Boniface VIII championed this position, but it can be traced back as far as the African theologian St. Cyprian of Carthage. See Alan Race, *Christians and Religious Pluralism*, (Maryknoll: Orbis, 1982), 10.

dialogical approach to other faiths as it carries with it a dialectical 'Yes and No' in terms of revelation and salvation.[11] In terms of revelation this approach, which is basically Theocentric, argues that there is original 'general revelation' which is an act of God (Romans 1: 18. 2: 12-16; Acts 14:15; 17:27, John 1). This form of revelation, they contend, is the revelation which other religions apart from Christianity have experienced. Such revelation is incomplete as it is only a preparation for the final self-revelation of God in Christ. To put in another way, general revelation is partial while revelation in Christ is complete and final.

On the question of whether adherents of other religions will have salvation, the answer is an emphatic 'No'. Adherents of other religions will have salvation only when they accept the salvific revelation that is only found in Christ.

Arguing on the possibility of revelation outside Christianity and salvation only through Christ, the inclusivist finds biblical justification in such stories as the conversion of Cornelius, and Paul and Barnabas address to a multitude at Lystra. On the conversion of Cornelius, they argue that in that story God's Spirit operated outside Christianity and yet at the same time required the adherents of other religions who had no prior explicit knowledge of God's self-revelation in Christ and his saving grace, to come to that explicit knowledge (Acts 10:35). On the story of the address of Paul and Barnabas before the multitude at Lystra, they argue that this text makes it clear that God has always made Himself partially known and in the last days He has made himself fully known in Jesus Christ (Acts 14:16-17).

Perhaps the text which provides the most explicit support for the inclusivist position is the story of Paul's speech on the Areopagus where he acknowledges the authenticity of the worship of the people of Athens at their altar 'to an unknown God' but goes on to explain and clarify the identity of the 'unknown God' as the one who created

---

[11] For more on this see Race, *Christians and Religious Pluralism*, 38-69.

the heaven and the earth and pointed them to the person of Jesus Christ whose resurrection is an assurance that God has appointed him to be judge of the world. Thus Paul introduced them to the God they had worshiped all along as unknown (Acts 17: 22-31). This view of Paul provides grounds for what some inclusivist theologians call 'anonymous Christians'[12] as the episode suggests that the people of Athens had been Christians without knowing that they were such until Paul made known to them the identity of 'an unknown God' which they had worshipped all along.

Protestant forms of inclusivist theology find solidarity in the Vatican II document, the *Declaration on the Relation of the Church to Non-Christian Religions (Nostra Aetate)* which alludes to the working of the Spirit of God in other religions or the concept of general revelation in other religions when it states: "The Catholic Church rejects nothing of what is true and holy in these religions. She has a high regard for the manner of life and conduct, the precepts and doctrines which, although differing in many ways from her own teaching, nevertheless often reflect a ray of that truth which enlightens all men.[13]

The Pluralist Model
The pluralist model of a Christian theology of religious pluralism is generally regarded as belonging to the liberal end of Christian theology. For the pluralist, knowledge of God is partial in all faiths including the Christian faith. In other words all 'higher religions'

---

[12]The post Vatican II Catholic theologian Karl Rahner is the leading exponent of the theory of "Anonymous Christian" See his books *Theological Investigations* Vols. 5 & 6 (London: Darton, Longman & Todd, 1966 & 1969, respectively). Also his essay "Christ in non-Christian Religions", in G. Gispert-Sauch (ed.) *God's Word Among Men* (Delhi: Vidyajoti, 1973).

[13]Austin Flannery, OP (ed.), *Vatican II. The Conciliar and Post-Conciliar Documents,* (Dominican Publications, St. Saviour's, Dublin, Ireland 1975), 739. To explore this strand further see Paul F. Knitter, *No other Name? A Critical Survey of Christian Attitudes Toward the World Religions,* (Orbis Books, Maryknoll, New York, 1985), 97-119.

(as some of them chose to discriminate between the different faiths) 'present some facet of God's truth.'[14] They opine strongly that there are several spheres of saving contact between God and man. In other words, "God's revealing and redeeming activity has elicited response in a number of culturally conditioned ways throughout history. Each response they contend is partial, incomplete, unique; but they are related to each other in that they represent different culturally focussed perceptions of the one ultimate divine reality."[15]

They argue for a theocentric theology of both revelation and salvation in which God, rather than Christ, is seen as the centre of the religious universe. Christology which is the bedrock of both the exclusivist and inclusivist models of theologies of religious pluralism, is thereby downgraded.[16] Christ becomes an 'example' rather than the normative 'way' of salvation. Pluralists talk of differences in modes of the divine reality, arguing that such allows Christians to be fully committed to Christ and at the same time fully open to other religions.[17]

Pioneered by theologians such as Ernst Troeltsch, W.E. Hocking and Arnold Toynbee, the pluralist model has also been championed by Paul Tillich, John Hick, and Wilfred Cantwell Smith. From the Roman Catholic side, Hans Kung is a key exponent of this position. Lacking Christian theological precedence or pedigree with an explicit New Testament base, arguments for tolerance of other religious positions has been the hallmark of this theological tradition.

Where to Begin with a Theology of Pluralism in the African Context

It is common knowledge that when one's body itches all over, the hand scratches the part of the body that itches most. We have said earlier that in the African religious environment Christianity and

---

[14] A. Toynbee, *Christianity Among the Religions of the World* (Scribner's, 1957), 111, cited in Race, *Christians and Religious Pluralism*,.72.
[15] Alan Race, *Christians and Religious Pluralism*, 77-78.
[16] Paul Knitter, *No other Name?* 172ff.
[17] Paul Knitter, *No other Name?* xiv.

Islam have the largest numerical following. What we should also say is that these two great missionary religions continue to rival each other for the soul of the African, and in their interactions raise a barrage of questions that theologians of Africa never had to face in the past but which African theologians of the 21st century cannot ignore.

We have also suggested that there is a need for African theological colleges to take the issue of religious pluralism seriously. This is not merely in order to satisfy intellectual, abstract requirements of theological thinking (important as that may be), but to help attend to existential problems which the leadership of the churches, and members of congregations face daily - and sometimes with increasing discomfort.

It is in terms of where it itches most and what constitutes the most existential problem within the religiously pluralistic continent of Africa that we would suggest that the teaching of Islam is taken seriously by African theological institutions. Parishioners are more likely to ask the theological specialist (pastors and priests) questions about Islam and its relation to Christianity, than questions concerning African Traditional religion or the rest of the world religions such as Judaism, Hinduism, and Buddhism.

In order to make a case for theological institutions to take Islam seriously, we would like to elucidate just two out of the numerous areas of importance in the Christian-Muslim encounter in the African continent that require theological insights to appropriately make such encounters meaningful both for the theological specialist and those that he/she ministers to.

Questions of the Essence of God

A recurrent question we often face when we move around Africa goes like this: Christianity alongside with Judaism and Islam are known and general accepted to be the three monotheistic religions or Abrahamic religions, as some choose to call them. That Christianity is an offshoot of Judaism is not contested, as Yahweh of the Hebrews is the same God Christians believe is the father of Jesus Christ.

Islam, on the other hand, argues that it is closely related to the previous revelation of Christianity and Judaism. Are both Christianity and Islam equally true? Do they have something in common? Where do they meet and where do they part? Questions that may seem elementary, such as whether the God who is the Father of Jesus Christ is the same God as Allah of the Muslims, come up all the time.

Apart from these questions that deal with the essence of the two religions, there are also questions that deal with salvation, the person of Christ in the Bible and Jesus of the Qur'ân, and so on. Another recurrent question goes like this: Did Jesus in John 14ff. promise the coming of the *paraclete* (comforter, or the Holy Spirit of Christianity) or did he promise a *pereclyte* (praised one, or Ahmad, invariably interpreted as Muhammad by Muslims) of Islam. These questions are as inconsequential for some as they are crucial to others.

Thorny Questions of Religious Rights and Freedoms
For the past few years the Shari'a debate in parts of northern Nigeria, which has led to a great loss of lives, has raised basic questions of religious rights and freedoms. We are limited by time and space in our discussion of this issue but even raising the question does make a strong argument for taking religious pluralism as it relates to Islam seriously in our theological colleges. What we can say within the constraints of this paper is that such issues will continue to surface not just in Nigeria but also in many other parts of Africa where Muslims constitute a majority or even an important minority. Currently, Kenyan Christians and Muslims are locked in the Kadhi Courts debate. As both Christian and Muslim communities have realised, the temperature of the discussion rises rapidly when it comes to the issue of religious rights and freedoms. These are emotive issues that have to be approached with care and full knowledge about what each other is communicating.

The issue of the Shari'a debate in Northern Nigeria and the Sudan, and to a lesser extent that of the Kadhi Courts in Kenya, demonstrates the need for an African theological reflection of what it means to live in a religiously pluralistic society. It also brings to the fore our contention that a theology of religious pluralism in Africa should begin with Islam. As recent engagements have shown, it would serve no good purpose if Christians were to ignore a theology of religious pluralism as it relates to Islam, and thereby engage in a venting of feelings about Islam and Muslims without full knowledge of what they are talking about.

Conclusion

In this presentation we have attempted to show that in a Christian 'theology of religions' Christian theologians attempt to account for the diversity of the world's religions, especially as these religions relate to Christianity. We have argued that a Christian theology of religious pluralism must be viewed from within a Christian framework. As Alan Race rightly points out, it is not possible for a Christian theologian to place his or her own faith in parenthesis while examining the faith of the other. To put it in another way, "What the Christian theologian must do is strive to listen attentively to the faith of the non-Christian as this is unfolded by the believer himself, without pre-judging that faith and without abandoning his own commitment as he/she proceeds.[18] A knowledge and understanding of what religious pluralism (and especially Islam) means for the African Christian theological student, we have contended, is an asset to the Christian faith and practice since it is only with a firm grasp of the issues that the questions from congregants can appropriately be answered.

As we have shown, there is no consensus on what constitutes an authentic Christian theology or religious pluralism. There is, however, a growing awareness of religious pluralism as a theological problem which African theological institutions must take seriously and to which they need to make a contribution. Such a contribution should not be isolationist but should take into account the three main

---

[18]Race, *Christians and Religious Pluralism*, 5.

ways of understanding religious pluralism which we have discussed above.

It is our prayer and hope that those who make decisions on theological education will take the issues we have put across seriously so as to make Christian theology relevant to the theological specialist and to priests and pastors who work in the field. Many years ago now, Wilfred Cantwell Smith recognised the importance of Christian theologians taking religious pluralism seriously when he wrote: "From now on any serious intellectual statement of the Christian faith must include, if it is to serve its purpose among men, some doctrine of other religions. We explain the fact of the Milky Way by the doctrine of creation, but how do you explain the fact that the Bhagavad Gita is there?"[19]

For his part, Canon Max Warren, then General Secretary of the Church Missionary Society (now Church Mission Society), having been concerned about the agnostic science of his day, recognised the challenge that other religions posed to Christianity. "[T]he confrontation between Christian belief and agnostic science will turn out to be more like child's play when it is compared to the present challenge to the church in the encounter between Christianity and the other world faiths."[20]

---

[19] W. C. Smith, *The Faith of Other Men*. (New York: Harper Touchbooks, 1972), 133.
[20] Cited by Race, *Christians and Religious Pluralism*, 3.

CHAPTER TEN

Approaches to Teaching Islam in the Twenty First Century

John A. Chesworth

Africa is described by Ali Mazrui as having a 'Triple Heritage', in that its culture has been influenced by African Traditional Religion, Christianity, and Islam. During the post-Colonial period Africa was seen as being the ideological battleground for the Capitalist West and the Communist East. With the collapse of Communism Samuel Huntington posited that the new global struggle could be seen as 'Clash of Civilizations', specifically citing the role of Islam in this global struggle and as a factor in the destabilisation of the world.

One of the main areas where this kind of destabilisation is occurring is Africa. Although wars no longer seem to be fought over political ideologies, Africa has remained a battleground in a religious struggle for peoples' hearts and minds. Yet again Africa is being used to play out a struggle between external forces. The present 'Battle for Africa', between Christianity and Islam is guided by external forces as much as the former battle between Capitalism and Communism.

What are the factors behind this battle? First of all, Islam and Christianity are both missionary religions. The Arabic word for outreach – *da'wa* means 'to Call' others to the faith; the Latin word *missio* – means 'to Send' and tell others about the faith. The institutional structures of both religions have an interest in propagating their version of belief: for Muslims these are Revivalists/reformers who are usually linked to Wahabbist ideas who seek a return to the 'Ideal State,' Muhammad's Medina; on the Christian side there are a variety of groups, some described as 'fundamentalist' who are externally funded and operated.

An example of one Christian group involved in such outreach is: *Christ for All Nations* (CfAN). Its leader, Reinhard Bonnke, a German who is a regular visitor to Tanzania and Kenya, regards "Africa as a field ripe for harvest." Ludwig comments on this approach: "[it] does not leave much room for dialogue with other religions. In Tanzania [Bonnke] has to refrain from direct attacks, but nevertheless he uses a 'powerful' militant language."[1]

Because Bonnke has spoken out against Islam some of his 'Crusades' have been cancelled in Nigeria and Mali because of fears of violence arising from his views. Paul Gifford discusses Bonnke's attitude to Islam and Muslims in Africa:

Bonnke is quite open that he is conducting a campaign against Islam, moving against the Muslim lands of North Africa. Of his Jos crusade, *Revival Report* says: "Muslims vie militantly for control of the city. That fact ... made the Jos crusade crucial for CfAN in its evangelistic commitment to drive upward into Africa." And elsewhere: "Jos was one of CfAN's most strategically important for advancing north into Nigeria's Moslem strongholds". This he considers his divine mandate: "We are even knocking on the gates of the Islamic fortresses, because Jesus has said 'Knock and it shall be opened unto you.'" Everyone understands exactly whom he is referring to when he writes: "We are gripped by a holy determination to carry out the Great Commission of our Lord, which is a command to attack the strongholds of Satan." The widely-heralded, seemingly unstoppable advance of Christianity, exemplified by Bonnke and

---

[1] Frieder Ludwig, 223, "After Ujamaa: Is religious revivalism a threat to Tanzania's stability?" in *Questioning the Secular State*, D. Westerlund (Ed.). London: Hurst & Company: 1996: 216-236.

his seemingly limitless resources, personnel and technology, appears as the ultimate threat to Muslims. To Muslims, Bonnke's aim is the elimination of every Mosque from Africa in the shortest possible time. This elimination is to be achieved through evangelisation and not through arson but in Muslim eyes the ultimate effect is the same, their cultural annihilation.[2]

In addition to Bonnke's views on Islam, Gifford also examines the methods of conducting outreach by large public rallies, including the sheer logistics and statistics involved.[3] He also analyses the content of sermons delivered in a series of thirteen meetings conducted in Zimbabwe.[4] Of particular interest is the account of the Nairobi Crusade conducted in Mathari Valley in February 1991. Gifford makes specific reference to how Bonnke deals with Islam:

> [By] definition Muslims can only be part of Satan's Empire. At Mathari Valley Bonnke welcomed all: "Whether Christian or not, Hindu, Muslim, it doesn't matter. Jesus loves you, Jesus loves you, Jesus loves you. He's willing to save and heal you, whatever your background, and I'm very happy you are here." The happiness arises from the possibility of their turning to Jesus. If they fail to grasp this opportunity, however, they remain in Satan's power and will be damned eternally.[5]

Bonnke's 'combine harvester' approach to evangelism, is not the only one that is used in Africa. Many Christian organisations are active in Africa, specifically seeking to win Muslims to Christ. Some are international such as Call of Hope/*Njia ya Uzima* [Way of Wholeness] and Life Challenge Africa. Others are locally initiated, such as Sheepfold Ministries, which began in Kenya and also works

---

[2] Paul Gifford, "Reinhard Bonnke's Mission to Africa, and His 1991 Nairobi Crusade," in *New Dimensions in African Christianity*, (ed. P. Gifford; Nairobi: All Africa Conference of Churches: 1992), 171; cf. idem, "'Africa Shall be Saved'. An Appraisal of Reinhard Bonnke's Pan-African Crusade," *Journal of Religion in Africa* 17/1 (1986): 63-92.

[3] Gifford, "Africa Shall be Saved", 63-65; Gifford, "Reinhard Bonnke's Mission", 157-60.

[4] Gifford "Africa Shall be Saved", 65-78.

[5] Gifford, "Reinhard Bonnke's Mission to Africa," 163.

in neighbouring countries, and *Biblia ni Jibu* [The Bible is the Answer] which is virtually a 'one man show' working in Dar es Salaam. They use a variety of approaches, including living amongst the Muslim community, the use of literature, training evangelists. Most, however, deliberately work with a low-key approach and in general avoid preaching campaigns targeting Muslims.

Any group considering evangelism amongst Muslims needs to consider the 'cost of conversion' for the new Christian. Discussing this with a long-term worker for *Njia ya Uzima*, who is from a Muslim background, it became clear that we held similar views and a concern for the care of converts. A church or group may decide to conduct outreach amongst Muslims, but all too often the question of care and nurture of the new Christian is seen as only spiritual. Little thought is given to the fact that a Muslim who becomes a Christian will be shunned by both family and community. They may be totally disowned, so that they turn to the church that has brought them to Christ for help and find platitudes rather than support.

In the twenty-first century there has already been a radical shift in world-wide perception of religions and their significance in current affairs. The events in the past few years within Eastern Africa - civil war in the Sudan, and the bombings in Nairobi, Dar es Salaam and Mombasa - serve to illustrate the tensions that are here. Events in Nigeria, such as the introduction of *Shari'a* in some states, raise tensions and questions. Here in Kenya questions concerning the status of *Kadhi* Courts have been raised by the Constitutional Review process.

Having demonstrated the need for more understanding of Islam and of Christian-Muslim Relations, this paper presents ways of teaching Islam in a theological school context and seeks to show how this can be done within an African setting.

Contemporary events illustrate both the reality of interfaith tensions and the need for Christians to understand Islam and the learn how to relate to Muslims. This paper seeks to outline issues within the African context which need to be explored and to provide conceptual and bibliographical resources which can help us to determine the content of a theological curriculum which takes this dynamic seriously.

What to Teach

In order to understand Islam and Muslims today it is necessary to understand something of the roots and origins of Islam. The subject areas important to consider within the context of Eastern Africa for an introductory course will include the following topics:

Introduction to the Study of Islam

Ascertaining how much the student already knows about Islam and its presence in East Africa often helps the student to realise how much more there is to know. This section also helps students to understand the reasons that Islam is being studied.

Pre-Islamic Arabia

To know what pre-Islamic Arabia was like informs our understanding of how the development of Islam was influenced by the Arabian culture, Arabian Traditional Religion, Judaism and the various Christian denominations that were present.

Life of Muhammad

For Muslims, the life of Muhammad is the model they aspire to live up to, especially the Medinan period, which is seen as the 'ideal society'. Because of this, it is important to present the critical stages of Muhammad's life so that students may understand the responses of present-day Muslims.

The Qur'an

This should aim at demystifying the Qur'an, explaining what is understood by *umm-l-kitab*, and describing how the Qur'an came to be in its current form. Explaining the main elements of the Qur'an, using examples of passages from the *Suras*, and especially those passages in the Qur'an which mention Jesus.

Sunnah and Hadith

Since the actions and sayings of Muhammad are at times considered to be more important than the Qur'an, they are critical to understanding legal decisions and the actions and opinions of Muslims.

Spread of Islam 632-1258

How Islam spread in the first five centuries after Muhammad and how that has shaped culture and commerce. This gives an insight into the Islamic mind-set and attitude to expansion of Islam as well as to the ways in which Islamic states govern their peoples.

Practice of Islam

Understanding the ways in which Muslims practice their faith, what they believe and the ways that affects other communities is very important. The areas that should be studied are:

Diin – Five Pillars of Religion
Iman – Beliefs in Islam
Dhimma – The ways in which Christians and Jews are treated under Islamic rule
Jihad – Explaining the concept of struggle, the ideal and the reality.

Jurisprudence

The legal structures of Islam including *Shari'a* and Kadhi Courts are often misunderstood. How legal decisions are made and the way that the courts work are especially needful with the Muslim call for the re-instatement of Kadhi Courts in mainland Tanzania and the reassessment of Kadhi Courts in the Constitutional review process in Kenya.

Gender and Islam
An awareness of the attitude to gender in Islam is very important. At an introductory level, it is a helpful exercise when choosing both Quranic passages and Hadith to use ones that illustrate the place of Women in Muslim society.

Islam in East Africa
This segment begins at the start of the 8th c. and includes the Portugese occupation, the Sultanate, the colonial period, independence, and the present. Also described are different Muslim groups present in East Africa, their locations and the influence of each group in the present situation.

Christians and Muslims in East Africa
Understanding the ways in which Christians and Muslims interact, as well as something of their tensions and difficulties is very important. Looking at Muslim Outreach Da'wa and the methods employed by them in outreach. Studying Christian Evangelism and witness. Finding out about Dialogue and how to use it at all levels of societal structures.

A suggested introductory course outline, together with bibliography is given as an appendix.

How to Teach Islam
It is all very well having an outline of what to teach. But teaching a subject such as Islam within the context of a Christian seminary needs both sensitivity and imagination. This is in order to encourage students to grasp the relevance of the subject to their situation and its importance to their future ministries.

Approaches
Lectures. The necessary facts about Islam must be put across in ways that are interesting and relevant to the students.

Audio-Visual Aids. The use of Videos and other information technology resources, are increasingly available with a range of material produced both by Muslims and by Christians.

Texts. Students should learn how to handle the Qur'ân and Hadith.

Visits. Much can be learned by a positive visit to a Mosque, where presuppositions on both sides can be challenged.

People. Arranging meetings with Muslims and Christian evangelists, in order to learn the challenges of outreach from both faith groups can be very helpful.

Resources

The acquisition of adequate resources is a major challenge to all of us in theological education. How do we obtain the material that we need to teach in an appropriate and contextual manner? Most of the resources that are most useful are too expensive for our institutions to be able to afford:

Books. Key texts on Islam are often too expensive for most African theological libraries. Many specialist books cost 5-6,000 shillings. However some publishers are producing books at less than 2,000 shillings. (See below for a bibliography of important texts relevant to the study of Islam in Africa.)

Journals. Journals are necessary as they keep us up-to-date with new trends and research – but they are very expensive. Some journals, however, are offering subscribers in Africa a more realistic cost.
- *Journal for Religion in Africa.* Even though it is published by Brill, subscribers in Africa pay the reduced rate of $58.
- *Islam and Christian-Muslim Relations-.* This resource is very expensive, $474 for Institutions. I discussed this with them and they are happy to offer it in Africa at around $90.

- *Journal of Quranic Studies*. This journal is £74 for Institutions and £37 for Individuals. The editor told me that they do not have a large enough subscription base to be able to subsidise the price.
- *Muslim World* published in Hartford, USA.
- *Islamochristiana* published by Pontifical Institute for the Study of Arabic and Islam (PISAI).

Magazines. Magazines published locally by Muslim groups provide useful information.
- *Al-Islam* published by Islamic Foundation in Nairobi.
- *The Guide* published by the Cultural Council of the Embassy of the Islamic Republic of Iran in Nairobi.

Videos. These are relatively cheap and readily available. Most Muslim bookshops stock them and many will make copies for you.
- *The Message* [Life of Muhammad – made by Muslims]
- Deedat vs. [Debates by Ahmed Deedat – South African Polemicist]
- *Mihadhara* [Muslims using the Bible to show the truth of Islam]

CD-ROMs. The value of CD-ROMs is that they carry a huge amount of information. For instance, *The Encyclopaedia of Islam* is 11 volumes and takes up a lot of shelf space. CD-ROMs do tend to be expensive. But some are very reasonable and affordable.
- *Encyclopaedia of Islam* - published by Brill, contains full text of the 11 Volume Series – expensive.
- *Historical Atlas of Islam* published by Brill, accompanies book of the same name and contains all the maps – expensive.
- *Alim*, a Muslim-produced resource, with the Qur'ân text in Arabic and English, also audio of recitation. It also includes an extensive collection of Hadiths and Jurisprudence. It costs around $100.

- *World of Islam* -- This is distributed by World Vision and costs $30. This includes the complete text of many books and useful teaching material.

Internet – Web-Sites. The Internet is an almost inexhaustible resource base. Information is posted, breaking news, opinions, texts of speeches, and articles can all be found. However it also has its problems. It is not always clear whether information posted on the web can be relied on. The ability to access information will also depend on whether your institution is connected to the internet, and how good a connection you have. The URLs given here are examples of sites that have been found useful in research. Some are Muslim sites, either actively propagating Islam, or simply informing. Some are Christian sites – some specifically set-up to inform Christians, others to attract Muslims and interest them in Christianity. Some are locally generated sites. Other sites include Newspaper Web-sites and the CIA!

- Islamicity http://www.islamicity.org
- The Young Muslims Association http://www.yma.org
- Sites about Ahmed Deedat and Islamic Propagation Centre International (IPCI) International Islamic Dawah Centre http://www.users.globalnet.co.uk/~iidc/iidci
- About Ahmed Deedat: http://home.virtual-pc.com/wipecrc/aboutad
- Ahmadiyya Movement   http://www.alislam.org
- Crescent Medical Aid   http://www.crescent-medical-aid.org/home.html
- Iqra Islamic Publications http://www.iqra.net
- Islam in Tanzania – text of various statements and articles plus lots of useful links, two on-line newspapers as well as chat room http://www.islamtz.org
- Answering Islam, A Christian-Muslim Dialogue and Apologetics   http://answering-islam.org

- Help for Muslims seeking the True Path http://www.aboutislam.com/default.htm
- Swahili texts http://www.swahilionline.com/links.htm
- Daily Nation http://www.nationaudio.com/News/DailyNation/Today/News/index.html
- Coastweek http://www.africaonline.co.ke/AfricaOnline/coastwk/980130/special1.html
- The CIA site on Kenya with facts about the country http://www.odci.gov/cia/publications/factbook/ke.html

For additional sites see two books by Gary Bunt: *Virtually Islamic: Computer-mediated Communication and Cyber Islamic Environments.* Cardiff: University of Wales Press, 2000 and *Islam in the Digital Age: E-Jihad, Online Fatwas and Cyber Islamic Environments.* London: Pluto Press 2003, which discuss the whole question of the use of the internet by Muslims.

The need for African Islamicists

How many Islamicists do you know? I suspect that the answer is 'not many.' How many are African? Probably even fewer. How many of them are working in Africa? At a recent meeting twenty-four papers were presented on Islam in Africa – only five were presented by Africans and only five of the presenters were actually living in Africa. Obviously there is a great need for African Christians to become experts in Islamics.

Conclusion

The future of Africa depends on its people being able to live together. Most Africans are either Muslims or Christians. Unless we train our students, the church leaders of tomorrow, to understand their Muslim neighbours and to relate to them, there is little hope for harmony in Africa.

Appendix 1
A Post-Graduate Course in Islam and Christian-Muslim Relations

St. Paul's, together with Programme for Christian-Muslim Relations in Africa[6] (PROCMURA), is developing a Post-Graduate Programme in Islam and Christian-Muslim Relations.

The General Objectives of the Programme
[1] The provision of necessary tools for Christian-Muslim positive engagement.
[2] Doing Christian mission in an interfaith milieu.
[3] Appreciation of the Christian-Muslim presence in Africa and its meaning for Christian living:

Course Duration and Structure
[1] The Post-Graduate Diploma (P-G Dip) is a 12 month programme. The Course consists of eight taught Modules worth 120 Credits and a Long Essay in the final four months.

[2] The Master of Arts Course in Islam and Christian–Muslim Relations (MA) is a 4 Semester programme in addition to the Eight taught Modules it includes a Dissertation Module worth 60 Credits

[3] Each semester will be of at least 15 weeks duration.

[4] The programme will concentrate on various aspects of understanding Islam and Christian-Muslim Relations.

[5] The overall structure of the course is: 8 Taught Modules each worth 15 Credits (For both Courses) 1 Dissertation worth 60 Credits

---

[6]The Programme for Christian-Muslim Relations in Africa (PROCMURA) is based in Nairobi and states as its purpose that it is dedicated to promote within the churches in Africa: 1. Faithful Christian witness to the Gospel in an interfaith environment of Christians and Muslims; 2. Constructive engagement with Muslims for peace and peaceful co-existence.

Semester One: 4 Taught Modules (60 Credits) Together with Research Methodology (Which is Mandatory for the MA, but no Credits are awarded).

Semester Two: 4 Taught Modules (60 Credits) Together with Selection and approval of Research Topic for MA only.

Long Vacation: PG Diploma Long Essay.

Semester Three and Four: For the MA Research done and Dissertation completed (60 Credits).

[6] To complete the PG Diploma a 10,000 word Long Essay is written. To complete the Master's a 20,000 word Dissertation is written.

Course Titles
FOUNDATION MODULE: INTRODUCTION TO ISLAM
To introduce students to an understanding of Islam in both its religious and cultural dimensions. To give an overview of the major concepts that shape Islam. Emphasis is given to the life of Muhammad and the Faith and Practice of Islam.

INTRODUCTION TO CHRISTIANITY
The course aims to develop the students' understanding of the essentials of Christianity. Giving an overview of the Christian scriptures, essential aspects of Church History and Theology.

QURANIC ARABIC
To introduce the student to the Arabic used in the Qur'an. To enable them to read the Qur'an, to understand basic Arabic grammar and to be able to use a lexicon.

QURANIC STUDIES

To allow students to examine in depth the origins and contents of the Qur'an. The approach includes an historical review of the interpretation of the Qur'an. It also identifies and examines the major themes of the Qur'an.

ISLAM IN AFRICA

To allow students to examine in depth the various themes concerning the spread and impact of Islam in Africa. The course gives an overview as well as seeking to cater for the background and experience of the individual student.

SUFISM

An overview of the development of Sufism from its origins. It examines the nature of Islamic Mysticism and studies some of the major Sufi orders with special reference to those prominent in Africa.

ISLAMIC HISTORY

The course aims to develop the student's critical historical skills and to enable them to gain an understanding of the sweep of Islamic history, together with the impact of the spread of Islam. Emphasis will be on the early centuries and the Islamic resurgence from the 18th Century onwards.

CHRISTIAN-MUSLIM RELATIONS

Students will examine themes concerning the origins and development of Christian-Muslim Relations. The approach includes an historical review looking at both positive and negative incidents and texts. It includes the teaching of the Qur'an about non-Muslims, and the earliest encounters. It identifies the major themes of discussion between Christians and Muslims. The contemporary situation in Africa, the impact of Islamic resurgence and the introduction of

Shari'a will also be studied. Regional studies will examine the situation in the areas represented by students.

ADVANCED QURANIC ARABIC
This course builds on the introductory course, enabling students to read and to translate passages from the Qur'an, also to improve the understanding of Arabic Grammar.

ISLAMIC THEOLOGY
Introducing the main themes of Islamic religious thought. Using an historical overview, to examine the development of the various schools of thought. To examine Islamic reform and revival from the 18th Century onwards, before looking at the contemporary situation.

ISLAMIC LAW (SHARI'A)
To introduce the principles and theory on which Islamic Law (*Shari'a*) is based. To gain an understanding of the development of Islamic Law and its interpretation and its interpretation. To introduce the different Schools of Law (*maddhab*) and the main variations between them. Reviewing the present situation in Africa, where different groups within the same region use different interpretations of Islamic Law.

GENDER ISSUES IN ISLAM
Allowing students to examine the sources of Islamic thought on gender relations, such as the Qur'an and Hadith. Studying contemporary interpretations of the early sources, particularly by Muslim feminists. To study the contemporary situation in Africa, the impact of Islamic resurgence and its effect of gender roles. Regional studies will be used to reflect the students' situations.

SUNNA AND HADITH

An introduction to *Sunna* and *Hadith*, examining how they were collected and classified. Studying a selection of texts looking at their interpretation and application, both historically and contemporarily.

RESEARCH METHODOLOGY

Designed to equip students with an understanding of the concepts, methods and tools of research in humanities and social sciences. In order to enable them to carry out a research project in a successful manner, then to present their findings in an acceptable form. The course will focus on, seminar presentations, extended essays and dissertations.

DISSERTATION

It is expected that the topic chosen will normally concern aspects of Islam and Christian-Muslim Relations in the African context.

Admission Requirements

Any candidate seeking admission to the Post-Graduate Diploma must have a minimum of a Lower Second Honours Degree (2.2), or a Grade Point Average (GPA) of at least 2.7 or the equivalent, in the system where they obtained their first degree.

Any candidate seeking admission to the Master of Arts must have a minimum of an Upper Second Honours Degree (2.1), or a Grade Point Average (GPA) of at least 3.0 or the equivalent, in the system where they obtained their first degree. Someone will qualify if they have a Post-Graduate Diploma from St. Paul's in Islam and Christian-Muslim Relations with an overall average of 60%. They are also given exemption of 4 modules.

The programme has been submitted for approval to the Commission for Higher Education in Kenya. It is hoped that the first course will begin in August 2004.

Appendix 2
A Bibliography of Books on Islam in Africa

Alkali, N. et al
1993   *Islam in Africa: Proceedings of the Islam in Africa Conference*, Ibadan: Spectrum Books Ltd.

Anglars, H.P.
1987   *Wana wa Ibrahimu: Wakristu na Waislamu*, 6th. printing. Tabora: TMP Book Department

An-Na'im, A.A. (Ed.)
2002   *Islamic Family Law in a Changing World*, London: Zed Books Ltd.

Azumah, J.A.
2001   *The Legacy of Arab-Islam in Africa: A Quest for Inter-religious Dialogue*, Oxford: Oneworld

Bakari, M. & Yahya, S.S. (Eds.)
1995   *Islam in Kenya,* Nairobi: Mewa Productions

Bennett, N.R.
1978   *A History of the Arab State of Zanzibar*, London: Methuen

Brenner, L.
1993   *Muslim Identity and Social Change in Sub-Saharan Africa*, L. Brenner (Ed.). London: Hurst

Brown, D.
1989   *Njia ya Nabii Muhammad: Wakristo waufahamu Uislamu,* Dodoma: Central Tanganyika Press

Caplan, A.P.
1975   *Choice and Constraint in a Swahili Community*, London: OUP (IAI)

Chande A.N.
1998   *Islam, Ulamaa and Community Development in Tanzania*, Bethesda: Austin & Winfield

Chesworth, J.

1999   *Muslim Affirmation through Refutation: A Tanzanian Example,* MA Birmingham

Chesworth, J.   2002   'Anglican Relations with Members of Other Faiths and Communities', *Encounter,* Number 1, 16-36

Chimera, R.
1998   *Kiswahili, Past Present and Future Horizons,* Nairobi: Nairobi University Press

Constantin, F. (Ed.)
1987   *Les Voies de L'Islam en Afrique Orientale,* Paris: Karthala

Cruise O'Brien, D.B. & Coulon, C.
1988   *Charisma and Brotherhood in African Islam,* Oxford: Clarendon Press

Farsy al, A.S.
1989   *The Shaf'i Ulama of East Africa, ca 1830-1970: A Hagiographic Account,* Translated, edited and annotated by Randall L. Pouwels, Madison: African Studies Program University of Wisconsin

Freitag, U. & Clarence-Smith, W.G. (Eds.)
1997   *Hadrami Traders, Scholars, and Statesmen in the Indian Ocean, 1750s-1960s,* Leiden: Brill

Gaudeul, J-M.
1990   *Encounters and Clashes Vols. I & II,* Rome: Pontifico Istutio di Studi Arabi e Islamici 2nd Ed.

1999   *Called from Islam to Christ,* Crowborough: Monarch

Goddard, H.
2000   *A History of Christian-Muslim Relations,* Edinburgh: EUP

Gray, J.
1962   *History of Zanzibar from the Middle Ages to 1856,* London: Oxford University Press

Griffiths, P.J. (Ed.)
   1990   *Christianity through non-Christian eyes*, Maryknoll: Orbis Books.

Guennec-Coppens, Le F. & Parkin, D. (Eds)
   1998   *Autorité et pouvoir chez les Swahili*, Paris: Karthala

Hamdun, S. & King, N.
   1994   *Ibn Battuta in Black Africa*, (With a new foreword by Ross E. Dunn), Princeton: Markus Wiener Publishers

Hansen, H.B. & Twaddle, M. (Eds.)
   1995   *Religion and Politics in East Africa* London: Currey
   2002   *Christian Missionaries & the State in the Third World*, Oxford: James Currey

Harries, L.
   1954   *Islam in East Africa*, London: UMCA

Hastings, A.
   1996   *The Church in Africa: 1450-1950*, Oxford: Clarendon Press

Hinton, M.J.
   1992   *Ministering Among Muslims in Africa: An annotated list of practical materials*, Nairobi: ACTEAIsnet

Hiskett, M.
   1994a   *The Sword of Truth: The life and times of Shehu Usuman dan Fodio* (2nd Ed.), Evanston: Northwestern University Press
   1994b   *The Course of Islam in Africa*, Edinburgh: EUP

Hjort, A.
   1979   *Savanna Town: Rural Ties and Urban Opportunities in Northern Kenya*, Stockholm: Department of Social Anthropology, University of Stockholm

Hoorweg, J., Foeken, D. & Obudho, R.A.
2000 *Kenya Coast Handbook: Culture, Resources and Development in the East African Littoral*, Hamburg: LIT Verlag Münster

Isichei, E.
1995 *A History of Christianity in Africa: From Antiquity to the Present*, London: SPCK

Kagabo, J.H.
1988 *L'islam et les <<Swahili>> au Rwanda*, Paris: École des Hautes Études en Sciences Sociales

Kane, O.
2003 *Muslim Modernity in Postcolonial Nigeria*, Leiden: Brill

Kanyeihamba, G.W.
1998 *Reflections on the Muslim Leadership Question in Uganda*, Kampala: Fountain Publishers

Kasozi, A.L.
1986 *The Spread of Islam in Uganda*, Nairobi: OUP

Kenny, J.
2000 *The Spread of Islam through North to West Africa 7th-19th Centuries*, Lagos: Dominican Publications

Kepel, G.
1985 *The Prophet and Pharaoh*, London: Al-Saqi Books

King, N., Kasozi, A. & Oded, A.
1973 *Islam and the Confluence of Religions in Uganda 1840-1966*, AAR Studies in Religion 6 Tallahasee: AAR

King, N.Q.
1971 *Christian and Muslim in Africa*, New York: Harper and Row

King, N.Q. et al. (Eds.)
1989 *Robin Lamburn - From a Missionary's Notebook*, Saarbrücken: Verlag Breitenbach Publishers

Khalid, A.
    1977   *The Liberation of Swahili from European Appropriation*, Nairobi: East African Literature Bureau

Kusimba, C.M.
    1999   *The Rise and Fall of Swahili States*, Walnut Creek: Alta Mira Press

Levtzion, N. & Pouwels, R.L. (Eds.)
    2000   *The History of Islam in Africa*, Oxford: James Currey

Lewis, I.M. (Ed.)
    1980   *Islam in Tropical Africa* (2nd Ed.), London: Hutchinson

Lings, M.
    1993   *A Sufi Saint of the Twentieth Century: Shaikh Ahmad Al-'Alawi*, Cambridge: Islamic Texts Society

Mandivenga, E.C.
    1983   *Islam in Zimbabwe*, Gwere: Mambo Press

al Mazru'i, A.A.
    1995   *The History of the Mazru'i Dynasty of Mombasa*, Translated and annotated by J.McL. Ritchie, Union Académique Internationale Fontes Historiae Africanae Series Arabica XI, Oxford: OUP on behalf of The British Academy

Mazrui, A.A. & Mazrui, A.M.
    1995   *Swahili State and Society,* London: James Currey
    1998   *The Power of Babel,* Oxford: James Currey

Mbillah, J.
    2002   'Inter-Faith Relations and the Quest for Peace in Africa', *Encounter*, Number 1, June 2002, 3-15

Middleton, J.
    1992   *The World of the Swahili an African Mercantile Civilization*, New Haven: Yale University Press

Mugyenzi, S.
    2000   'Christian-Muslim Relations at Crossroads in Uganda', *The Anitepam Bulletin* No. 28 November (2000), 1-9

Muhsin, A. (al-Barwani)
    n.d.   *Jifunze Kusoma Kiarabu: Kwa Wiki Tatu*, n.p.d.
    nd   *Let the Bible Speak*, no publishing details

Nimtz, A.H.
    1980   *Islam and Politics in East Africa: The Sufi Order in Tanzania*, Minneapolis: University of Minnesota Press

Njozi, H.M.
    2000   *Mwembechai Killings and the Political Future of Tanzania*, Ottawa: Globalink Communications

Nurse, D. & Spear, T.
    1985   *The Swahili: Reconstructing the History and Language of an African Society, 800-1500*, Philadelphia: University of Pennsylvania Press

O'Fahey, R.S.
    1990   *Enigmatic Saint: Ahmad Ibn Idris and the Idrisi Tradition*, Evanston: NUP

Oded, A.
    1974   *Islam in Uganda: Islamization through a Centralized State in Pre-Colonial Africa*, Chichester: John Wiley & Sons Ltd.
    2000   *Islam and Politics in Kenya*, London: Lynne Riennar Publishers Inc.

Pouwels, R.L.
    1987   *Horn and Crescent: Cultural change and Traditional Islam on the East African Coast 800-1900*, Cambridge: Cambridge University Press

Prins, A.H.J.
   1961   *The Swahili-Speaking Peoples of Zanzibar and the East African Coast (Arabs, Shirazi and Swahili), Ethnographic Survey of Africa East Central Africa XII*, London: International African Institute

Quraishy, M.A.
   1987a   *Textbook of Islam Book 1*, Nairobi: Islamic Foundation
   1987b   *Textbook of Islam Book 2*, Nairobi: Islamic Foundation

Radtke, B., O'Kane, J., Vikør, K. & O'Fahey, R.S.
   2000   *The Exoteric Ahmad Ibn Idrîs: A Sufi's Critique of the Madhâhib and the Wahhâbîs*, Leiden: Brill

Rasmussen, L.
   1993   *Christian-Muslim Relations in Africa*, London: British Academic Press

Said, M.
   1997   *The Life and Times of Abdulwahid Sykes (1924-1968)*, London: Minerva Press

Salim, A.I.
   1973   *Swahili-Speaking Peoples of Kenya's Coast 1895-1965*, Nairobi: East Africa Publishing House

Sambano, B. (Translator)
   1979   *Ushirikiano Kati ya Wakristo na Waislamu*, Dodoma: Central Tanganyika Press

Salter, T. & King, K. (Eds.)
   2000   *Africa, Islam and Development: Islam and Development in Africa – African Islam, African Development*, Edinburgh: Centre of African Studies

Sanneh, L.
   1996   *Piety and Power: Muslims and Christians in West Africa*, Maryknoll: Orbis

1997 *The Crown and the Turban: Muslims and West African Pluralism*, Oxford: Westview Press

Shepard, W.E.
1996 *Sayyid Qutb and Islamic Activism: A Translation and Critical Analysis of Social Justice in Islam*, Leiden: E.J. Brill

Soghayroun, I.E.
1981 *The Sudanese Muslim Factor in Uganda*, Khartoum: Khartoum University Press

Stamer, P.J.
1996 *Islam in Sub-Saharan Africa*, Estella: Editorial Verbo Divino

Sundkler, B. & Steed, C.
2000 *A History of the Church in Africa*, Cambridge: Cambridge University Press

Tayob, A.
1999 *Islam in South Africa: Mosques, Imams, and Sermons*, Gainesville: University Press of Florida

Trimingham, J.S.
1949 *Islam in the Sudan*, London: OUP
1952 *Islam in Ethiopia*, Oxford: OUP
1959 *Islam in West Africa*, Oxford: Clarendon Press
1962 *A History of Islam in West Africa*, Oxford: OUP
1964 *Islam in East Africa*, Oxford: Clarendon Press
1980 *The Influence of Islam upon Africa* (2nd Ed.), London: Longman

Udoma, P.L.
2002 *The Cross and the Crescent: A Christian Response to Two decades of Islamic Affirmation in Nigeria*, London: St. Austin Press

Ward, K & Stanley, B (Eds.)
2000 *The Church Mission Society and World Christianity 1799-1999* Richmond: Curzon

Watt, W.M.
    1989   *Muslim-Christian Encounters: Perceptions and Misperceptions*, London: Routledge

Westerlund, D. & Rosander, E.E. (Eds.)
    1997   *African Islam and Islam in Africa*, London: Hurst

Westerlund, D. & Svanberg, I. (Eds.)
    1999   *Islam Outside the Arab World*, London: Curzon

Whiteley, W.
    1969   *Swahili: The Rise of a National Language*, London: Methuen & Co Ltd

Wright, M.
    1971   *German Missions in Tanganyika 1891-1941: (Lutherans and Moravians in the Southern Highlands)*, Oxford: Clarendon Press

el Zein, A.H.M.
    1974   *The Sacred Meadows (A Structural Analysis of Religious Symbolism in an East African Town)*, Boston: Northwestern University Press

Appendix 3
Sample Course Description: Introduction to Islam

OBJECTIVES
To introduce students to an understanding of Islam in its religious and cultural dimensions. To give an overview of the major concepts that shape Islam. Emphasis is given to the life of Muhammad and the Faith and Practice of Islam.

COURSE OUTLINE
[1] Introduction to the Study of Islam
[2] Pre-Islamic Arabia
- Cultural context of pre-Islamic Arabia
- Religious context of 6th Century Arabia

[3] Life of Muhammad (570-632)
- Birth until his 'call' – 570-610
- 'Call' and Muhammad in Mecca – 610-622
- *Hijra* and Muhammad in Medina – 622-632

[4] The Qur'an
- The formation of the Qur'an
- Introduction to the Qur'an
- Jesus in the Qur'an
- Women in the Qur'an

[5] Sunna and Hadith
- Introduction
- Examples of Hadith – Women in Hadith

[6] Faith and Practice of Islam
- *Diin* – Five Pillars of Religion
- *Iman* – Beliefs in Islam
- *Dhimma* – The treatment of the People of the Book under Islam
- *Jihad* – What it means in theory and practice

[7] Jurisprudence
- Introduction to *Shari'a*

[8] Islam in East Africa
- From 8th Century to 1490s
- 1490s-1698 – Portuguese occupation
- 1698-1890s – Omani occupation
- 1885-1960 – Colonial Period
- 1960s – to date – Independence and post-Independence

[9] Different Groups within Islam
- Sunni
- Shi'a
- Ibadi
- Sufi
- Ahmadiyya (Qadians)

[10] Christian Muslim Relations in East Africa
- *Da'wa*
- Evangelism
- Dialogue

Suggested Bibliography
REFERENCE BOOKS
Bewley, A.   1998   *Glossary of Islamic Terms*, London: Ta-Ha Publishers
Esposito, J.L. (Ed.) 1995 The Oxford Encyclopaedia of the Modern Islamic World, Vols 1-4, Oxford: OUP
Rahman, F.   1979   *Islam* (2nd Ed.), Chicago: University of Chicago Press

INTRODUCTIONS TO ISLAM
Abdalati, M.   1985   *Islam in Focus*, Nairobi: Islamic Foundation
Cragg, K.   1965   *Call of the Minaret*, London: Collins
Jomier, J.   1988   *How to Understand Islam*, London: SCM

Maududi, S.A. 1980 *Towards Understanding Islam* (Revised Edition), Birmingham: UKIM Dawah Centre
Ruthven, M. 1997 *Islam: A Very Short Introduction*, Oxford: OUP

THE ARABIAN AND HISTORICAL SETTING
Kennedy, H. 1986 *The Prophet and the Age of the Caliphates*, London: Longman
Lapidus, I.M. 1988 *A History of Islamic Societies*, Cambridge: CUP

THE LIFE OF MUHAMMAD
(Together with the books listed above)
Al-Ismail, T. 1988 *The Life of Muhammad*, London: Ta-Ha
Guillaume, A. 1955 *The Life of Muhammad: A translation of Ibn Ishaq's Sirat Rasul Allah* (13th Impression), Karachi: OUP
Motzki, H. (Ed.) 2000 *The Biography of Muhammad: The Issue of Sources*, Leiden: Brill
Watt, W.M. 1961 *Muhammad – Prophet and Statesman*, Oxford: Clarendon Press

THE QUR'AN
'Ali, 'Abdullah Yusuf 1997 *The Holy Qur'an - New Revised Edition*, New York: Amana Corp
Esack, F. 1997 *Qur'an, Liberation and Pluralism*, Oxford: Oneworld
Gätje, H. 1996 *The Qur'an and its Exegesis* (New Ed.), Oxford: Oneworld
Mawdudi, A.A. 1995 *Towards Understanding the Qur'an*, Nairobi: Islamic Foundation
Parrinder, G. 1995 *Jesus in the Qur'an* (New Ed.), Oxford: Oneworld

Rahman, F.　　1994　*Major Themes of the Qur'an*, Minneapolis: Bibliotheca Islamica
Watt, M.W. & Bell R.　1970 *Introduction to the Qur'an*, Edinburgh: EUP

HADITH, SUNNA AND SHARI'A

Burton, J.　　1994　*An Introduction to the Hadith*, Edinburgh: EUP
Coulson, N.J.　1964　*A History of Islamic Law*, Edinburgh: EUP
Doi, A.R.　　1970　*Introduction to the Hadith*, Lagos: Islamic Publications Bureau
　　　　　　1984　*Shari'ah: The Islamic Law*, London: Ta-Ha
Siddiqi, M.Z.　1993　*Hadith Literature*, Cambridge: Islamic Texts Society

ISLAMIC DENOMINATIONS

Baldick, J.　　1989　*Mystical Islam an Introduction to Sufism*, London: I.B.Tauris
Daftary, F.　　1998　*A Short History of the Ismailis*, Edinburgh: EUP
Haeri, F.　　1993　*Sufism*, Rockport: Element Books
Momen, M.　　1985　*An Introduction to Shi'i Islam: The History and Traditions of Twelver Islam*, New Haven: Yale University Press
Trimmingham, J.S. 1998 *The Sufi Orders in Islam* (New Ed.), Oxford: OUP

CHAPTER ELEVEN

Biblical Reflections on a Panel Discussion on 'Disability'
Report of a Panel Discussion

Grant LeMarquand

A highlight of the theological consultation which took place in Limuru in June 2003 was an afternoon given over to a panel discussion on a topic rarely addressed in church contexts in Africa – the plight of so-called 'disabled' people. Four speakers, each of them with a particular disability, but each of them tremendously gifted individuals, discussed their experience of living with a disability within an African context.

Samuel Kabue, a World Council of Churches consultant on this subject, highlighted the concerns of disabled people as far back as antiquity. In some African cultures, for example, disabled people were not allowed to gather fruits and roots alongside those who were not disabled. He pointed out that, with the coming of the agrarian era, since food was plenty some was given to the disabled as charity. In the colonial and post-colonial periods, this idea of charity spread to governments and churches, and food, clothes, blankets and other necessities were distributed to the disabled. What was often missing, however, was any sense that people who were blind, or hearing-impaired, or lame could make a positive contribution to society.

In 1981 the United Nations declared an International Year of Persons with Disabilities. Between 1983 and 1992 the United Nations devised an action plan to meet the needs of the disabled. These plans, however, were rarely implemented by national governments, especially in cash-strapped Africa.

The church has often cared for the disabled in matters of physical needs. The Thika School for the Blind, for example, was established by the churches. Surprisingly, however, the churches have sometimes neglected the spiritual needs of the disabled.

Two more members of the panel, Mr. P. Were and Mrs. Jane Miano proposed that any curriculum for ecumenical theological education should include an awareness of the need for the churches to be involved in advocacy for the disabled, in building the capacity of disabled persons, and in building awareness in the community of the needs and gifts of disabled people.

The final speaker was the Honourable Joyce Sinyo. She argued that there should be sensitivity about disabilities in the theological curriculum. She based this on the fact that Jesus in his ministry was sensitive and responded with love to both the physical and the spiritual needs of the disabled. Thus, our curricula should reflect the love of Jesus for the disabled.

The entire panel discussion was moving for most participants. It was clear to all present that the presenters had opened a window on a world that our institutions often neglect. A lively discussion took place later in the consultation in which some members told stories of former students at St. Paul's who had struggled to study theology and to be ordained, but who today were exercising fruitful ministries for the kingdom of God. Their disabilities, in fact, had become for them an opportunity for the gospel.

A Biblical Reflection

In the context of our consultation several of the major problems of the disabled were raised and discussed: problems of access to facilities for people who are on crutches or in wheelchairs, problems of stereotyping of disabled people, of assuming that a disability in one area meant lack of any abilities to share with the world, and problems of access to education.

One problem struck this observer as especially disturbing, perhaps because I am a biblical scholar. A member of the consultation related a story about a friend who was disabled, but who had sensed that God might be calling him into the ordained ministry. Sadly, some biblical texts were presented to this person as barriers to their pursuit of ordination. In particular, there is a passage in Leviticus which discussed the requirement for the Old Testament priesthood.

> And the Lord spoke to Moses, saying, "Speak to Aaron, saying, None of your offspring throughout their generations who has a blemish may approach to offer the bread of his God. For no one who has a blemish shall draw near, a man blind or lame, or one who has a mutilated face or a limb too long, or a man who has an injured foot or an injured hand, or a hunchback or a dwarf or a man with a defect in his sight or an itching disease or scabs or crushed testicles. No man of the offspring of Aaron the priest who has a blemish shall come near to offer the Lord's food offerings; since he has a blemish, he shall not come near to offer the bread of his God. He may eat the bread of his God, both of the most holy and of the holy things, but he shall not go through the veil or approach the altar, because he has a blemish, that he may not profane my sanctuaries, for I am the Lord who sanctifies them."
> (Lev 21:16-23)

This passage has been quoted and used to exclude people with various disabilities from leadership positions in the church. Before we discuss this text, it might be helpful if we put another Old Testament passage on the table which could also be used to exclude disabled people.

According to 2 Samuel 5, when David was approaching Jerusalem the Jebusites mocked David, saying that he could not possibly capture such a stronghold: "even the blind and the lame will ward you off" (2 Sam 5:6). The Jebusites were wrong, of course. David captured the city and made it his capital. The story informs us that because of this incident "The blind and the lame shall not come into the house [i.e. the temple]" (2 Sam 5:8).

So we have two Old Testament texts, one legal and one narrative, both of which exclude disabled people from worship and worship leadership in the temple of God. Of course, from the perspective of the Old Testament purity tradition this exclusion was understandable for 'symbolic' reasons. According to Gordon Wenham, "The idea emerges clearly that holiness finds physical expression in wholeness and normality".[1]

As Christians, however, we must insist on reading the Bible as a unity. Taking one verse or one passage out of its context in the overall story of scripture can have disastrous results. It is often said that 'anything can be proved by scripture' and this is true if proper care is not taken to read every passage in the light of the whole biblical narrative.

In the case of these passages from the Old Testament we can see this: in the context of the Hebrew people God appears to have allowed certain cultural traditions which were imperfect to, nevertheless, be vehicles for his revelation to his chosen people Israel at that time. We can still learn something from those traditions. In the case of the exclusion of the disabled, these texts still teach us that God is holy and perfect and that human worship will always be the offering of imperfect human beings.

But the biblical story does not end with Leviticus and 2 Samuel. The centre and goal of the biblical story is Jesus Christ and every part of scripture must be read in the light of that centre. Biblical interpretation must be Christocentric. So what is there about Jesus that will help us to put these Old Testament passages in context? Several texts must be mentioned here briefly.

First, as was mentioned already by the Hon. J. Sinyo in her contribution to the panel, we must look at the healing ministry of Jesus as a ministry which welcomed and loved people with various diseases and disabilities. There is no need to list all of the relevant biblical texts here. In fact there are so many that it would delay us unnecessarily. It is enough to mention that Jesus healed people who

---

[1] Gordon Wenham, *The Book of Leviticus* (NICOT; Grand Rapids: Eerdmans, 1981), 292; cf. his important article "Christ's Ministry of Healing and His Attitude to the Law," pp. 115-26 in *Christ the Lord: Studies in Christology presented to Donald Guthrie* (ed. H.H. Rowdon; Leicester: IVP, 1982). The idea of holiness as 'symbolic' is based on the work of social anthropologist Mary Douglas, *Purity and Danger: An Analysis of Concepts of Pollution and Taboo* (London and New York: Routledge, 1984 [1966]).

were blind, deaf and lame. In performing these miracles Jesus not only restored them to health and wholeness, but he also restored them to the community. Since they would not have been able to worship in the temple with their disability (2 Sam 5:8), their healing was the removal of a barrier which separated these people from the worshipping community and from access to the presence of God in the temple.

Secondly, we must examine briefly a neglected text from the gospel of Matthew. Each of the synoptic gospels mentions that Jesus, during the last week of his life, entered Jerusalem on a donkey and then went to the temple. Only Matthew mentions that while Jesus was in the temple he not only performed a prophetic denunciation of the place by overturning the tables and driving the animals and people out, and not only did he spend time in his final week teaching in the temple – he also healed. It is worth seeing the verse as Matthew records it for us: "And the blind and the lame came to him in the temple and he healed them" (Mt 21:14). Notice the wording: "the blind and the lame". Clearly this is an echo of 2 Sam 5:8.[2] Jesus has just ridden into Jerusalem as people shouted "Hosanna to the Son of David" (Mt 21:9). But this Son of David does not come, like his ancestor, to conquer with the sword, but to heal and teach and, finally to die for the sins of the world. Something greater than David is here. David excluded 'the blind and the lame', Jesus welcomes and heals them. Texts which exclude the disabled from ministry cannot be used by those who claim that they follow this welcoming Jesus.

In fact Jesus' teaching from an earlier part of the gospel stories has already hinted that the kingdom of God which is breaking into the world in the ministry of Jesus will have a very different attitude to disabilities and deformities. Consider this text,

> And if your hand causes you to sin, cut it off. It is better for you to enter life crippled than with two hands to go to hell, to the unquenchable fire. And if your foot causes you to sin, cut it off. It is better for you to enter life lame than with two feet to be thrown into hell. And if your eye causes you

---

[2]See, for example, R.T. France, *Matthew* (Tyndale New Testament Commentaries; Grand Rapids: Eerdmans, 1985), 302.

to sin, tear it out. It is better for you to enter the kingdom of God with one eye than with two eyes to be thrown into hell.

(Mark 9:43-47)

Jesus is not only welcoming of the disabled; he says that only the disabled will get into the kingdom! Since we all sin, the only way to get into the kingdom is to remove those parts of our bodies that cause us to sin – the kingdom, it seems, will be filled with the blind, the maimed and the lame (See also Luke 21:12-24). Of course we must recognize that Jesus was using hyperbole, exaggerated rhetoric, to make a point. We are all in need of God's grace and mercy. None of us is without sin and all of us need God's forgiveness. To be a Christian is to know that you are a part of the walking wounded, not a part of the pure and perfect.

In fact, it should be remembered that salvation is in the cross. It is because Christ became deformed for us on the cross that we are saved. Salvation is not a matter of attaining perfection, but a matter of allying ourselves with the crucified one, the one who was pierced, and bruised, and torn apart for us. According to the book of Revelation Jesus has carried those wounds into heaven for us (Rev 5:6). He is not ashamed of his wounds because they are our deliverance.

The first African convert to Christianity learned this well. In Acts 8 we read of a deformed man, a eunuch. God cared about him so much that he sent Philip to share the gospel with him. When Philip arrived on the scene he found the man reading from the Old Testament. The passage he was reading was from Isaiah 53:

> Like a sheep he was led to the slaughter
> and like a lamb before its shearer is silent,
> so he opens not his mouth.
> In his humiliation justice was denied him.
> Who can describe his generation?
> For his life is taken away from the earth.

(Acts 8:32-33; cf. Isaiah 53:7-8)

The deformed eunuch was reading about one who had become deformed for him.[3]

The Bible is clear. If we take the time to read the whole story, God's love extends to all, abled and 'disabled'. The very helpful panel discussion at the Limuru consultation has left us with a challenge: will we as theological institutions help the churches to reflect the ministry of Jesus by welcoming, encouraging, and empowering the disabled? In Jesus' parable it is the maimed, the blind and the lame who are invited to feast (Lk 14:13, 21). Can *we* turn them away?

---

[3] As Wenham points out (*Leviticus*, 297), the "extension of God's grace to eunuchs and foreigners had already been anticipated in Isa. 56:4-8".

CHAPTER TWELVE

Theological Education and the Youth in the Family, Church, and School

Josphine Gitome

During one of the worship services in my local church, a drug-addicted youth who was poorly dressed and dirty entered the church while the speaker was preaching. All eyes turned to the boy. The preacher immediately stopped and called the boy forward for prayer. The young man hurriedly walked out looking very intimidated.

Was that right procedure to handle this situation? He had not waited to develop a relationship with the young person and did not even ask him whether he wanted to be prayed for. There is an increasing number of youth with serious problems in our society, but it is doubtful whether our theological institutions today treat this issue adequately. The young people in church-sponsored schools and Christian families are struggling with issues requiring guidance and counsel. My own research among the youth in the P.C.E.A. church in Kikuyu Parish revealed a need for individual guidance and counselling that was not always forthcoming.[1] In this paper, we shall examine various contexts for youth ministry showing the type of challenges that youth face and the need for a theological curriculum to address these needs.

---

[1] J. Gitome, "Pastoral Care and Counseling to Educate Young Adults in the P.C.E.A. Church: With Special Reference to Kikuyu Parish" (University of Nairobi M.A. thesis, 1989).

Youth in the Family

Most young people spend less than 20% of their time with their parents due to their engagement at school or college. Formal education itself may alienate children from their families. In the past families, neighbors, friends and peers facilitated guidance and counseling for the youth. In modern society we have delegated what was previously done by family and neighbours to the formal education sector or schools. The traditional roles of the family and other support structures are therefore minimized or neglected.

We must however note that, inasmuch as youth culture may be influenced by urbanization and modernization, the African traditional worldview still holds an important place in the thinking of African people. This is evident from the fact that well-schooled Africans still hold to traditional beliefs especially when dealing with issues of health and affliction, birth and death etc. Laurenti Magesa, for example, points out that some youth resort to traditional healers when they are faced with a challenge they perceive the Christian faith cannot help them overcome.[2] For this reason alone, we must ask, 'how can theology address this issue?'

It is imperative to seek to understand the African worldview if this question is to be adequately addressed. The coming of missionaries into Africa brought with it a western form of education, which largely ignored the existing forms of African traditional education[3] and at times even directly undermined it. As a result, most African church leaders have been trained for many years in a theology framed in the western worldview. There is an urgent need for a paradigm shift if theological education is to be relevant to the youth in Africa today. As we examine an African approach to morality among youth, we find in African tradition a wealth of material to draw on. The theological student must be adequately prepared in a

---

[2] See Laurenti Magesa, *African Religion: The Moral Traditions of Abundant Life* (Nairobi: Paulines, 1998).

[3] This was largely informal: social norms, religious beliefs and practices; family life, individual's roles and responsibilities and special trades were learned from family, specialists, peer groups and elders as one grew up.

theology of culture so that he or she becomes skilled in integrating the informal education of the African communities into pastoral guidance and counseling.

For example, in traditional sex education, the age group, community sanctions, ritual celebrations, and social support from the elders, all play a part. The church needs to explore ways of integrating these 'African traditional resources' into youth programs in the church so as to be able to deal more effectively with issues of human sexuality. The youth are struggling to understand their sexuality and at the same time to cope with all sorts of modern societal pressures. Catechism and learning the Ten Commandments by heart are not an adequate preparation for these struggles. The issue of sexual purity and especially sex outside marriage is, for example, a case in point. It is obvious that many Christian youth have not been able to maintain virginity until marriage. This is evident from the increasing number of young couples whose first child is often born before the first nine months of marriage are over. Could we say they have not studied and understood the Ten Commandments? Do their respective communities or churches consider a couple who are engaged as already united such that they can relate sexually, or are they expected to observe purity according to Christian teaching? Most of the church youth show ignorance in this matter. Some youth I have talked to in seminars assume the engagement ceremony to allow the two to meet intimately. The church needs to address this issue especially in this era of HIV/AIDS pandemic.

Today's youth are encountering a lot of change due to urbanization and modernization. The family members need to understand that the world in which young people are growing up is not the same world their parents grew up in. Think about a rural family with a teenager in high school. The parents' world entailed a daily routine with little exposure to the 'modern' world, but the teenager has the electronic mass media at his or her disposal. Through the media, the youth receive more and more exposure and the opportunity of interaction with the modern world. This makes the youth attracted to modern or western cultural values, sometimes without understanding the concepts behind them.

In most parts of the modern world, family life is in crisis due to divorce. Divorce is becoming a common phenomenon that youth have to live through. The emptiness of having to live with one parent at a time or being denied access to a parent is a new problem in Africa. Without both parents as consistent role models modern young people are growing to hate family life and some consider living single as an option. Scientific developments even offer the option of having a baby without a marriage partner! Our theology needs to face these realities while looking for ways to preserve and uphold the ideal of family life as God ordained it. Christian counselors in the church today need more practical skills to deal with tense and difficult marriage relationships among church members. The youth in the churches today need thorough pre-marital guidance so that they can learn to appreciate the joys of Christian marriage in spite of the bad examples from some of their parents. Is the church structure prepared to provide such counsel and education?

Unemployment in the cities makes the situation of young couples complicated. The pastoral worker must be aware of such acute problems, which reduce many people to poverty. Some unemployed people end up abandoning faith, becoming hostile to the common *mwanachi* and engaging in alcohol and drug abuse, prostitution, and crimes, which, of course, only worsen their world. What has the theological curriculum to offer to this scenario?

Some families today have members in different denominations, which needless to say, at times live under one roof. Some family members may be involved in sects, cults, the occult or even 'devil worship.' Ndirangu records how the search for love, wealth, fame, and power has led some on the wrong path.[4] The church should be capable of providing clear teaching and direction on these issues.

Unfortunately this is not always experienced by the youth. The challenge to theological education includes preparing clergy to deal

---

[4]Ndirangu, *The Youth in Danger* (Uzima, Nairobi), 2000

with the parents of a youth lured into the occult. Does our current theological education even address the issue of occultism? Religious pluralism is a threat to parenting teenagers and the clergy need the skill to guide both the teenager and the family.

Youth in the Church

There is some comfort in seeing that so many youth have found hope in the Bible and church attendance. But does our theological education address the youth ministry holistically?

My research indicates that many do not find their needs met in the routine Sunday service program and that they are especially bothered by the churches' emphasis on collecting building funds during the service.[5] In most of the churches I studied, there exists a 'Youth Service' started in response to meet the youths' need for participation in leadership roles. Even then, the elders supervised it so closely that the youth lacked room for free self-expression. Where the youth leader allowed room for extempore prayers, some youths expressed themselves freely to God by speaking in tongues. But this was normally controlled and such a leader was denied further chance of leading the service. Through responses to a questionnaire I also learned that the youth were dissatisfied with most preaching, especially because of the preachers' tendency to dwell on the sinful life of the youth and condemning their favourite leisure activities. When asked about participating in the Lord's Table most of the youth said they were confirmed members but did not participate because according to several sermons they had listened to they felt condemned. Instead of seeing the parish minister for guidance they suspended themselves from the Lord's Table even before the church suspended them.

On the level of education my observations indicated that young people are more educated than most church leaders. This means that they felt that an evangelist or church elder has very little to offer. They therefore do not go to them for counseling. Many seek counsel

---

[5]Gitome, "Pastoral Care."

from age mates and some move to new religious movements. The mainline churches, therefore, lose young people who could have been trained to lead the church. Those that remain in leadership are often the elderly. How is the theological curriculum addressing this need? The neo-Pentecostal churches seek to satisfy the young who feel left out in the present social set-up of the church.[6] The marginalized often find Pentecostalism a refuge. But my observation indicates that some do so only for a short while and then emptiness emerges, especially if the young person is unemployed. When the time for settling down in marriage comes, the need for daily upkeep at times supersedes the spiritual need. Some have moved from the fellowship into the secular world and concentrated more on the eradication of their poverty, pursuing whatever trade provides livelihood even when such trade may not be compatible with faith previously confessed.

All is not lost and some churches are just doing fine. It is possible to borrow a leaf from the way some of these churches are handling their youth. Their strategy is in training, where they have recruited and trained youth pastors. The youth easily identify with such a person. In the Parklands Baptist Church,[7] for example, the relationship of the youth and their patron is so intimate that they fully participate in programs designed for them.

Youth at School

In school (where young people spend 80% of their time) church leaders could participate in the pastoral programme of the schools within their parish as a starting point. Some do, but others have neglected this important ministry. At times the church minister is overwhelmed by immediate parish duties and easily forgets the schools in the parish. There is an historical dimension to this issue. J.N.K. Mugambi indicates that when the Kenyan government took

---

[6]J.N.K. Mugambi, "Pastoral Care for Youth and Students" in D. Waruta, and H. Kinoti, eds. *Pastoral Care in African Christianity* (Nairobi Acton, 1994), 114.

[7]Nairobi, Kenya.

over the running of schools but allowed missionaries to participate in school and vocational education in their sponsored institution, this participation actually became marginalized.[8] Most Protestant clergy retreated to the church. The Church, therefore, does not exercise significant influence on the religious and moral education in public schools and colleges.

Some para-church organizations visiting the schools have become popular among the youth because they address such issues such as music, the occult and new religious movements and the 'prosperity gospel.' The negative result, however, has been the disparity seen between the para-church organization and the parents' church. The faith introduced at school by these groups is often over-spiritualized such that when the youth leave school, they are unable to face the reality of life. The para-church groups sometimes alienate the youth from their family and their home church. In the past this alienation has led to mushrooming new churches increasing by the day. But they have also born bad fruit in strained parent-child relationships.

Church leaders need to consider recruiting persons of good moral standing as full-time teachers or social workers who are trained in pastoral guidance and counseling. Such staff could be given the task of ministering to the needs of students in schools within the parish. Such people could work closely with the school but need not be a part of the teaching staff so that they may have enough time to develop a rapport with students. They should be answerable to the school administrator as well as the parish clergy within the area. In the past, guidance and counseling teachers have not had any link with the church. Caution must be taken to avoid much confusion of faiths among students in cases where two or more denominations within the parish have seconded a worker to the school.

In conclusion let us remember that the energy of youth has always posed a challenge to people in authority. Attempting to do pastoral work with young people in Africa without an adequate

---

[8]Mugambi, "Pastoral Care for Youth and Students," 153.

understanding of the realities of youth culture today is a grievous mistake. Theological education is relevant only if it addresses ministry in the perspective of the youth's practical needs. By so doing the youth will be brought closer to God and to the churches used by God for the extension of the kingdom.

CHAPTER THIRTEEN

Challenges of Theological Education in the Twenty-First Century

Sammy Githuku

The purpose of this paper is to highlight briefly some of the challenges of theological education in Africa today. Constraints of time and space would inhibit a detailed discussion of all the issues on this topic. I hope, however, that the few issues raised will provoke a worthwhile discussion in this symposium. I must acknowledge at the onset that the issues raised in this paper are based on personal observations during my seven years of teaching at theological colleges in Kenya. But these issues may be true of many other theological institutions on the continent of Africa. Some institutions are probably working on these challenges already. I have therefore assumed that the issues raised in this paper are common to most denominational and ecumenical theological colleges today.

Generally, it would be agreed that one of the objectives of theological colleges is to assist their students grow as ministers of Jesus Christ. This aim is sometimes not clearly articulated by the theological colleges and the Churches. If one poses some questions: "Where is the emphasis given during training? Is it in the intellectual training or in the spiritual and character building? Is it in both?" Most theological colleges will claim that they lay emphasis on both, but more often the spiritual development of the students is not emphasized in most of our schools. At present, above everything else, most theological institutions are academic institutions. Their tendency is to put an emphasis on academic standards sometimes to the detriment of ministerial training or character building.[1] There is not, at present, a healthy balance between the academic and the practical.

This insistence on academic standards narrows the primary aim of theological education to facilitation of intellectual growth. The students, for their part, work hard for better academic results because, in the end, this is what receives recognition.[2] Quite often, theological colleges and the sponsoring churches take the spiritual maturity of their students for granted. The colleges assume that the respective churches see to the spiritual maturity of their students while the churches, on the other hand, assume that the colleges are undertaking this responsibility. Unfortunately the reality is that neither body is fulfilling this responsibility adequately. Some students who join theological colleges for training have no personal experience of the world and its real challenges.[3] They are still "infants" in spiritual and life issues. Some of the students may have impressed their churches by their active participation in the church youth groups, fellowships, or singing, but spiritually they are "children" requiring serious nurturing. While theological colleges may wish to help their students develop physically, academically, and spiritually, they simply do not have adequate resources.

The result of this situation, therefore, is that most theological colleges do not fully take part in the formation of the future priest. Since neither the churches nor the theological colleges take full

---

[1] Some colleges, for example, have their degrees offered or sanctioned by public universities. One reason for this is to ensure that their academic standards are nationally or internationally acceptable.

[2] At the St. Paul's graduation ceremony, it is the quality of academic work which tends to be recognized.

[3] Today there are more and more students joining theological education immediately following their secondary education. These candidates can be as young as eighteen when they enrol for theological education and about twenty-one at their graduation.

responsibility, formation is often left to chance. Older, mature students, depending on their past experience, may graduate feeling well prepared but younger students may graduate feeling insecure, unsure of their vocation, possibly confused about their faith, and in many cases critical of the institutions of the church.

One of the challenges of theological colleges, therefore, is to incorporate into the programme of studies courses and experiences in which spiritual formation of the students is enhanced. We must abandon the belief and assumption that because the students have been chosen for the ordained ministry by their churches, that their old patterns of life are totally displaced and that they are somehow (magically!) mature. Theological colleges have the responsibility to further personal formation and enhance obedience in Christ. This is a life time task, of course. Maturity may be encouraged, however, through Bible study, teaching on the habits of the Christian life and life in prayer. In such a programme students focus on listening to what the word of God says to them in the light of their work in the world.[4] It might be assumed that, because theological colleges teach biblical studies and have regular devotions, the spiritual aspect is adequately captured. Unfortunately this is not the case. Theological colleges should aim at making "saints". They must therefore be transformed into places where students are trained to grow into the habits of priestly life.

Primarily, theological colleges train students for the ordained ministry. There are denominations for example, that ordain their students deacons while in their second year and into priesthood in their final year.[5] Others do it immediately at the end of the three or four years of theological training. Either way, sometimes this is done

---

[4] Other activities that would enhance spiritual growth would include retreats, training in various forms of prayer, reading books that deal with spiritual development. The appointment of spiritual directors for students should be encouraged.

[5] Some churches have a period of internship, in which a student who graduates from a theological college spends a whole year, before ordination, under an experienced minister.

without consulting the theological colleges on the suitability of the candidate. This explains how sometimes theological education is understood: It is a guarantee for the ordained ministry. In the end the churches find out that they have ordained candidates who during their years of training did not grow to the maturity of a minister of Jesus Christ.

A further challenge is that although churches own theological colleges, these institutions are not systematically used to equip the lay church workers. Theological colleges are solely used for training for the ordained ministry. In this new century, theological colleges and the Churches must move away from this mode of training. They should also admit and train lay men and women who have a call to serve the church in ministries other than the ordained ministry. These men and women should be equipped with theology to enable them correctly respond to other needs of the church. There is more to the church than celebrating sacraments! This wall separating theological colleges and the rest of the church world should be demolished by admitting into their programmes men and women who are specialists in other secular disciplines for short and full time courses. These men and women will be of better use in the local churches after completion of their studies. A second advantage is that they will also bring the realities of the world into the theological colleges. This would awaken students to the realities that await them after training and initiate useful dialogues with church workers of other disciplines.

A third challenge to be addressed is that of context and relevance. A careful study of the curricula in most theological colleges will reveal that they are geared towards the established churches in the rural areas. The outlook of these curricula is mainly pastoral. Most courses are only done at an introductory level.[6] It is a fact, however, that most of the rural population in Africa is migrating to the urban centres. The life style and the challenges of the urban centres call for

---

[6] Religious Studies, Pastoral Care, Pastoral Counselling, African Theology, African Traditional Religion, Philosophy, Christian Ethics are some of the courses which are taught for only one semester.

a different type of ministry. This must be reflected in theological education curriculum. Let us compare the two cases:

In the rural areas, congregations speak their mother tongues. Their time is well defined by seasons and common activities. They have more time to listen. In most cases they are of the same ethnic group, the same background and engaged in the same occupation. The community support for an individual Christian is enormous. Life is less stressful with few problems.

In cities and towns, on the other hand, life is full of complexity. People are very busy. They work for long hours and hence have very little time to host the minister for a visit. Occupations are diverse. People live more of an individualistic life with very little community support. There is less use of the mother tongue and more use of English, French, or Kiswahili. People are crowded together in slums with poor sanitation facilities.

At present the churches deal with these differences of rural and urban congregations by appointing priests with higher theological education in towns and those with lower theological education in the rural areas. It must be pointed out, however, that higher theological education is not the same as specialised education. A priest may have two degrees in theology but not be specialised in any one practical area of the ministry. Most of our students have been born and brought up in the rural areas. They have little conception of what life is like in the slums, for example. It is not surprising to find a student who has graduated from a theological college who finds it difficult to express what he or she has learned in English within a Kiswahili setting such as we find in most urban areas[7].

Urban congregations call for a different type of ministry. At present our current curriculum unfortunately does not offer specialised training that can equip theological students to enable them cope effectively with the urban needs that they will encounter

---

[7]This may not be true of Tanzania where most people are conversant with Kiswahili, but it is certainly true of Kenya. Competence in languages should be emphasised in our curricula.

after their training. The curriculum lacks important subjects such as 'Evangelism' and yet the urban centres are 'ripe for harvest.' We lack courses on different types of counselling[8] although urban life is life lived in stress. We need to include in our curriculum courses which are appropriate to the rapidly expanding urban context.

Theological colleges and the churches cannot afford to ignore these concerns. We could perhaps gain help in this area by admitting students for theological education who already have knowledge or even professional expertise in such specialised areas. If including such courses in specialised areas of the ministry is difficult, then perhaps theological colleges could develop particular emphases and offer specialised courses to students from other theological colleges. It is not an overstatement to claim that some courses offered in the theological education curriculum are not relevant to the challenges of life that the students are expected to meet after training. This is our fourth challenge. I believe that theological colleges should be more flexible in the types of courses offered, and only those courses that are relevant to the needs of the churches should be taught. Courses such as 'Theology of Early Church Fathers', 'Karl Barth's Church Dogmatics', 'History of British Methodism' may or may not be of relevance in the life awaiting the students in the community. Courses should be evaluated for their relevance, and time spent on courses judged less relevant should be shortened to allow more time for the more relevant courses. Such courses might include 'Theology of Development', 'Crisis Management', 'Peace and Reconciliation', 'Law', 'Mission and Evangelism', 'Elementary Accountancy', 'Ministry to the Poor', 'Ministry in the Context of HIV/AIDS' to propose but a few.

It might be argued that all courses offered in the current curriculum are important to the future ministry of the students. A method of discernment and evaluation must be sought to determine how relevant a course is. One criterion for deciding which courses

---

[8] One semester of pastoral counselling currently offered in the curriculum is not adequate to make a priest a qualified counsellor.

are relevant is to insist that before any new courses are offered the tutor provide a detailed introduction justifying how the course is relevant and important to the life of the church and Christian today. This should be submitted to the students and fellow tutors for discussion and adoption before it is taught.

Research and evaluation poses a further challenge to theological institutions. For the time I have been in the ministry I have not witnessed a forum in which the church leaders and the theological colleges come together for the purpose of evaluation. During such an exercise, exchanging ideas, sharing new challenges in the ministry, evaluating the performance of the students that graduate from theological institutions every year, and evaluating the performance of tutors would be done. Often theological colleges take for granted that they know what the churches want. The churches on the other hand assume that theological colleges know their needs. These assumptions are wrong. Theological colleges should take upon themselves the responsibility of reshaping the mission of the theological vocation for the sake of the church in the twenty-first century. One way through which this evaluation could be enhanced is research. I would propose that a research paper in a current relevant area in the life of the church be a graduation requirement for every student. This would enable the theological institutions to advise the church on its changing mission in the world today. A forum could also be held in which the churches could inform the theological colleges of new challenges they are facing in their ministry that require research, while the colleges, on the other hand, could share their findings through research with the churches. If this is adopted, theological colleges will assume more responsibility for shaping the mission of the church in the world by providing the training that men and women in the churches actually need.

Several theological colleges are seeking to be 'Christian Universities'. This is usually done by introduction of new faculties into the college. In a country in which there are limited university education opportunities, this is a noble course. However, this must be done cautiously following proper guidelines. First, if these universities are successful, it is likely that within a short time the students and faculty members in these new faculties will out number those in theology. If our institutions are to remain Christian the 'Faculty of Theology' must remain central in the administration of the university lest theology be reduced to a mere (and marginal) department. Secondly, students of these secular faculties bring with them new standards of behaviour. When the theology faculty and other faculties share educational and residential facilities this may prove problematic. Proper guidelines should be drawn on how these new faculties will co-exist with that of theology - and the latter should not subordinate.

Finally, the cost of education is high and this has affected theological education in several ways. Let me highlight two major issues. First, some churches have given up college residential accommodation for their sponsored students. Some of these students hire small rooms in the estates and painfully struggle to meet their daily needs. Most of them, and especially the married ones, live in want. Moreover they are on their own. Neither their sponsoring churches nor the colleges monitor their way of life outside of the campus. In a country where poverty is so rampant these students are not insulated from its effects. The effects of this trend will be evident not long from now. The colleges and the respective churches must urgently address this challenge in the new century. Second, the supervised practical experience of students while in training has been reduced or done away with. Some colleges have no funds to post and supervise the students during their training. Students are therefore graduating with little or no supervised practical training. A few hours in a night club or four days in a factory is not enough practical experience to prepare a student for the challenges to be faced in his or her ministry. This situation can be overcome either by introducing a year of 'In-Ministry' training or, if the finances are totally restrictive, by reorganising the number of courses to accommodate a semester of internship for all students[9]. During this semester students would participate in supervised and tested practical experience such areas as in hospitals, prisons, homes of the aged, and AIDS orphans.

In the foregoing pages, I have reflected on some of the challenges that face theological education in Africa today. The issues pertaining to the selection of candidates for the ministry, curriculum, context and relevance may have to be discussed afresh every year. Evaluation of our effectiveness in training for ministry must, therefore, become a deliberate and ongoing task.

---

[9]For those colleges that use the Semester calendar, students could do at least thirty units in three years. If all the students did six units per semester, they would be able to cover thirty units in two and a half years. The other semester could be used for supervised practical training.

CHAPTER FOURTEEN

Residential and Distance Approaches to Theological Education

Godfrey Nguru

Introduction

In the last two decades we have witnessed drastic changes in political socio-economic systems internationally and here in Kenya. We saw the fall of the Berlin wall, which for many decades divided East Germany from West Germany, leading to the creation of a united German state. We saw the collapse of one of the world's super powers, the Soviet Union, and emergence of several independent states from what used to be known as the Union of the Soviet Socialist Republics. These events have left the U.S.A. as the only super power to 'police' the world. The recent war in Iraq waged by U.S.A and Britain against the strong opposition from the rest of the international community is clear evidence of the changed international political scene.

On the continent of Africa, we saw the dismantling of the Apartheid system in South Africa and fall of several dictatorial governments, including the Kenya system only last year. We have witnessed the clamour for democratic space and for freeing of the airwaves. People have demanded and in many countries won the freedom of expression and association. In many parts of Africa, including Kenya, this has led to a more liberalized economic system without the price and market controls that characterized earlier decades.

This democratization and liberalization of the political and social economic system have to a great extent affected higher education. The otherwise elitist and closed public university system has opened up to more students through what has come to be called "parallel programmes" mainly for private or self-sponsored students. This change has been forced on universities by the need to generate additional income to make up for reduced government grants. We have witnessed the proliferation of extension and long distance programmes by public universities where educational centres have been opened up in small urban areas to service students who cannot travel to larger campuses. Various forms of partnership have been formed between public universities and other post-secondary institutions in order to offer degree courses, a development which was unthinkable two decades ago. Moi University in Eldoret, for example, has partnered with the Kenya Institute of Management to offer the M.B.A. degree. All this has happened alongside stiff competition from overseas institutions of higher education, many of them for several years now, conducting aggressive campaigns to attract Kenyan students to their campuses. Many of these institutions, including some from South Africa, regularly run expensive advertisements in the daily press in the effort to enroll new students. Some foreign universities have launched partnerships with tertiary institutions in Kenya to offer the degrees of these foreign institutions. Others, like the University of South Africa (UNISA), are directly offering their degree programme to students in Kenya through distance education.

All this is happening while most theological institutions in this country are still stuck to a traditional, onsite residential system of education.

In this paper the term 'higher education' will be used to cover all studies and training activities at the tertiary level. It encompasses universities offering classical disciplines (arts and science faculties, including theology) as well as specialized branches (agriculture, engineering and technology). Furthermore, the concept incorporates traditional post-secondary school institutions such as polytechnics, teacher training colleges, theological colleges, and other vocational schools. Consequently, 'higher education' embodies all forms of vocational institutions, including theology.

The Residential System

It is probable that the majority of us at this conference received formal education through the traditional residential mode of educational delivery. In this mode the classroom has been thought of as a place in which the teacher gives information and the student takes it all in. Traditionally, the teacher is the library and the authoritative source of all knowledge and information. The student is the passive recipient of this information. The student may be in class but does not speak much. The student is considered an empty vessel without ideas of his own or her own, and with no experience or skills to be shared with the class. The student simply waits to be filled. The all-knowing teacher is expected to fill these students with information and skills. The teacher thus gives information and does not allow the students to ask questions or to think for themselves.[1]
The traditional system has been onsite or residential. It is basically a closed system in which the institution will tell the learner what to learn, the objectives to be achieved and how he or she will be assessed. In this system, learning takes place in a specific place, at specified times, and at the pace set by the institution. Learning methods and sequence are also set by the institution which decides who will help the student and what sort of help can be received. The learner's wishes or preferences are not taken into account. Most university charters have a clause such as "The University will decide what will be taught and who will teach".

The St. Paul's United Theological College B.D. degree programme is a classic example of this type of education. Their

---

[1] On this mode, sometimes called the 'banking method,' see especially Paulo Freire, *Pedagogy of the Oppressed* (Revised ed.; New York: Continuum, 2000).

sending churches carefully select students who attend the programme. They come to the College campus in Limuru for a specified period of either two or three years. Here they follow a prescribed curriculum, and a specific timetable, and only receive their degree if and when they meet certain specific standards.

A major drawback of this traditional system is that it limits access to theological education to only a few selected people – this at a time when the churches in Kenya need more trained leaders - but St. Paul's currently produces only about thirty graduates a year. Another drawback is that this system assumes that all students have the same learning needs and can move at the same pace, which cannot be true. Such a system keeps away many adult learners who, due to their occupation or employment or the need to support families, cannot study full-time or relocate to Limuru to pursue three years of theological education.

Distance Education

Today the approach to education has changed greatly. It is now widely recognized that people are not just vessels waiting to be filled with knowledge and information. They bring minds of their own and knowledge based on past experiences. It has therefore been recognized that the traditional approach of educational delivery has not always been the most effective or efficient. Just as there has been a desire within the secular world for institutions of higher education to open their educational space, so it is in the area of theological education. According to Bikas C. Sanyal[2] innovations in educational delivery systems in the universities have come about because of a variety of reasons: the constraints of financial and physical resources; the availability of new technology that can be put to use in education; the internationalization of higher education; new clientele: employed, part-time and mature students. These factors have led higher education to new ways of delivering educational programmes.

---

[2]Bikas C. Sanyal, *Innovations in University Management*, (Paris: UNESCO, 1995).

According to The African Network of Institutions of Theological Education Preparing Anglicans for Ministry (ANITEPAM), Theological Education by Extension (TEE) is simply one part of distance learning.[3] The terms 'distance learning' and 'distance education' are at times used interchangeably. Some, however, prefer to use the term 'distance education' to speak of the whole process of teaching and learning. Other terms used include open learning and flexible learning.

'Open Learning' refers to opening up learning opportunities to a wider range of people and enabling them to learn more congenially and productively. In his book *Exploring Open and Distance Learning*, Derek Rowntree has defined open learning as "arrangements to enable people to learn at the time, place and space which satisfies their circumstances and requirements."[4] He goes on to explain that the emphasis is on opening up of opportunities by overcoming barriers that result from geographical isolation, personal or work commitments, or conventional course structures which have often prevented people from gaining access to the training they need. Rowntree identifies four characteristics of open learning: a programme tailored to student wishes and at an acceptable price; a programme when and where it is wanted and which proceeds at the student's pace; a system which enables a student to set his or her own objectives, choose the content and sequence of the programme, and decide when and how learning will to be assessed; a system flexible enough to enable the student to decide how he or she wants to learn (with others or on your own, from books or from video, with emphasis on theory or on practice).[5]

Open learning is therefore taken to refer to an educational system, which provides learners with some control regarding how they learn and the pace at which they learn. Open learning may also

---

[3]"Understanding Distance Education," *The ANITEPAM Bulletin* 32 (2001): 11.
[4](London: Kogan Page Ltd., 1992), 14.
[5]Rowntree, *Exploring Open and Distance Learning*, 18.

involve learners having some control of what they learn and how (or if) their learning will be assessed.

ANITEPAM (the African Network of Institutions of Theological Education Preparing Anglicans for Ministry), similarly, defines open learning as a situation where individuals are able to enroll in a programme regardless of age, the ability to attend class, status in respect of employment (in or out of work), the extent to which they are tied to the environment, financial status and ability to meet the cost of fees and other incidental costs of study, and previous educational qualifications and attainment.[6]

In such a system there would be a need for support systems, which can provide counsel and advice to students first on what to study and then in assessing his or her own progress. Such support can come from a variety of sources, including professionals (tutors), and peers (mentors, family, and friends). This support could be made available at a variety of places and times and through various means (by face-to-face encounter, by letter, telephone or e-mail).

'Distance learning' refers to learning while at a distance from one's teacher – usually with the help of pre-recorded or packaged materials. In this situation learners are separated from their teachers in time and space but are still being guided by them. It is a mode of education in which communication must take place through means which are alternative to the traditional setting of the classroom, such as the post, electronic mail, audiotapes, or two-way radio.

Distance education systems have been established to deal with increasing educational needs that cannot be met by traditional systems. Hence local needs and local environments have influenced distance education systems.

The best-known distance learning systems are part of what is now known as the distance education movement. This movement embraces hundreds of worldwide schools, colleges and universities who cater to learners studying at a distance. The Open University in the U.K. was the world's first University to teach only at a distance

---

[6]"Understanding Distance Education," 14.

and admitted more than 24,000 students in its first year. Among the many unusual features it pioneered were admission without qualifications, degrees built up from credits obtained by taking a number of modular courses, and a team approach to developing courses. In 1992 the undergraduate programme at the Open University had 77,000 students enrolled. It is estimated that more than one and a half million people have studied with the Open University. African examples of similar projects include the University of South Africa (UNISA) and the Open University in Tanzania.

Of course, not all distance learning systems need be particularly open. Theoretically distance learning need not be open at all. There are various types of distance education programmes which could be contemplated.

'Correspondence Studies' is a mode of education that has existed for about a hundred years. This form of learning uses printed materials, which may or may not be supported by radio, television, short face-to-face sessions, tape recording, telephone, video, and computer use. 'Home study' was a term once commonly used in North America to describe this kind of distance education. 'School of the Air' or 'School Broadcasts' also are other examples that used programmes based on providing instruction through radio and television.

This type of educational delivery system has been developed into what have become known as 'Virtual Universities.' An example of this is the 'Africa Virtual University' (AVU). This is an interactive instructional telecommunication network established to serve African countries. Magdallen Juma states that the mission of the AVU is to use the power of modern information technology to increase access to educational resources throughout Sub-Saharan Africa.[7] She goes on to say that the objective of AVU is to improve the quality and relevance of science, engineering and business instruction in Sub-

---

[7] Magdallen Juma, "The African Virtual University Project: The Case of Kenyatta University, Kenya," in *Higher Education in Africa: Achievements, Challenges and Prospects* (Dakar: UNESCO, 1998), 534.

Saharan Africa. The second objective is to expand enrolment levels and to support and encourage African universities to develop curricula that could be broadcast to other African countries. The growth of new technologies has made possible the creation of virtual universities in which quality professors, libraries, and laboratories can be shared. In Anglophone Africa there are now twelve receiving sites: Addis Ababa University, Kenyatta University, Makerere University, Uganda Polytechnic Kyambogo, Martyrs University – Uganda, Open University of Tanzania, University of Zimbabwe, National University of Science and Technology – Bulawayo, University of Cape Coast, Kumasi University, and the University of Ghana.

The AVU at Kenyatta University started in 1998 with four courses (Mathematics, Calculus, Physics and Internet). The Mathematics course was transmitted from New Jersey Institute of Technology. The courses in Physics and the Internet were transmitted from University of Dublin. Each transmission session is video-recorded for use later on, either for purposes of revision or for viewing if a student has missed a lesson. Juma concludes that, "The African Virtual University (AVU) network offers a lot of hope for Universities in Africa to share resources, expand enrolment levels in science, and build capacities in technologies, which is a prerequisite for economic development."[8]

The advent of the Internet has revolutionized higher education in many ways. Through the Internet one is able to access volumes of information from various sources such as websites and libraries. At this point it is even possible to undertake doctoral degree via the Internet. Many of us are now familiar with e-mail as a way to facilitate faster communication. Within Kenya, for example, it is now possible to communicate with all the twenty-eight dioceses of the Anglican Church of Kenya. The use of new information technologies in higher education based on the Internet has only recently begun. Pressure to increase teaching productivity has led to research into the use of computer-based learning and has been found to be effective when

---

[8]Juma, 548.

properly supported by an open learning infrastructure. According to Sanyal, the advantages of this type of learning include: an ability to tailor learning to suit the student's pace and needs, an ability to simulate the learning experience through one-to-one feedback from the instructor and through on-line discussion groups, and cost effectiveness. Even the possibility of a deeper learning by doing is sometimes available in the classroom setting. In this system the teacher now plays the role of interpreter, guide and course developer, rather than simply lecturer. Information technology can also be used for more efficient tracking and assessment of students.[9]

Having listed the possible advantages of this type of learning, it is also important to note that there are problems with it. The programme lacks, for example, face-to-face peer or teacher contact, it often entails a huge learning curve especially when the student is beginning, and the lack of appropriate library or other facilities may disadvantage the student. The organizing institution may also find it hard to set up and begin the successful running of such a programme. The cost of acquiring computer equipment, its maintenance and upgrading or updating the systems, expertise needed to set it up and run it, are some of the many hurdles that may undermine the effective delivery of the programme. However, theological educators in Africa today could do better to tackle these challenges than be stuck with the old ways of doing things, and face certain doom.

Conclusion: The Way Forward for Theological Education

It is now widely accepted that the centre for Christianity is shifting to the South, and particularly to Africa. On the other hand it has also been said that the African Church is like a river, which is several miles wide but only one inch deep. The only way to correct that situation is for theological education to supplement programmes that are being offered through residential institutions to increase their enrolment and the number of graduates released each year to serve in the growing Church.

---

[9]Sanyal, 281.

Theological institutions must wholeheartedly embrace new technologies in their education programmes. Though this may be expensive at the beginning, it will eventually pay off in the way it enriches research and instruction delivery of their academic programmes. St. Paul's has made a start through St. Paul's Institute of Life Long Learning (SPILL). The first programme to be run from the Institute is the post-graduate Diploma / MA in HIV/AIDs and Pastoral Care, which will employ a number of different distance learning models. The programme begins in June 2003.

In the introduction of educational innovation there are certain obstacles to be faced. The first of these obstacles is the resistance from 'traditionalists' from within the faculty. Writing about the Africa Virtual University Juma observed that "Academicians tend to be conservative and any new innovation in education such as AVU is bound to evoke resistance."[10] Many lecturers are reluctant to abandon their investment in teacher-centred education and many see new innovations and technologies as a threat to their job security or professionalism.

Another obstacle to the implementation of educational innovation is lack of resources. The initial investment in these innovations can be heavy. The African Virtual University was funded by the World Bank. Rarely would theological institutions be able to find the kind of money required to set up a 'Virtual Theological College' system. But it is quite possible to start small with equipment and materials that do not cost a lot of money.

Finally there are problems and obstacles due to lack of technical expertise. In Africa we still lack the people with adequate training and experience to install and maintain new technologies. Qualified (and affordable) computer technicians are hard to come by. At this point theological institutions are thus forced to depend on expatriate staff to meet these needs.

---

[10] Sanyal, 537.

But in spite of these obstacles if institutions of theological education are to survive and grow in the 21st century and if they are to remain relevant and meet the demands of a fast-growing Church, they have to embrace innovation and new technologies wholeheartedly.

CHAPTER FIFTEEN

The Way Forward for Theological Education in Africa
Final Reflections from the Limuru Consultation on Theological Education

We, 45 church leaders, students, and theological educators gathered at St. Paul's United Theological College, Limuru, to celebrate one hundred years of faithful ministry, give thanks to God for the opportunity we have had to reflect on our vocation in theological education.

In our deliberations we have rejoiced in our unity in Christ as well as in our diversity as people of different ethnic and racial groups, both genders, various denominations and different abilities. We have also recognized the variety of gifts and talents that we are and have within the body of Christ.

Several crucial issues have impressed themselves on us during our time together.

HIV/AIDS

We have heard over and over again of the seriousness of the HIV/AIDS crisis in Africa. This crisis is not merely an issue, but an emergency which demands a response. In light of this:

- We rejoice in the launching of a new Post-Graduate Diploma and MA programme in Pastoral Care and HIV/AIDS at St. Paul's.

- We encourage the churches and theological institutions of Kenya and Africa to formulate clear, theologically-informed and pastorally sensitive policies as we face this crisis.
- We should consider implementing examinable courses on HIV/AIDS not only at St. Paul's, but in all other institutions and programmes of theological education including TEE programmes, residential programmes and any forms of distance learning.
- Continuing education programmes for clergy, lay leaders, and congregations should be implemented in all of our churches.
- We encourage theological institutions of our member denominations who run TEE programmes to offer their help to the Organization of African Instituted Churches to help them to formulate appropriate HIV/AIDS programmes of their own.
- We encourage these programmes to be as practical and informative as possible.
- We should consult as widely as possible with different religious and secular groups to build support structures for these programmes.
- The library at St. Paul's should work towards developing an information resource centre on HIV/AIDS by gathering information including books, governmental and non-governmental policy statements and documents, and any other existing research. This information should be made accessible to the public.
- We recognize that different ethnic groups in Africa have particular cultural impediments which work against the fight against AIDS and we encourage research and cultural sensitivity when training and teaching in this area.
- We recognize that abstinence before marriage and the faithfulness of both partners within marriage is the most certain way to avoid the transmission of HIV. At the same

time, we encourage the use of condoms in situations in which their use will save human lives.

Biblical Interpretation

We recognize the centrality and authority of scripture in the life of the church and in theological education. Therefore,
- We encourage deeper reflection on the meaning of the Bible in its original context and in African contexts.
- We encourage the collection of works of biblical interpretation by African scholars and the use of these works by teachers and students at St. Paul's and other institutions of theological education.
- We encourage staff development in the area of biblical studies so that Kenya can become less dependent on expatriate teachers in this area.
- We suggest that St. Paul's hold regular and on-going courses for pastors and lay leaders on the interpretation of the Bible and on preaching.
- We recognize the need for local translations and revisions to take place and we encourage interaction between scholars and translators to achieve more accurate and accessible translations.
- We suggest that those preparing for ministry give attention both to learning the original biblical languages and to the preparation and critique of sermons in the vernacular.

Ecumenism

We rejoice in St. Paul's long history of ecumenical cooperation. At the same time we recognize that we have not achieved the unity for which Jesus prayed (John 17). Therefore,
- We encourage the continuation of St. Paul's as an institution which welcomes students and faculty from a a wide variety of denominations.

- We recognize that although our identities are divided along denominational lines, our primary identity is in Christ.
- We wish to resist the division of Christian bodies into spheres of influence and encourage greater cooperation between churches.

The Marginalized

We have listened this week to the stories of some who are marginalized within our society and our churches because of gender, disability, or age.

- We affirm that all people are created by God in his image and that God hates nothing that he has made. The gospels witness to Jesus who loved people of all ages, and who reached out to those who were considered outcasts.
- We resolve to examine our facilities, our policies, and our attitudes in order to remove barriers put in the way of the disabled.
- We encourage the development of programmes within our theological institutions to train our students to reach out to the disabled, to children, to youth and to the aged.
- We encourage the recruitment and welcome of women to train for the various ministries of the church.
- We confess that our poor reading of scripture has sometimes served to marginalize people further, and we commit ourselves to more careful study of the whole biblical story.

Theological Content and Modes of Delivery

We have had healthy discussions on the nature of the task of theology and theological education and we have been challenged to take advantage of the many available modes of delivery available.

- We encourage our institutions to pursue the academic study of theology without losing sight of practical training for mission and ministry.

- We encourage initiatives which indigenize theological reflection so that students are able to perceive the relevance of their studies for the African and global contexts.
- We encourage tutors to include works written by Africans in their study and teaching.
- We encourage the development of residential and extension education for all levels of training for ministries in the church and we welcome future possible developments in education involving internet resources.
- We encourage the opening up of theological education to any who are interested, whether or not these students are sponsored by a church body, without losing sight of our vocation to train men and women for 'professional' ministry.
- One of the goals of theological education is to provide the churches with leadership. We recognize that in places the church is in a leadership crisis and we recommit ourselves to leadership training which is both theologically sound and practical.

Contributors

Mr. **John Chesworth** is head of Religious and Missiological Studies and a lecturer in Islam and Christian-Muslim relations at St. Paul's United Theological College. He is a graduate of the University of Birmingham where he did his M.A. in Islamics and is now a Ph.D. candidate.
[P.O. Private Bag, Limuru, Kenya]

Professor **Musa W. Dube** teaches Biblical Studies at the University of Botswana and is a HIV/AIDS Theological Consultant at the World Council of Churches. She is a graduate of the University of Durham and of Vanderbilt University and the author of *Postcolonial Feminist Interpretation of the Bible* (2000) and *Other Ways of Reading: African Women and the Bible* (2001).
[P.O. BOX 355, Gaborone, Botswanna]

The Rev. Dr. **Joseph Galgalo** is a senior lecturer in Systematic and Contextual Theologies at St. Paul's United Theological College. Galgalo, a graduate of St. Paul's and of the University of Cambridge is a minister with the Anglican Church of Kenya and a member of the Inter-Anglican Theological and Doctrinal Commission.
[P.O. Private Bag, Limuru, Kenya]

The Rev. **Sammy Githuku** is a lecturer in Hebrew and Old Testament studies at St. Paul's United Theological College. He is a graduate of St. Paul's and of McGill University, Montreal, Canada, and a PhD candidate at the Catholic University of Eastern Africa.
[P.O. Private Bag, Limuru, Kenya]

Mrs. **Josphine Gitome** teaches in the Religious Studies Department of Kenyatta University and is a graduate of the University of Nairobi.
[P.O. BOX 43844, Nairobi, Kenya]

The Rev. Dr. **Grant LeMarquand** is Associate Professor of Biblical Studies and Mission at Trinity Episcopal School for Ministry and a former lecturer at Wycliffe College in Toronto and at St. Paul's. He is a graduate of McGill University, and of Wycliffe College in the University of Toronto. He is the author of *An Issue of Relevance: A Comparative Study of the Story of the Bleeding Woman (Mk 5: 25-34; Mt 9:20-22; Lk 8:43-48) in North Atlantic and African Contexts* (2004).
[311 Eleventh St, Ambridge, Pa 15003, U.S.A.]

The Rev. Dr. **Johnson Mbillah** is the General Advisor to the Programme for Christian Muslim Relations in Africa (PROCMURA). He is a graduate of the University of Birmingham and is a Presbyterian Minister.
[PROCMURA, P.O. Box 66099, 00800 Westlands, Nairobi, Kenya]

The Rev. **Peter Mageto** is a doctoral student at Garrett-Evangelical Divinity School. He is a graduate of St. Paul's and is an ordained minister of the Methodist Church of Kenya.
[8909 Forest View Road, Evanston, IL 60203, U.S.A]

Ms. **Maryann Mwangi** is the co-ordinator for HIV-AIDS program of St. Paul's Institute of Life Long Learning and also lectures in social studies at St. Paul's College. She is a graduate of the University of Delhi and of the University of Jamia Milia.
[P.O. Private Bag, Limuru, Kenya]

The Rev. Prof. **Godfrey Nguru** (Principal of St. Paul's United Theological College 1999-2004) is currently the Vice Chancellor of Daystar University, Nairobi. He is a graduate of the University of

East Africa, Makerere University College, and the University of Tennessee. He is an ordained priest of the Anglican Church of Kenya.
[Daystar University, PO Box 44400, Nairobi, Kenya]

The Rev. Dr. **Nyambura Njoroge** is the Executive Secretary of the Ecumenical Theological Education Programme of the World Council of Churches. She is a graduate of St. Paul's and of Princeton and is ordained in the Presbyterian Church of East Africa.
[The World Council of Churches, P.O. Box 2100, 1211 Geneva, Switzerland]

The Rev. Dr. **Jonas Pazstor** has taught at St. Paul's United Theological College, the Reformed Theological Academy, Debrecan, Hungary, and the Faculty of Theology of Károli Gáspár University. He is a graduate of Pázmány University, Budapest, the University of Edinburgh and of the University of Manchester and holds doctorates from both Princeton Seminary and Károli Gáspár Reformed University. His many publications include *A misszió theologiája* [A Theology Mission] (Debrecen: Ref. Theologiai Akadémia, 1980).
[Karcag Utca, 23 Alberty Lua, Budapest H-1116, Hungary]